The Moon Belongs to Everyone

ELIZABETH MACLENNAN was born in Glasgow, into a family with strong Highland connections. After reading History at Oxford and training for the stage at LAMDA, she began her career with a highly praised Joan in *The Lark* for Granada Television, and a run in the West End in John Bowen's *Little Boxes*. However – after many more successes, including leads in BBC television plays and several movies, Elizabeth opted for a very different kind of theatre. With her husband, John McGrath, and her brother David, she founded the 7:84 Theatre Company. At first this was based in London, touring all over Britain, but soon she helped to found 7:84 Scotland, and went back to live there.

7:84 toured over the whole of Scotland, taking new plays in a vivid new style to audiences, usually of non-theatre-goers, in the places they would normally go for their entertainment – the clubs, village halls, Community Centres and small theatres, as well as the biggest theatres in the land. 7:84 demanded not only acting skills, but also total involvement in all areas of its work, as well as dancing, singing and the playing of musical instruments. From 1971 to 1988 Elizabeth committed herself wholeheartedly to this theatrical, political and organisational commando course. At the same time she brought up three small children, with all that that involves. This book is the story of that adventure, and of the cruel ending to her work in 7:84 Scotland with the threat of Arts Council cuts.

She writes: 'Recently new work has taken me to film all over Europe, alongside Greeks, Czechs, Slovenes, Serbs and Croats, Basques and Spaniards. It has brought home to me most vividly the value of our distinctness. More and more in terms of culture, it is the "powers that be" who call the tune. The story of the "piper" is often either neglected or distorted. In this book I have tried to tell a small part of that story.'

A Day Off. 7:84 Scotland and 7:84 England foregather
outside Dumbarton in 1975 for a game of football (Scotland v. England).

The Moon
Belongs to Everyone,

Making Theatre with 7:84

ELIZABETH MacLENNAN

Methuen

First published in 1990 in Great Britain
by Methuen London, Michelin House,
81 Fulham Road, London SW3 6RB
Copyright © 1990 by Elizabeth MacLennan

The author has asserted her moral rights

A CIP catalogue record for this book
is available from the British Library

ISBN 0 413 64150 3

'The Moon Belongs to Everyone' from
'The Best Things in Life Are Free'
by DeSylva, Brown and Henderson used
by kind permission of Redwood Music Ltd,
14 New Burlington Street, London W1X 2LR

Photoset by Rowland Phototypesetting Ltd
Bury St Edmunds, Suffolk
Printed and bound in Great Britain
by Clays Ltd, St Ives plc

Thanks to the following for the use of their photographs:
Studio Edmark, Oxford, page 36
Barry Jones, pages 45, 59, 65, 72, 80
John McGregor, pages 91, 100
Freeway Films, page 97
Antony Brannan, pages 110, 118, 155
Finn McGrath and Jac Heyer, page 126
Sean Hudson, page 143

The posters reproduced on pages 62, 64 and 74 were designed by
John Byrne, on pages 99 and 145 by X3 and
on page 169 by Annette Gillies.

Cover picture taken from
Demonstration, 1931, by Käthe Kollwitz

Contents

The beginning of Wildcat

Acknowledgements

I would like to thank all those whose letters, speeches and interviews I have quoted, for their permission to use their words and their work; in particular Ena Lamont Stewart, Clive Barker, Annie Inglis, Colin Mortimer, Nick Redgrave, Dave Mac-Lennan, Adrian Mitchell, Bill Riddoch, Linda MacKenney and Peter Holland.

I acknowledge gratefully quoting from letters from Bill Speirs and 7:84 board minutes and papers. To all those whose remarks and conversations I have recorded, my thanks and I hope they don't mind.

My encouragement came from many directions. From John who went away to write himself and managed not to look over my shoulder till I had finished – a great act of faith and friendship. From Sue Townsend, Annette Gillies, Mary-Ann Coburn, Alannah O'Sullivan and Aly Bain who said 'Do it'; Clive Barker, Susan Basnett, Olga Taxidou and Shelagh Fraser who made helpful comments and said 'Carry on'. My thanks to Annie Davis for deciphering, typing and long-standing friendship, and to Trish Nicoll and Susie Brown for typing. To Tony Brannan and Barry Jones for permission to use their great photographs with regret that we could not fit in more. Especial thanks to Geoffrey Strachan of Methuen, to Louise Moore for good humoured editorial help and to both of them for asking the right questions.

To John McGrath, my major 'influence' and life partner, whom I have quoted frequently herein – most of this book is for him, with lasting love.

To Finn, Danny and Kate, our children to whom this book is dedicated, along with their generation upon whom we place our highest hopes, for permission to use their diaries, experiences and comments extensively, and for their resilience which kept me going – my loving thanks.

My thanks lastly to *all* the members of 7:84 who made it go on happening, individually within and outside the company; our supporters in the arts organisations and communities – Highland and Lowland; local authorities; trades unions; women's groups; schools; officials and individuals at the grass roots within the towns and villages; and to the audience for making it such a 'good night out'.

While I hope this book may be helpful to theatre students, it is not intended primarily for specialists. It deals with both the personal and public part of a working life. To me and to many women they are equally important. It is above all addressed to our audience, past, present and future. I hope it will continue the dialogue with them and particularly with the women among them, onstage and off, who have supported me so strongly. Our struggles and our joys are shared, and no official history can erase them.

Priorities

1974, BBC RADIO (SCHOOLS)
'The important thing in any creative act is joy.'

W. H. Auden

DECEMBER 1987, BBC RADIO

'So you are saying you are prepared to pay more in taxes
to maintain a health service which will allow you to stay alive
longer?'
   'Yes, I am. And so are quite a lot of other people.'
   'But where will this end? One's got to draw the line
somewhere.'

MARCH 15, 1988, RADIO 4

'The course is designed to explain to children HOW they
should buy and WHAT they should buy. The late
secondary school group must realise they are an
IMPORTANT MARKET. And know how to fulfil that role.'

Introduction

We began serious discussions about starting a theatre company to recreate a form of popular theatre and tour it to working class audiences and their allies during 1968. This was the Year of the Events in Paris, the big Grosvenor Square demonstrations against the Vietnam War, the gunning down of the students at Kent State University, the shooting of Bobby Kennedy, Civil Rights marches in Derry, the Russian invasion of Czechoslovakia and Che Guevara's guerrilla struggles in Bolivia.

Many people want the theatre to be a mysterious place, inexplicable, full of nuance, ambiguity and fun. They want it to transport them away from everyday life, problems, questioning, 'squalor', having to think. Many feel theatre should be comfortable, comforting, expensive, supportive of middle-class values, decorative, a fun experience, a giggle, a gasp, a good cry. The lights go down, you shut off your critical faculties and wade into the weight-supporting shallows and feel the sand of passing sensations between your toes. If you're lucky you can down a stiff drink in the interval, or eat chocolates and ice-cream at the same time. Why not? What right has anybody to tell other people how to enjoy themselves?

Many people in the business feel that the leisure industry is there to provide work and pay mortgages for performers, writers, cameramen, musicians, propmakers and so on. If you rise to the top of the pool, the world's your oyster; posh parts, fancy clothes, chat shows, the Cotswolds, Roseland, Hollywood, the white Rolls Royce, the nanny with tax problems, title, friends with royalty – well, why not?

In our discussions other questions arose. You might ask yourself, as I did, has anybody ever said anything to you in a theatre that really made a difference to your life and attitudes? Is that as important? Is there a choice? Does that kind of theatre need additional skills? Is it available round where you live? Was it ever? If so, do people go, do they enjoy it? If not, why not? Is thinking boring? Do you see yourself as part of the experience happening on the stage or outside it? Why is Shakespeare respectable? Why do some people not go to the theatre at all? Where *do* they go, why, what for? Are they right to feel excluded? Which kind of experience and set of class values are you part of? Is it more or less artistic? Does questioning imply lack of respect? Why is music popular? Should the audience leave their politics in the cloakroom? If so, why? Can politics be fun? Is there a blacklist? Is joy class-based? One kind of fun for some classes, another kind for others. . . .

Why do we need writers? Is there such a thing as a reactionary laugh? Is there such a thing as a socialist actor? Should performers leave their politics behind at the stage door? Should theatre make money? Raise money? Be cost effective? Be subsidised? Which skills, which audience? Is it permissible to break the rules and still be an artist?

To this last question history says, emphatically, Yes. But who is saying No in the 90s? In whose interest?

Is the position of the theatre artist improving as a result of 'market forces', or getting worse? Do audiences get what they want, deserve, feel entitled to?

*　*　*

7:84 Theatre Company was started in 1971

Now it is in danger of being written out of history, along with most of the popular oppositional theatre of our times. It is fighting for its life. Then the political tide was in our favour and it was more acceptable, even trendy to be oppositional. Now its funding is threatened, it receives patronising reviews which talk of 'falling standards, crude agit-prop', and academics vie with each other to explain its demise.

Today alternative and oppositional theatre has become fragmented, competitive. Rampant individualism has set companies against each other, as each dons the appropriate funding mask, be it 'new writing', 'community' or 'touring product', the acceptable survival kits for anything even mildly critical of the status quo, the barriers erected to prevent people bursting onto the pitch or becoming part of the main action.

While the students in Beijing and Prague demonstrated their need to speak freely and express their desire for change, here in Britain that need is projected as inappropriate for our present culture which requires above all affirmation of the status quo, of the idea that the rich are entitled to get richer, the poor poorer. By all means let the arts celebrate this 'diversity', but not challenge it. The cultural tanks and personnel carriers are ready to crush any of that.

But this kind of theatre has been around since Aristophanes. It is an awesome tradition, the popular tradition, and will outlive its present insecurity. Should working people's lives be reflected on the stage, why should the theatre speak for them?

*　*　*

It is my intention in this book, as a performer and founder-member of both 7:84 Theatre Companies, to examine from some of my own first-hand experience the values and impact of this other kind of theatre – not to devalue the achievements of the bourgeois theatre, whose apologists are legion, but because otherwise in all the clamour of the New Realists our voice may not be heard. I shall be contentious, partial. Where possible I shall use records I kept at the time, and try to share my own feelings of excitement in the process. It is not an official history: inevitably many productions and people involved will be left out. Nor will I attempt to do full justice to the history of the remarkable English 7:84, for, apart from anything else, its story – like my own – is not over yet.

*　*　*

The story has several beginnings: there is the beginning of my life, roots, influences, where I came from, and a bit about my education, training, early

2

work; there is the beginning of the original 7:84 and its subsequent growth; then the beginning of the Scottish 7:84.

The middle period falls into two sections. The first is the highly confident time of *Little Red Hen, Out of Our Heads, The Trembling Giant*, and others in Scotland, and three mighty McGrath plays in England – *Fish in the Sea*, the enormously successful *Lay Off* and *Yobbo Nowt*; the growth and excitement of the English company band; other new companies starting and the growth of a popular theatre movement throughout Europe.

The second half of the middle period was perhaps the busiest and most successful of all, and coincided, surprisingly perhaps, with Thatcher's first term of office. There is a mythology grown up that the 'heady, early days' of 7:84 finished in the early 70s. But 7:84 continued to function throughout the 80s, performing much of its boldest, most innovative work to ever-growing audiences, and dealing with many of the questions they urgently wanted raised.

Had Thatcher *not* been re-elected in 1983, 7:84 might well have continued to grow and develop within a strong cultural revival in Scotland. But a forceful, independent culture with a popular voice became undesirable. Thatcher began her long march through the institutions, attempting to undermine and destabilise them, and to bring Scotland in line with the Tory majority in the south, by restructuring schools, universities, the hospital system, the social services, the Arts Council, and, not least – and most devastatingly – the trades unions.

It is against this background that the last section of the book unfolds, which I have called The Squeeze, and it brings me up to the present.

There are, happily, always exceptions: the momentous arrival of *glasnost* and *perestroika*; for me, the birth of a new child, critical success, the challenge of doing my one-woman show, *The Baby and the Bathwater*, and the discovery of an exciting emergent popular theatre in Canada and Australia through touring abroad in the late 80s with 7:84; international solidarity through touring in the Soviet Union, forging links with the Cinema Actors Theatre of Tblisi, and the knowledge that theatre movements like 7:84 were being taken up and developed all over the world, and may even continue here, albeit in different forms, and unaware of their connections.

* * *

It's a long way to Tipperary

There is a general perception that if you try to do something 'totally new' in the theatre, it might 'last' for a couple of years, but it will inevitably 'burn out', and those taking part will 'move on' (and by inference UP) to, well, Higher Things – the RSC, the National, television, their own comedy series perhaps, or, if they are really masochistic, their OWN company. The idea of moving OUT from Higher Things and INTO impoverished, touring theatre, which was the situation in my case, is considered downright perverse.

However, when we started 7:84 we did not say to ourselves as we set off to Hull University, say, or Fraserburgh Town Hall, 'Ahah, this is my red brick road to the Land of Oz,' (although the thought might occur perhaps when the lights failed or the electrician was catapulted across the room by a near-lethal switch) – no, we said, 'This is going to be a great show and I'm going to enjoy doing it.' It was good while it lasted, but I was thankful to get home to my own bed, a decent hot meal. Touring is an enormous pressure. It can also be a great release, challenging every part of the imagination.

In our precarious business most actors have to respond to the demands of the marketplace, and fear of becoming pigeon-holed, stereotyped, even these days blacklisted, keeps them flitting like butterflies. So I am clearly an oddball, hanging in all these years; or, as my dear Aunt Effie put it – I was forty at the time – 'The trouble with you is that you're a permanent adolescent.' So many people have said to me on the road, 'Don't you ever feel like settling down?'

In 1990 I had worked in the theatre for thirty years. After the first eleven years we made the decision to start our own company; to find the audience, the money, the circuit, put on new plays, question the norm, learn, find more money, keep going, bring up three children, keep going. Success, struggle, exhaustion, renewal. Well over thirty tours. An average of perhaps sixty gigs per tour (the early ones were longer), hundreds of benefits, line-runs in vans, new friends, company meetings, dirty coffee cups, smoke-filled rehearsal rooms, children growing up. An extended dialogue with the most extraordinary audience a performer might be privileged to get to know, to be criticised and cherished by.

In addition to describing how these events came about I have kept a diary of 1988 – for me a traumatic year – an attempt to make sense of events. Sometimes chunks of my past appear in it, and they are there as they occurred to me at the time. Here is how it begins.

* * *

Diary, March 1988

9 March, Edinburgh
Breakfast with Hugo Medina from Chile. And old friend from 1974 – he fled from Santiago after being imprisoned and tortured during the coup; a fine actor, he helped to start the Teatro Popular Chileno *in exile in London, but went back to Chile a few years ago. I haven't seen him since.*

He tells me eighty-three actors and Chilean artists are on a list and have received death threats. Many others, previously non-aligned, have associated with them, and they are here touring a play in Europe to draw attention to the situation in Chile. Contrary to their government propaganda, things are NOT getting better. They have meetings with Edinburgh District Council, Lothian Regional Council, and the Scottish TUC later, in Glasgow. They will go back to Chile.

Hugo has been in London. Everything in England has been cut, he says; how is it here in Scotland? We are waiting for our funding to be announced, I tell him, things are hard, but it IS different here; the consensus, a Labour majority in Scotland. The theatre is confident, feels young, optimistic, perhaps, but bold; there are lots of new groups touring, maybe a basis for action in the 90s. In SPITE of the devastation of the working class since Thatcher, we can build on that. There is at least cultural confidence, there is a huge audience, the writers are there, the talent.

One: Beginnings. The Sixties

Hey diddle de dee

I was born and grew up in Glasgow. More of that later.

At the end of my second year at Oxford in 1958, I 'starred' in an Oxford Theatre Group revue at the Edinburgh Festival Fringe, with Ken Loach and Dudley Moore. That autumn, in the first stage adaptation of James Joyce's *Ulysses*, I worked with John McGrath for the first time. I played Molly Bloom. For the 1959 Edinburgh Festival he wrote the part of Shirley the social worker in *Why The Chicken* for me. It was to be the first of many. The same evening I performed in another late night revue for the Oxford Theatre Group, with Giles Havergal and Alan Bennett. These two opposite kinds of performing – extrovert 'variety' and 'serious' acting – have attracted me ever since. Not until we started 7:84 in 1971 was I able to combine the two.

In autumn of 1959, having got my degree in history, I went to LAMDA – the London Academy of Music and Dramatic Art – which was as that time run by Michael MacOwan and Norman Ayrton. Both became friends. From Michael I learnt respect for the text, from Norman respect for the expressive power of the body. I was influenced by Vivian Matalon who taught 'scenes' and had worked in New York with Sandford Meisner. This contact led me to an interest in the Group Theatre and their development of Stanislavski's techniques. Later, I became very interested in their experience as a company. I was taught Voice by the formidable Iris Warren, and then by her pupil Kristen Linklater.

It was at about this time that I found out, to my surprise, that many 'professionals' are suspicious of writers, and frightened of 'clever' women.

Among the overseas students I made several lasting friends: Pearl Padamsee from Bombay, Janet Suzman from South Africa, and Yael Drouyanoff from the Habima Theatre in Israel, with whom I shared a flat. Donald Sutherland was there, having trouble with speaking 'proper' English, and terrible trouble with Restoration Comedy. Ellen Knox, from Vassar and New York, a classmate of Jane Fonda, and very witty in her disparaging New York way, also shared with me for nearly two years.

I left before the end of my two-year course, because John Dexter had set up a professional production of *Why The Chicken* with the intention of bringing it into the West End. He threw me in alongside the youthful Terry Stamp – in this version I played his Cockney girlfriend – Melvyn Hayes, Peter Gill and, eventually, Michael Caine. It turned out that John Dexter did not direct it, due

5

to some strange manoeuvres at managerial level. To everyone's surprise, Lionel Bart, who had been one of the investors in the production, did. The play changed a great deal 'on the road'. Some of these changes were inspired by the impresario Binkie Beaumont, who appeared one dark night in Wimbledon with an orange face, and West End values. The show never did reach the West End, 'dying the death' at the Golders Green Hippodrome. During the run Terry Stamp was spotted by Peter Ustinov for *Billy Budd*, and Michael Caine by Cy Enfield for *Zulu*. I had learnt a bit about what the West End was looking for.

I went to Dundee. During the summer break after my first year at LAMDA, I had worked as a Student ASM at Dundee Rep for twenty-five shillings a week. At that time, I rang John and told him about an extraordinary actor there called Nicol Williamson. When I went back in 1961 to work with Anthony Page on Viktor Rozov's *In Search of Happiness*, I played Nicol's wife. Anthony had directed me in Oxford in my very first term in a stunning production of *The Changeling*.

Dundee in 1961 was quite grim. A lot of the audience in the old theatre, now burnt down, wore felt hats and sat with their hands clasped and their lips pursed. But they went.

Elizabeth MacLennan as Masha in Chekhov's *The Three Sisters*, Richard Eyre's production at the Royal Lyceum Theatre, Edinburgh. *Left to right*: Antonia Pemberton, Elizabeth MacLennan, Angela Pleasance.

6

Anthony had assembled a galaxy of talents: Peter Gill, Edward Fox, Glenda Jackson, and of course Nicol, amongst them. I stayed in digs in Broughty Ferry with Kate Binchy.

I went back to London in October to play in a comedy with Alfred Marks for Rediffusion, and made the front cover of the *TV Times*. It was my television debut. By now I had an agent and was soon going up for lots of interviews and auditions at the BBC and all the television stations.

I took part in many productions, among them 'You in Your Small Corner' by Barrie Reckord, playing a Cockney girl who fell in love with an educated West Indian – I think one of the first television plays with an overt sexual relationship between a white girl and a black man, sensitively directed by Claude Whatham. It brought me good reviews, and not a few obscene phone calls.

A film director called Ken Hughes saw me in this and offered me my first film, *Sammy*, to star opposite Anthony Newley as a cigarette girl. There was a lot of press interest: 'Oxford blue-stocking gets big film role', 'Liz B.A. becomes a leading lady', sort of thing. I was only shown one scene of the script, but as my agent was enthusiastic and said it was OK, I said yes.

They didn't show me any more of the script until the Friday afternoon before shooting was to start. It was full of strip scenes, utterly sexist, and badly written. I rang my agent. 'I don't want to do this. It's not what it was cracked up to be.' I turned it down.

A couple of months later I was offered the part of St Joan in Anouilh's *The Lark*, again for Claude Whatham at Granada. It was probably my most prestigious job to date, with a very strong cast. It was to go out 'live'. Nicol played the Earl of Warwick. I had gastro-enteritis during the final rehearsal, and just made it to the end of the show. There was a nurse standing by throughout the transmission. In spite of this it got very good notices. Robert Kemp, the Scottish playwright, reviewing for *The Scotsman* said my Joan, who 'might well have attended classes at the Sorbonne . . . achieved moments of intense pathos, and was exactly what Anouilh must have intended.'

My first experience of film was opposite Rod Taylor, in an adaptation of A. J. Cronin's *Shannon's Way*. It was for the CBS Dupont Show of the Week and claimed to be the first Anglo-American co-production on ITV.

'Walk a Tight Circle' was an extraordinary play, written for the BBC by John Hopkins at the height of his powers. I had a very complex character to play, very emotionally demanding. The director, Vivian Daniels, tried to get me to actually break down in a photo session, and I was angry with him, but we grew to appreciate each other greatly. I played in 'The Truth About Alan' opposite Ian McShane, and Robin Phillips. It was by John Bowen, and the start of a lifelong friendship with him.

For ATV's 'Love Story' series, I worked in a comedy opposite James Villiers, and a piece by Michael Hastings, with Norman Rodway, called *The Emotional Machine* and in the same month an 'Armchair Theatre' with Alec Clunes, directed by that great stylist, and another lifelong friend, Philip Saville.

In amongst all these, I was doing episodes of series like 'Dr Finlay's Casebook', 'Z-Cars', 'No Hiding Place'.

I was still working in the theatre whenever possible. There were two productions I remember with interest: one was a Royal Court Sunday Night

7

production at the Embassy Theatre of another Michael Hastings play – *The World's Baby* – in which I was fascinated by Vanessa Redgrave's methods, and enjoyed working with Freddie Jones and Peter Bowles. The other production took place at the British Drama League – a first play by an American, Robert Weingarten, directed by Garry O'Connor, with stage management, lighting, sound effects by the 'technician' who had just left Cambridge, one Richard Ayre, now the director of the National Theatre in London.

I have outlined this part of my life in the first half of the Sixties to make clear that when it came to starting 7:84 and going on the road to make theatre for working-class audiences, I had to make a real choice. I enjoyed this part of my work, and still do enjoy television and film work. In the mainstream theatre at this time I wanted to work with Peter Brook, but didn't. Later I wanted to work with Buzz Goodbody, but didn't. Apart from that, I was lucky, worked hard, and worked almost continuously.

* * *

1966. Young, busy, freelance actress, four years married to John McGrath, living in leasehold house in West London. Hair appointments, classes, interviews, lunch appointments, dinner parties, visits to shows, films, friends. 'The Forsyte Saga' was on the telly, Edward Bond starting at the Royal Court, the *Royal Hunt of the Sun* at the National Theatre. We watched silent movies with Ken and Shirley Russell. Jeanne Moreau made me cry in *Moderato Cantabile*. The year began in the Highlands, and ended with our first baby, Finn, born 11 December in two hours forty minutes, and beautiful.

Ronald Eyre directed John's new play, *The Bofors Gun*, at the Hampstead Theatre Club. It opened on 12 April to wonderful reviews from Harold Hobson, Alan Brien and most of the other critics. We canvassed furiously for my brother Bob's Labour candidacy in March in Caithness and Sutherland, and on 1 April, while I was filming up a Welsh mountain near Llanrwst, I heard the results on the radio in the catering van – he was in by a majority of sixty-four. Jubilation. Another, stronger Labour Government.

We did occasional touring performances for the poet Michael Horowitz and his magazine *New Departures*, with Tamara Hinchco, and Margaretta D'Arcy, and once or twice, memorably, with Stevie Smith, pale and very, very interesting. On one occasion, after there had been complaints about the unreliability of the promise 'transport will be provided', Horowitz sent a Rolls Royce to collect us from the Earls Court Road, and Donal Donnelly and I felt as though we were taking part in a bank job. He was performing two Beckett mimes. I was doing McGrath's *Tell Me Tell Me*, a short play for two women. It takes an impoverished poet to deal with transport problems. . . .

On the opening night of BBC2, I played Madge Wildfire in a dramatisation of *Heart of Midlothian* with Fulton Mackay, Archie Duncan and other stalwarts of the Scottish scene. Michael Billington wrote, 'I like Elizabeth MacLennan going stark mad in a Tam-o-Shanter.'

Troy Kennedy Martin was perhaps our closest friend. He and John had worked together for several years, starting up 'Z-Cars' and breaking new ground with 'Diary of a Young Man'. Johnny Sekka and his wife, Cecilia, were frequent callers – soon he was to do John's *Bakke's Night of Fame*, again directed by Ronald Eyre, and again at Hampstead. Johnny was always our first foot at New Year.

8

John's sister, Moira, came to stay with us, helping with the babies and enjoying London.

In many respects a golden year, it gives a small idea of the kind of life we led. But on 1 July a tragedy ; Pauline Boty, painter, actress and dear friend, died of cancer, aged twenty-seven, when her baby, Boty, was only months old. We were all desolate. A group of us tried to look after her husband, Clive Goodwin, as best we could.

I last saw Clive when we went to Grunwicks together with John, and Howard Barker. Clive said this was the part of London where he grew up, and it was somehow surprising. But the fact that he was THERE was not. Shortly after that he also died tragically and is still badly missed, by both the left, and progressive theatre and television. A rare species, the committed organiser, energiser, an impresario with originality, imagination and wit.

Clive and Pauline's flat was the place where many formative meetings and discussions took place at that time, from where *The Black Dwarf* magazine was run, where Christopher Logue held court, and Tony Garnett, David Mercer and others got encouragement and practical support. Clive was simultaneously immensely fashionable and fashion conscious, revolutionary, not afraid of ridicule and full of enthusiasms – for new painting, new writing; for 'dolly' girls, jokes and surprises; for action, food, new sensations – it was not at all surprising to see him a few years later striding across the bridge in Dornie, Wester Ross, to see a performance of *The Cheviot* in the village hall, in his smart shorty mac and Italian shoes, and dancing at the Ceilidh afterwards.

It was he who suggested the name 7:84 from the statistic in *The Economist* that 7 per cent of the population of Great Britain owned 84 per cent of the wealth.

We made frequent trips to Birkenhead, to John's cousin Sheila's wedding and to show off the baby Finn to his grandparents. With seven girl cousins, there were a lot of McGrath family weddings around this period.

In January '67 the student Jan Palach set himself on fire in Czechoslovakia. We very concerned about what would happen there.

I continued to go to dance classes, to shop at Biba; Finn walked before he was one, and was the apple of my eye. John went to Helsinki to film *Billion Dollar Brain*. I was in something else in which I was fitted with a dress which had been worn by Gladys Cooper. We went on holiday to Provence, to a village house we rented for ten pounds a week, and we ate a lot of fresh sardines. My brother Ken was twenty-one and we sent him a ticket to come and join us. Troy had discovered this nirvana advertised in a post office window in Brondesbury. I went back to rehearse in Glasgow for a BBC play with a young Tom Conti.

In 1967 I did some filming for a few days where I was a nurse and Donald Sutherland was the patient – I don't remember what film it was, but they called me back to re-shoot a tiny bit months later and by this time Danny was a noticeable bulge, the nurse's costume was a tight fit, and they had to shoot over my shoulder – which they would have done anyway given the Donald Sutherland factor. John seemed to be working for months on a script for Fred Zinnerman of Malraux's book, *Man's Fate*. Zinnerman used to ring us up at 7.30 am to ask how many pages John had written the night before.

Before we knew where we were it was 1968 and Danny was born four days early, on 2 January, brought on, John and everybody maintained, by a particularly good New Year celebration at our house. Already hungry and very energetic, with huge brown eyes.

When Danny was three months old I was catapulted into a West End transfer of John Bowen's play, *Little Boxes*. We opened in the Duchess Theatre after only seven days' rehearsal. The rest of the cast had already played in it at Hampstead, but I was replacing Angela Thorne who had other commitments, and had to work fast, especially as it was farce, and technically quite demanding. It was a very brave play, and certainly 'ahead of its time' – about two girls in a lesbian relationship coming out and their parents' reactions.

I met Noël Coward after one performance of *Little Boxes* – he came to the wardrobe room two floors up at the Duchess Theatre which also served as my dressing room. I was happily ensconced with the young wardrobe mistress and her washing machine where Danny (three months old at the start of the run) could come in with John and see me between shows or get fed.

'So this is where they've hidden you,' he smiled. 'Well I enjoyed your performance. You are quite good, aren't you?' People in the profession at that time called him The Master, and it was a bit like a royal visit.

On the Sunday Harold Hobson's review came out. He had been kind to me before in *Why The Chicken*, but this was over the top. He concluded:

'Elizabeth MacLennan makes to her wilfully uncomprehending parents a singularly beautiful speech, idyllic in its delicate perversion, in which she tries to explain how two girls came to love each other . . . So manifest were Miss MacLennan's pain and yearning in delivering it, that on Thursday it left the audience bemused and thoughtful and in a way exalted, freed for at least a moment from the self-righteous burden of conventional judgement . . . Denied the understanding for which she has made her high, courageous bid, her face seems blasted with ecstasy and terror. As I looked at her, with the accumulated force of the whole evening and the united strength of her colleagues supporting her, I felt the same awe with which I watched the exquisite and solemn conclusion of Samuel Beckett's first play. All evenings and all triumphs end; even so the memory of Thursday will not soon vanish, nor its triumph fade.'

Years later Hayden Murphy said in a review that I had the capacity to make people change their minds – reviews like these mean a lot.

In May John went to Paris to take part in the 'évènements' – the students' uprising of May '68. He was very involved with the students at the Beaux Arts and with Jean Jacques Lebel, instigator of street 'happenings'. Martin Luther King was shot that summer. These events made a lasting impression on us. We became involved in the anti-apartheid movement.

In September I played Masha at the Edinburgh Lyceum for Richard Eyre's remarkable production of *The Three Sisters*. The work he was doing at the Lyceum at this time was exciting. I worked again for Richard Eyre at the Lyceum in 1970 in his production of John's play for the Edinburgh Festival, *Random Happenings in The Hebrides*. We stayed in a rented flat near the Botanic Gardens;

the boys played in the gardens with my brother David's friend from the deep south of the USA who was avoiding the draft. Here in Britain big demonstrations against America's war with Vietnam were happening regularly. Danny, aged three, defended his brother from the street bully – 'You leave my big brother alone.' The children had become close and protective of each other which stood them in good stead when we started touring together the following year.

John Cairney played my brother in *The Hebrides*, and his voice resounded off the grid above the stage when he sang 'Scarlet Ribbons' – I thought he must have inherited something from the great Martin Harvey. John Thaw gave a convincing picture of a devious Labour MP. The play is a bridge between the kind of writing in *The Bofors Gun* and the later McGrath 7:84 plays.

Then back to London.

I felt very at home in London in the Sixties, in the way that as a foreigner you can alight on a city that seems to suit you. Almost all my friends had come there from elsewhere, usually the north, or Ireland, and had other roots to go back to.

I liked and still like the anonymity of London, the extraordinary variety. People had a very clear idea of London's function as a market place for ideas and talent, innovation and opportunity. I did NOT like Londoners' provincialism about 'The North', or their widespread indifference towards old people, children, death and many of the values of working-class life.

My own parents were still mostly in Scotland, although my father's work for the Royal College of Obstetricians and Gynaecologists took him to London quite a bit and they were always passing through on their way to give lectures in Australia or the States. My in-laws, to whom I had become very close, came from Birkenhead to stay with us from time to time. They were happy to help us with the children for short periods such as studio days or the production week before a show opened.

I put down my own very strong familiar roots there in that house off the Earls Court Road. That neighbourhood, and the wider circle of our acquaintances, brought many lasting friendships.

These roots were quite difficult to tear up, even when I later felt I had to.

Two: Get Me Out of This. 1971

I had already begun to question the kind of bread-and-butter work which was available on television and feel the need to be less of a 'commodity', to be able to work in a committed way, as part of an ensemble. For nearly ten years I had worked with many of the best directors of the time and in many new challenging and controversial single plays. I had turned down a film and a long-running lead in 'That Was The Week That Was'. Probably a mistake! I had played opposite many remarkable actors. For all that and in spite of the demands of two small babies, I found myself inexorably pulled back to the theatre.

The day-to-day 'production line' of television did not appeal. I tried to write about my feelings about this kind of work at the beginning of 1971.

I called it *Paid to Crouch*.

WEEK ONE

Monday My agent's secretary rang: I had been offered a part in a regular TV series – a leading part in one episode. No script available as yet, not yet written. She gave a description of the director's secretary's description of a character – who later turned out to be my character's husband. I asked to see the script when it came out. It was to be two weeks' work at my usual rate for that type of programme.

Wednesday The script arrived.

Friday Rang my agent, told him the part was not very exciting. He pointed out that work was scarce, and that it was now only eight half-days' work for the same money, and that it would be repeated and probably sold abroad (i.e. more money later) and that I couldn't afford to be choosy at the moment. I said I would think about it over the weekend. He said, 'They start on Wednesday, but don't appear to be all that anxious.'

Over the weekend I read the script again: an ordinary series episode, boring, full of clichés, resembling life as seen on other TV series rather more closely than life as it is lived. There was now a long character description of the part I was to play which was calculated to appeal to a vain actress, but bore no relationship to what the character actually did. I had not worked on TV for ten months, needed the money, decided to do it.

WEEK TWO

Monday Told my agent's secretary I'd do it. Agent rang back to say, 'I hear you've decided to Prostitute Your Art.' (He was pleased.)

Tuesday He rang again. I was to get even more money, and rehearsals were now not going to begin until the following Monday – i.e. six half-days' rehearsal.

WEEK THREE

Monday The new BBC rehearsal block was a seven-storey, prefabricated building, with three rehearsal rooms on each floor – twenty-one pieces of TV fiction were being manufactured here every day. In spite of this the place felt empty. A man in a peaked cap opened the door.

The lifts facing me opened and seven men with seven slices of toast came out. One said, 'You can get breakfast here too.' Found out which room was for me, went there – nobody there. Waited. The script editor arrived first. He was worried that the script was too long and that the regular actors in the series put him down.

Note: in some series of this kind the 'regulars' can afford to adopt a superior attitude to the writer, the script, the director, the other actors, the floor staff and particularly the audience – in fact everybody but the cameraman, upon whom a certain amount depends.

The director arrived with some of the other non-regular actors. To his annoyance the star was forty minutes late. We were given a piece of paper with the other actors' names on it. Actors are always nervous before a read-through.

Read-through inaudible. Most actors muffed words over two syllables, except the star, who enjoyed pronouncing the Latin quotations. Director's only comment: we must cut twenty minutes. The producer – a wizened BBC old-timer – took the director on one side and told him to cut 'Bugger' and a reference to the *Guardian*. The author was not present. The director and script editor then cut all material – like character-establishment, motivation, colouring – that was not pure plot. It was still too long. They then made sure that we all addressed each other by our proper names so that the audience would know who we were talking to. And they cut all long words – all except the Latin.

After lunch we went through the cuts, and got sent home. Before leaving some of the actors tore out all the pages of the script they were not in, and threw them away.

The director had seemed extremely irritable all day. He was annoyed with the star, the standard of the script, the objections of the actors to the cuts, and the producer. He seemed to regard actors having difficulties as obstacles to the smooth running of the show. He was under stress, having to turn one episode off the line every three weeks.

Tuesday Twenty minutes' work. 'Blocked' (did the moves of) one one-page scene. Changed the moves twice. Director's comment: fine, the feeling's there. As I was leaving, a problem arose over a scene about mistaken identity – the two actors cast were totally dissimilar. Director: why don't all actors come the same size?

Wednesday One hour's work. Blocked two more scenes. Actors lethargic. There was no difference between the energy the actors use to read the papers and the energy with which they apply themselves to the text. Something was clearly expected to take place, but not in rehearsal. Presumably in the studio.

Thursday Finished blocking scenes. Pointed out tentatively to the director that my character had a tendency to talk like a policeman. He looked baffled. He did not actively object, however, when I changed 'according to his story' to 'he said', 'I suspect' to 'I think', 'juveniles' to 'young men' and a few other such. He was more concerned about the producer coming to a 'run through' the next day; nobody knew their lines, in fact were still making them up.

Friday 'Hard day's work' – i.e. began at nine and finished at two. (They usually finish at two.) After three hours' going through the scenes – mostly line rehearsals, in a despondent attempt to put down the books before the producer came – we had what is known as a Technical Run-Through. Present: producer, script editor, camera crew, and, making his first appearance, the author.

These people wandered around the room with maps of the studio trying to follow the action as it moved from one part of the floor to another, peering at the actors – when they caught up – from a distance of approximately three feet. The floor manager gave hand-signals to spring into life, about six inches from the actors' noses. The wardrobe supervisor and the make-up girl talked to each other throughout, ignoring everything.

After this, the director seemed pleased, and smiled for the first time. The wardrobe supervisor, whom I had tried to contact four times unsuccessfully, now took me to the TV centre where we failed to find anything suitable so we went shopping, again with very little success. It looked as if I was going to have

13

to wear my own clothes. She had no time to find the right clothes because she was busy working on the next episode's film sequence.

Saturday The director had seemed puzzled by my attitude in two scenes I had with a policeman – a 'regular'. I felt that the character I was playing, when questioned by this policeman, in this way, would not reply like a detective in a witness-box, but would find him comic, or at least be flippant in her replies to cover her embarrassment. The woman had committed no crime, and the policeman was being oppressive and intruding on her privacy in a decidedly flat-footed way.

After a run-through on the Saturday morning – with about one hour of rehearsal time to go – the director, quite aggressively, accused me of 'obstructing the police' in what was 'routine questioning'. He seemed to think that I was getting at him personally – in other words, he identified with the policeman, to the point of using police jargon. He maintained that the way I was playing it threw an unpleasant light on my character, and would lose her the audience's sympathy, while I sensed that he was actually concerned about the image of the policeman – possibly subconsciously, or possibly as a result of comment from the producer.

When I said that it was 'routine questioning' from the point of view of the policeman, but from hers the questions were inept and intrusive, he said, 'It doesn't matter what you think – they know him, they don't know you,' and asked me to smile at the policeman, at least, before delivering the lines. I said I didn't want to be 'sympathetic', I wanted to be believable. The real issues were: the need to be charming in a relationship with the police in order not to make them appear ridiculous; the need for a female lead in any series to show due respect to the male heroes, in as decorative a way as possible; the need for a visiting actress not to upset the star's relationship with the audience; and hostility towards actors who speak their mind – particularly if they threaten established images.

I said I'd try and do what he wanted. Fortunately that was the end of rehearsal.

WEEK FOUR

Monday In the studio. Six hours' work. At this point the actors become objects while the director goes through the play for the benefit of the cameraman, lighting men, sound men, etc. This also involves being moved backwards and forwards, inch by inch, into positions which are most convenient for the cameras, but which subtly alter the relationships between the characters supposedly worked out in rehearsal.

As I waited, squatting, for a hand to be shaken in my face implying ACT, a boom-operator, also squatting over his boom, quipped, 'Do you like crouching?' To which I replied, 'Do you?' A few of his mates laughed, which annoyed him. To prove his manhood, he said, 'That's not the point – you get paid to crouch.'

In the restaurant I noticed technicians and actors almost always sit apart, and whenever possible patronise each other. The technicians are under the impression that the actors get more money for less work – forgetting that Equity has eighty per cent of its members unemployed. Actors tend to look on technicians as grey little men, rarely craftsmen, rarely 'artists'. This distinction is borne out by the parking arrangements. As I went in I was asked if I was Staff or Artist? I tried saying I was both, but was told THAT was impossible.

Tuesday Recording Day. Ten hours' work. Staggered through the episode with stops, then ran through with less stops and in costume. Director's Acting Notes: remember the new moves, keep the pace up, we're two minutes over. Good luck everybody, see you in the bar afterwards. An hour's break. Record.

A few breaks for technical reasons. All over in an hour and a half. At this point it is part of the ritual for everyone to go to the bar, swear eternal friendship, exchange telephone numbers, drink too much, and wander off into the night, muttering, 'Well, it pays the rent.'

As I left the television centre, I wondered if I would ever go back. I hadn't drunk anything, but felt extraordinarily euphoric driving down the road.

When we started 7:84 a few weeks later I would be paid (albeit inadequately compared to this), not to crouch but to stand up. I haven't regretted it.

Three: Beginning 7:84. 1971-1973

John had begun working at the Everyman Theatre in Liverpool, determined to build the audience he wanted, and with the triumph of his musical, *Soft or a Girl*, in 1971, he and their director Alan Dossor succeeded spectacularly. They built on it, with another six of John's plays being presented there during the next three years, *Fish in the Sea* amongst them. The Everyman became alive with excitement and was very influential throughout the country. I got to know a little more about Merseyside, and about working-class audiences. John talked a bit to the actors Gillian Hanna, Gavin Richards and to Nick Redgrave the young, enthusiastic prop-maker and set-builder about starting a company.

We also talked to Sandy Craig, a recent philosophy graduate from Edinburgh University, and friend of my brother David, about helping to book a tour and run an office from our front room. Sandy had never worked in the theatre – he had only just come out of university – but he cared about it a great deal and had a first class head, and a flair for communicating his enthusiasm. No amount of experience can substitute for those qualities, plus an ability to learn from the specifics of the touring experience.

Sandy's family lived in North Wales, near Mold, the small town where for a while John had gone to school, and where his parents now had a small cottage to which we used to escape at weekends. John wrote all of *Fish in the Sea* there. It was a wonderful place to write, totally quiet, and usually very wet. During the days I tramped the hills and fields around with the boys and made them bows and arrows. In the evenings we would sit and plan with Sandy, and with my brother David.

David had got his first theatre job in stage management at the Gardner Arts Centre in Sussex the previous year, in a production of the David Caute novel about Winstanley and the Diggers, *Comrade Jacob*, which John had adapted for the theatre. Victor Henry had played Winstanley in it, a characterisation of

15

luminous saintliness and power. He had also starred in John and Troy's series 'Diary of a Young Man' on BBC. Victor was ready to start work with the new company.

Gillian Hanna had had a great success as Bessie Braddock at the Liverpool Everyman and had worked happily with John on his short plays under the title 'Unruly Elements' when they were first performed there. She was willing to join us. Gavin Richards was keen, too, but not free of commitments until the following year. He would join us then if we were still going. . . . Roger Sloman was eager to join when he was free.

Michael Wearing, a close friend of Victor's, agreed to stage manage. A perfectionist and, at times, an essential prop to Victor, he exhibited enormous patience and had a sharp and vigilant class awareness and no time for bullshit. Above all, he had an excitement about the quality of the writing which committed him to the project. This zest for good writing has informed his very impressive track record as a producer ever since.

Feri Lean joined us to manage the box office, accommodation and much else. It was her first theatre job too, and she remained committed to it through considerable strength of character and a saving sense of humour, for the next seven years. Later that year she married David and the two of them plus John and myself became a formidable, close foursome, now sharing more and more of our work and aspirations, stress and ties of all kinds.

Trees in the Wind
'Wind will not cease even if the trees want rest.'

This is not a reference to the digestive problems arising from the touring diet, but a quotation from Mao Tse Tung from which derives the title of the first 7:84 play by John, which opened in August 1971 in the converted Cranston Street Church Hall on the Royal Mile at the Edinburgh Festival, and turned out to be the start of the whole thing.

Up until this time, our discussions about starting a new company had tended to get bogged down over the question of a building and creating the right environment. We talked a great deal about this with Clive Goodwin. There had been much discussion of 'ensemble' and the working of companies ever since the *Encore* days – the theatre magazine which Clive helped to start and which is sadly missed.

John had been briefly involved with Centre 42 in the early 60s. An attempt by a number of writers, including Doris Lessing, to make working-class theatre with trades union involvement, it became largely associated with Arnold Wesker.

Both Arnold Wesker and John had gained formative early experience at the Royal Court Theatre and acknowledge their debt to the encouragement of George Devine. Both wanted however to reach out to their own audience – the working class and its allies. But there was an important distinction between the approaches adopted by Wesker with Centre 42 and John with 7:84. Their view of theatre is different but not entirely opposed.

Wesker argued passionately for a humanist kind of socialism. Although his own family were Communist in the 30s his own position was more compatible with Fabianism, the theatre of the Co-operative Movement, the idealism of

William Morris and Robert Tressell. He worried about Stalinism, about English caution, but did not want to stray too far from the middle-class theatre's naturalistic forms. Beattie in *Roots* owed more to Stanislavski and Mahler than Brecht or the Beatles. Wesker's was an elevated view of art, deeply felt and shared, not surprisingly, by many of the arts establishments of the day.

John, however, found much to admire in working-class culture and drew inspiration from the popular forms of Grimaldi, the music hall, the Marx Brothers, carnival and live music. He liked Boulez *and* the Beatles. As a director he related to Meyerhold, Piscator and Felsenstein in theatre; Robert Flaherty, Jean Renoir, Jean Vigo and Eisenstein in film. His definition of the committed artist was closer to that of Sartre than that of William Morris. His theatre would follow on from the Workers Theatre Movement and the early Theatre Workshop, from a revolutionary not a reformist perspective. It would use popular forms but in new, challenging ways, making demands of the audience from a position of trust.

Their differences were articulated in an exchange of unpublished letters – sharp, at times highly critical, but ultimately fraternal and aimed however painfully at producing more better theatre. John attacked Wesker fiercely over *Friends*:

'Your cultural ideas pre-suppose the status quo but you know that for them to succeed we need a completely new kind of society. Are we going to create a revolutionary culture or are we going to sit on our arses and moan about the backwardness of the people?'

Wesker retaliated:

'What is revolutionary art? Art whose forms are different from anything we've seen before . . . or using bourgeois art forms to say revolutionary things? I've never encountered working-class art . . . I don't subscribe to the affected notions that music hall was art or that pop music is art. . . .'

Similar arguments took place within Unity Theatre, Theatre Workshop and hopefully will go on within every new generation of popular theatre makers. Nevertheless Arnold Wesker and John retained respect even affection for each other.*

This kind of critical respect is as unfathomable to many of our enemies as the diversity it represents. They prefer to look for splits.

Another friend and influence was Sean Kenny, who had designed John's production of James Joyce's *Ulysses* at the Oxford Playhouse which was the start of the professional association of all three of us.

---

* When in 1988 7:84 was under threat of closure by the SAC, Wesker wrote to them in its defence:
'If I had been asked which theatre groups would *not* come in line for withdrawal of Arts Council funding I would have placed 7:84 Theatre Company Scotland at the top of my list. If a group of such proven talent, professionalism and dedication is not deemed worthy of Arts Council support, then Arts Council policy is incomprehensible. I travel a great deal, to many parts of the world. Time and again 7:84 crops up. John McGrath is a unique writer. There is no one producing the kind of exploration he is making into theatre language and content . . . you cannot be contemplating rewarding fifteen years of devotion to a special public with dismissal.'

In many of these circles discussion continued about What Kind of Theatre? But we felt we couldn't wait any longer for a building, or for someone else to do something. We had to get plays written, and take them to wherever working people and their support, students, young people, would go – be it theatre or community hall, working man's club, trades council, cinema, school, park, canteen. The priority was the PLAY and the AUDIENCE, and the rest would follow. We would INVENT the necessary organisation. We would have to work for peanuts, and subsidise it ourselves.

What else was happening in '71 and '72? What was the climate in the theatre? The Living Theatre had been over from New York with their hyper-realistic production of *The Connection*, a strange experience in a West End theatre, but hypnotic. The Welfare State International had been touring around Yorkshire for three or four years. They, like us, began without benefit of Arts Council support. The People Show was beginning to tour. David Hare, Howard Brenton and Malcolm Griffiths were on the road with Portable Theatre, opening up the new university theatre circuit. And the climate in the universities was increasingly politically aware.

On 27 October 1971 the first issue of a new weekly photo-news magazine, produced in London, came out: *7 Days*. It was started by a group of writers and journalists from *The Black Dwarf*, *The New Left Review*, *Free Communications Group*, *Cinema Action*, *Gay Lib*, and *Women's Liberation*. It was owned by a trust which included Stuart Hood and John Berger. Its declared enemy was:

'Capitalism, the State and the ruling class groups that control the two. It will critically analyse the performance and supporters of social democracy, uncover exploitation, present the background to world developments, fight racism and back the struggles of immigrant and oppressed groups, encourage community action, and debate questions of sexuality and the family.'

John was on its collective. These issues were also central to the thinking of the group with whom we planned to start 7:84.

In Scotland four magazines supported by the Scottish Arts Council were widely read by students and intellectuals – *Akros*, *Gairm* (the Gaelic writing forum), *Lines Review* and, perhaps most important, *Scottish International*. Bob Tait, its editor, came to *Trees in the Wind* to interview John, who says it is still the most perceptive interview he has ever had.

In the October 1971 issues of *Scottish International*, there is also an article by the Professor of Economics at Strathclyde University, Kenneth Alexander, at that time a director at Fairfields Ship Yard. He reminds us that a young Nicholas Ridley was wielding the knife at UCS – the Upper Clyde Shipyard – where the work-in had just taken place that was to become the inspiration and model for so many subsequent factory work-ins from the Lucas plant to Lee Jeans and Caterpillar in the 80s.

The Citizens Theatre were performing *The Three Sisters* and Joe Orton's *Loot*. They still had two theatres. In The Close they were putting on Genet's *The Maids* and a play by Donald Howarth called *Three Months Gone*. Liz Lochhead had not long graduated from the Glasgow School of Art and had started winning poetry competitions. Adrian Henri was performing live with the

Liverpool Scene. Albert Hunt was working in exciting new forms at Bradford Art College.

Clive Barker, who had been Festival organiser of Centre 42, was one of our many links with Joan Littlewood, with whose early touring work our own had so many connections. In 1959 I had crept off and auditioned for her while I was at LAMDA, having attended a dress rehearsal of *The Hostage* while I was a student with Sean Kenny who designed it. At the audition she had asked me to tell a story, which I did, and to sing a song. We talked about the old 'pierrots' summer shows in Stonehaven. Joan seemed to know where that was, which surprised me at the time, as I didn't know as much about her early work then as I subsequently have learnt from her audience (some of whom we shared) and from getting to know Ewan MacColl during our Clydebuilt season. She liked my song, but she told me to go back to LAMDA and pick up as much as I could, which I did.

Nothing good is ever wasted in theatre: That song was later used in John's play, *Little Red Hen*.

* * *

So there we were, after working independently in theatre, films and TV for ten years, rehearsing *Trees in the Wind* at LAMDA, and setting up a tour from our front room, now 7:84's office.

I had been fiercely independent, determined not to be defined as daughter of, wife of, sister of. (And now mother of!) I have since realised that is an impossible dream, particularly if you are an actress, which is already a stereotype anyway, and it is part of the job to continually defy stereotypes that won't go away without a long struggle – in my case, having been at Oxford, I was of course 'blue-stockinged bombshell' (sic), and then, after LAMDA, 'lovely, green-eyed leggy Liz' (the *Express*), and in addition of course, daughter of, wife of, sister of. You rarely see male actors defined as 'father of', 'brother of' or 'husband of' as though that explained them satisfactorily.

Anyway – here we were, working together in a lifestyle which involved 7:84 and its plans and problems twenty-four hours a day, often to the exclusion of everything else. I became used to endless meetings, people staying, lack of privacy, shortage of money, lack of sleep and confiding in my children from a very early age. We were paid £18 a week, rising to £20, and there was no such thing as touring allowance. Without drawing attention to it John and I subsidised everything for years.

For the month in which they were actually building the theatre in Edinburgh, that is, erecting the three stages on which the action of the play would take place, converting the rest of the space (the word 'venue' was later invented by 'trained' theatre bureaucrats) and building seating on scaffolding, David, Sandy and Feri were paid £5 per week and hoping somebody would feed them. They did a magnificent job.

Victor Henry, disciple of Yat Malmgren, was a great 'mover', with a huge reservoir of energy on stage. He also liked to talk. Getting going in the mornings was sometimes a problem, but once launched into the play's very demanding monologues, we had our work cut out.

Trees in the Wind is about the ritual provocation by a deeply cynical, negative man of three young women trying in different ways to make a positive future. We were all required to read a great deal, as actors are in most McGrath plays.

Deborah Norton, who played the Maoist, Carlyle, had to read a lot of Mao, and also to read several passages more from the stage. The attentive silence which greeted these was later proof of the fact that audiences like ideas, indeed as much as emotion. Her concentration was impressive, her dry sense of humour essential. There was considerable interest in Maoism and what was happening in China at the time. President Nixon had just made his historic visit to Peking and 'Normalisation' was in the air. . . .

Gilly Hanna played Belle the social worker, vulnerable and tough at the same time, and I'm sure the experience fuelled her later feminism.

I had to immerse myself in the atrocities of Vietnam and the recent involvement of British troops in Ireland, and create the character of Aurelia, a young, radical feminist partly based on the American Valerie Solanas who wrote a book called SCUM (the Society For Cutting Up Men). Aurelia has the capacity to become possessed by man-made atrocities, but her plans to combat this man's world bring her into confrontation with the Marxist cat-burglar and 'Demon King', Joe, played by Victor. Henry, Victor and I enjoyed these epic confrontations, in which neither was victorious and the audience obliged to think hard.

Elizabeth MacLennan as Aurelia and Victor Henry as Joe
in *Trees in the Wind* by John McGrath, at the 1971 Edinburgh Festival.

The play's outstanding characteristic, which thrilled audiences and critics alike, was the coruscating brilliance of the language and its wild humour, particularly in the sections called the 'Songs' – The Song of Knives at Throats, The Song of Driving Mad, and The Song of Why They'll Never Know. Alex Norton saw us perform a couple of these in the bar at the Traverse Theatre at lunchtime during the Edinburgh Festival and said that it was the most exciting theatre he had ever seen and he couldn't wait to work with us.

The play also contains some of John's finest monologues, and some beautiful lyrical writing. It was billed as a piece of theatre which aimed to raise consciousness and at the same time provide a Good Night Out. It was the first use of that phrase to describe what we were trying to do, and it certainly did.

The programme, two sheets of A4, records thanks to Richard Demarco who had given us enthusiastic support, David Treisman who helped with research, Mao Tse Tung, John Prebble, Karl Marx, Valeri Solanas, 'J' (the author of 'The Sensuous Woman') Chou en Lai (quoted in the play), Gramsci, William Blake, Harold R. Isaacs, Richard M. Nixon, the *Guardian*, the *Evening Standard*, *Daily Mirror* and the walls of Paris in May 1968.

We opened the play at the end of August to critical acclaim – eventually. As Alan Wright of *The Scotsman* wrote, it was 'the best-kept secret of the Festival'. We were not very good at PR. But people found out about it, and by the Saturday night of the second week, we had our first full house. We played to full houses for the rest of the run.

Two years later Victor was mortally injured in a hit and run accident while he was walking down the road in London with some friends. He was taken to hospital and remained severely and irrevocably brain-damaged for thirteen years. I visited him in the intensive care immediately after – wake up, you can't fool me – and he squeezed my hand and smiled beatifically. He could smile beatifically in the play too and melt the hardest of flinty hearts, even as he played the 'Demon King'.

About ten years after the accident we received a letter from an insurance firm – would you care to put a value on this person, in terms of his potential earning capacity etc., etc. as an artist? John replied, 'Priceless, the sky is the limit. Probably the finest actor of his generation.' I think some sort of settlement was eventually reached. His sister Margaret and her family kept up their bedside vigil for years, and eventually his parents both died, never losing hope, but heartbroken.

Of course some people would have paid NOT to have to sit in the front row and have Victor's gimlet-eyed accusations thrown in their teeth – Sandy Dunbar, then Director of the Scottish Arts Council, for one. His energy and feeling of danger were sometimes almost too much . . . but he was, to me and to most of the audiences, unforgettable; an extraordinary talent.

Four: My Own Beginnings

As a child I stood nose-high at the polished wooden counter in James Hunter, Grocers, back shop, Bryes Road, Glasgow, watching the sugar (white) being carefully shovelled into 2lb brown paper bags, folded with immaculate symmetry and tied with string at the top. My strawberry-pink hat was secured under my chin with elastic, gaiters well buttoned, gloves also secured by elastic, passing up one coat sleeve and down the other, and under the hat a hair ribbon. Called Elizabeth after my Highland great aunt Lizzie Ross, my most immediate link with the fighting Ross women. She kept the hotel in Rogart, East Sutherland – croft, pub, and four letting bedrooms. With no children of her own, she regarded my father Hector, her nephew, as the son she would like to have had: a medical student at the university in Glasgow, and such a grand, big, handsome fellow too.

My Granny Mac lived a couple of streets away in a flat in Caledon Street, and gave us Sunday breakfast, piano, and the Congregational Church. She did a good line in eggy-bread, but her mother had been English so she called it French toast. She always wore a hat – sometimes I helped to choose – secured with an alarming pin, one of a collection bristling on her dressing table. She had powder in a crystal bowl, which was applied in clouds, and then wiped off. I held her gloved hand as we got on the 24 tram which took us down Sauchiehall Street to the Elgin Place Church.

After breakfast she played us the piano, and my brother Bob and I looked forward to these sessions. Chopin, Mendelssohn and Gilbert and Sullivan were her favourites, and Selections from Merrie England. As we got older it was she who took us regularly to concerts at the St Andrews Halls, and encouraged my love of music. She was beautiful and talented and had been a pianist before she married R. J. MacLennan, writer, journalist, comedy script writer of reviews and sketches, and subsequently Editor of the *Glasgow Evening News*. He died young, while my father was still at school. Granny Mac was brilliant.

Sometimes we visited my other grandparents on Sundays, in Balmoral Place, Stirling, beside the Kings Park. Grandpa Tom Adam was a small, erect, stern-looking figure who had 'been in the Boer war' (medical corps) and had an impressive white moustache and not a hair on his shining head. My mother once told me he shaved it because he didn't like the curls. His family, farming people, were not well-off – his uncle was a dry-stane dyker in Dunipace.

Tom left school and worked as a teacher to allow the rest of his family to complete their education. He then was supported by his wife, Margaret, while he himself qualified in medicine at Glasgow and then worked in public health, rising to become the Medical Officer of Health for Stirlingshire. He passed on to his eldest daughter – my mother, Isobel – a lifelong passion for social justice and preventative medicine.

Granny Adam had thin bone china and kept things very polished, mats on polished floors. She gave us milk in a fine pink glass. Grandpa Adam ate his porridge with precision, moving the plate round, bite by bite, to make a perfect, ever-diminishing island in the milk. I watched, mesmerised. I read most of Walter Scott from their glass-fronted bookcase behind the sofa. He took cold baths, and had heard Mr Gladstone speak. He was a Liberal. In his much-loved garden he softened, and gave us tiny tomatoes to eat from the greenhouse and chives that edged the path to nibble. He played rounds of golf regularly until he was in his eighties.

* * *

I started travelling as a baby, the day before war was declared, when people thought anything might happen, and children were bundled off to the country for safety.

My father took my brother, myself and a young children's nurse, Bet Erskine, to a tiny village in Inverness-shire, Whitebridge, to remain there for the first six months of the war. We had stayed there the previous summer in a cottage. There is a picture of me sleeping in a drawer.

My parents remained working in Glasgow where I was born and grew up, but they came to see us when they could get away. They were both doctors; he was a gynaecologist, and my mother worked in public health. They met at Glasgow University where they were students together, she had pigtails down her back, being not quite seventeen. They were engaged for seven years, during which time my father became President of the Union, and took part in student strike-breaking (during the General Strike) and my mother, for a brief period, joined the Conservative Party.

Then they did their 'house' jobs in London and Glasgow – he was a house surgeon at the Chelsea Hospital for Women, and she worked at the Children's Fever Hospital in Willesden. She said she spent all her spare time going to the theatre. But they both gained their formative clinical experience at home in the Glasgow of the 1930s, and as a direct result of this experience my mother became a socialist.

I think I inherited a commitment to working to change things, to questioning the status quo, and to fighting for what I believe in from both my parents. For although my father remained, by today's standards, a very mild Tory all his life, he would have been appalled by the present dismemberment of the health service. I was too young to remember the details of its being set up, but I remember well the passion with which they both defended it.

And they knew what they were talking about. My father's research was into contracted pelvis, a form of rickets which was widespread in Glasgow at the time, and produced among the highest maternal and infant mortality rates in Europe. He had delivered hundreds of babies by candlelight in tenements with a stair-head lavatory, and my mother had treated unvaccinated children with polio, diphtheria, TB – the killer diseases they struggled to eradicate before free milk, innoculation and decent housing were made priorities by the post-war Labour government.

My father's research had some influence on the Beveridge Report. It also had some effect on the recognition of the need for free milk for expectant mothers, vitamin supplements in their diets, the proper training of midwives, and the provision of proper pre-natal and ante-natal care in the post-war period. Most of the work of that generation – including the work of my mother and her contemporaries in preventative medicine – is now in danger of being swept away, and the effects will take several generations to recover from.

My first home was a tenement flat in Hillhead at 15, Sutherland Street. Now that street has been demolished.

When I was one we moved to Dowanhill Street where I grew up. While we were in Whitebridge my father had a shelter constructed in our basement. It occupied half of what had been a billiard room, and was supported by railway sleepers. As we slept at the top of the house I can remember sirens wailing, and being carried downstairs half asleep, clutching my gas mask with Mickey Mouse face, and a pillow. There were four beds and a cot down there, three battery hens in a sort of hutch, vats full of pickled eggs, and a cupboard with pots and pots of jam. There was also a large game of skittles and a pile of suitcases. Before we went downstairs my parents would fill the bath with water.

On one occasion after the siren had gone my mother went to the door to see if my father was come back from the hospital, and saw what looked like two Canadian servicemen leaning against our gable end to shelter from the rain – and the raid. 'Come in out of the wet,' she said, and from their position lined up along the gable came what seemed to us about twenty soldiers as they trooped down to our basement; we bounced out of bed while they played skittles and terrified the hens.

By the time I could walk there were definitely Germans in the cistern in the

23

bathroom. I had to sit on the toilet with the door open, so that I could jump up, pull the plug and run-like-mad before they leapt out and got me. My brother collected bits of shrapnel and we picked holes in the sticky stuff they had put on all the windows.

When we were bigger we played in the back lane or the wasteground beside our house. My big friend Ann Cochrane walked on the wall where the railings had been taken away for the war effort and a huge red sandstone block fell on her foot and you could see the bone. A bomb fell in their street. On the night of the Clydebank blitz, we could see the sky at the end of our street red with flames.

We left the very next morning for our next period of evacuation, this time to a house between Edzell and Brechin where we stayed for a year with another family with three children. My recollections of this period are unhappy. I missed my home. I think I was jealous of the youngest children; they played under a table in the nursery, and I remember feeling excluded.

The next adventure was much more exotic, and I remember it vividly. For about six or eight weeks we were the guests of the Noble family at Ardkinglas on Loch Fyne side near the village of Cairndhu in Argyll. It was a Fairytale Castle. In each wing lived a branch of the family, and there were some more evacuee children living on the estate. There were several complete worlds living side by side.

In the big house, where we stayed, they had a governess, and I had some lessons from her with the rest of the children. There was a wonderful tall aunt called Daisy, who looked a bit like Vita Sackville-West, had large hats and wispy, grey hair, and was generally carrying a trug with spinach or daffodils in it. She maintained a large walled garden, which no doubt kept us all healthy, and did a lot of cooking for what must have been a big establishment, no doubt very under-staffed by the pre-war standards of that class. I know the whole family washed up after dinner.

We had lunch all together in the huge dining room at a long table looking out over the garden – there must have been about eighteen adults and children of all ages. There were a number of family portraits on the walls; I remember sitting at the table opposite a fabulous creature called Anastasia who bred deer-hounds, and worked around the estate. Her cheeks and hands were red and raw, she wore dungarees and ate piles of tatties. Immediately behind her place at the table was a formal portrait of her, painted on the occasion of her being presented at court, in a silky white evening dress, with gloves, translucent complexion, and ostrich feathers in her hair. I was fascinated by the contrast. Years later I was introduced to her cousin at a party, when we were at Oxford. Yes, we've met. I remember you threw a jellyfish at me on the shore at Loch Fyne. You must have been about four.

The children divided into groups of age, although class might have come into it. The superior – or at any rate *older* – children had a club, which they called the BIG BEEFIES, and used to pass secret messages and make raids on us 'wee ones' from their Headquarters which were the dovecot. I was considered too young to join them, so I promptly retaliated – I think my first recruit was called Clive, who was about three or four – by starting the WEE BEEFIES; we had our own secrets that were bigger and far Better. On one memorable occasion, which we after celebrated in rhyme, we raided the opposition's fortress, pulling up the gardener's ladder which had given us access. We fired stones through the pigeon holes with fearful taunts, and then had to be rescued by one of our number when the ladder fell down; we thought we would have starved to death if they hadn't come along. Overall, apart from the narrow escape, it was a triumph.

Meanwhile I suppose the parents were getting on with their own war efforts. . . .

By four I was well settled in Glasgow and going to 'wee' school at Miss Dick's. She sat us at a round table, we did the basics, recited tables, and used an abacus. She asked my mother to do something about my Glasgow accent, which was odd because that was where we lived. We listened to 'Children's Hour' on the wireless. My brother and I used to imitate the high-pitched BBC English of the announcer and laugh – 'We present "Bellay Shooooz" from the novel by Nail STRITFIELD.' But I loved the books, even if they did talk like that.

Later on during the war my mother started the Blood Transfusion Service in Scotland, and travelled all over the country, sometimes taking us with her, which I enjoyed. The best trips were in the ambulance, with crates of empty blood bottles clanking. Quite often we got to stay in a hotel, the Cairndale in Dumfries, where they had stiff white table napkins and great big silver cutlery, in rows, and I loved the head waitress, Marie. She gave us cushions to sit on in the big dining room, and pudding with a blob of artificial cream on the top. Myrtle Girotti, the manager and our friend, had a box full of beads and necklaces that she let me dress up in; she and my mother smoked Gold Flake and when I was bigger Joe, her husband, taught me how to sail on the Solway Firth. But at this time Joe was away fighting in North Africa, getting an MC and a wounded leg, while Myrtle ran the hotel.

At six I went to Laurel Bank School (for Girls) and for a time shared a desk with Ann Biles, who later also turned into an actress and became Ann Kirsten. We learnt French and Bible and Elocution, and Maths (which I didn't like) and Latin and History (which I did), and we had our heads inspected, and learned skipping rhymes and got gravelly knees. In winter we were kept off school when it was too foggy to see across the road. Fog was very common in Glasgow then and there were no lollipop men and women to see you across. We would set off with scarves over the nose – smelling the coal-dust – and the nuns flapping up our street from Partick would loom up out of the darkness and disappear up the hill to Notre Dame. You could hear the hooters on the river at teatime and memorably at New Year, and the trams clanking past the end of our street all through the day.

I played a lot with my cousins. You could 'dreep' into Ashton Lane from their garden, and there were coal carts pulled by horses there, and not a single trendy restaurant. I went to Saturday morning pictures at the Grosvenor Cinema and collected a signed photo of Roy Rogers and Trigger. I wanted red hair like Greer Garson in *Little Women*, and read all the Anne of Green Gables books. I went to the baths, to the ice rink, to ballet class, was a bridesmaid twice and had to go to bed with my hair in pipe cleaners in order to be curly for it.

We performed plays on the landing, with our audience sitting patiently on the stairs. Entrances from three bedrooms, the bathroom (with Germans in the cistern) and one walk-in cupboard where my mother kept Everything. I got a bit fed up having to play the minister in an old brown tweed skirt of my mother's when my cousin Deirdre got 'married' (by me) to my brother (which she seemed to think was a great idea at the time) and then having to rush round the happy couple to be the bridesmaid as well – still in the old brown skirt, there being no time to change. While she, of course, was decked in the finest net curtain carrying flowers. Not that I wanted to get married or anything boring like that; oh no, I was going to be a concert pianist, at least, or at any rate a doctor like my mum.

As for plays, I preferred more adventurous scenarios altogether, preferably with *me* as the Scarlet Pimpernel, and *them* in tumbrils, doomed to die, or as Grace Darling, frantically rowing across the stormy seas of the landing in a cardboard box to the flickering torchlight of the waiting shipwreck. Just a minute, I'm coming, hold on tight. (This gleaned from a book I had, called *Stories of Great Women*.)

Sometimes we would go with my father on his evening rounds, visiting patients. We enjoyed the hurl, petrol still being scarce for trips. I remember sitting in the dark car outside listening to 'Dick Barton, Special Agent' on the car radio. It was scarier in the dark. Years later I did a play by John Hopkins in which Noël Johnston played my father and I told him this. He laughed. It took a little while to get used to our new relationship, without Jock and Snowy, the other heroes of that series.

But my introduction to the world of showbusiness, as for so many people in Glasgow, was the Carnival at the Kelvin Hall, the circus, and – most important – the pantomime.

My first pantomime starred Harry Gordon, a famous Aberdonian comic, and Will Fyfe, who were a great comedy duo. My grandfather had in fact written material for both of them and for another lesser-known comic called Willie McCulloch, but I didn't find that out till much later. This was also my first experience of that great Glasgow institution, the Alhambra Theatre. Later on I enjoyed the 'Five Past Eight' shows, starring Jack Radcliffe and Jimmy Logan and sometimes Stanley Baxter. When I was seventeen Jimmy Logan moved nextdoor and first-footed us. We became good friends. He was devoted to my dad and vice-versa.

That was the kind of theatre where I immediately felt at home; it was often spectacular but always vernacular. The humour was recognisable, it was happening all around anyway. There was always music, usually sentimental – my father usually cried at these bits – you felt it was all happening for your benefit, like a birthday party for the whole audience. You could join in, laugh out loud – it was popular theatre. I found the love songs a bit stilted, but the rest was for me.

The other unforgettable experience I owe to my mother. I must have been about seven at the time. She kept me up late to go to the Kings Theatre to see an extraordinary American actress called Ruth Draper; she was what they used to call a Diseuse. She worked on her own, with no set and practically no costumes. She just took us by the hand and told us stories, and we were spellbound. The particular story I remember was of the liberation of France as witnessed from a field in Northern France by a French peasant woman, seeing the British planes start to come over. Ruth Draper did not cry – she told the story. *We* all cried.

Some years later I saw my first West End play which starred Mai Zetterling and Dick Bogarde and a lot of other people with orange faces. I thought he was very lovely and sexy, but it was by Anouilh and they all seemed to be suffering a lot, and there were lots of nuances, and they wore very expensive clothes. There were many curtain calls at the end, with the leading lady and the leading man gazing at each other as though they couldn't bear to part, and they bowed very, very low, to the audience, and I realised we were onto something quite different. It's a far cry from Castlemilk Community Centre or Kinlochbervie Village Hall – or indeed as I later discovered, a few light years from Joan Littlewood's company at Stratford East, whom I saw doing *The Hostage* at the Theatre Royal, where I felt instantly at home.

But at this point, apart from going to weepy films and shows, I was enjoying school and practising the piano a great deal, inspired by David Mackie, pupil of Tobbias Matthay, stickler for forearm rotation and Mozart. His lessons were a high point in my week. Later on I enjoyed playing duets – with a fair degree of competition – with my father's colleague and friend, Ian Donald, the pioneer of ultrasound in pregnancy. He was a frequent guest at our house and we shared a passion for music, especially for Bach which he played with great abandon and not a few bum notes, as I was fond of pointing out. 'All right then, show me,' he would cry and then pounce on me for my part, and the session would disintegrate in hilarity. He was a wonderful man and a great influence.

Perhaps equally influential – but in a quite different way – was my father's best friend, Hector McNeil, Labour MP for Greenock, with whom all the issues of the post-war political scene were argued out in our house, my father usually, but not by any means always, taking the opposite side. Hector certainly had a big effect on my brother Bob, whose grasp of international politics from an early age was formidable. Being a little bit younger – how important that seems when you are small – I was less informed; I remember Hector discussing the implications of the Jan Masaryk 'suicide' with my mother and being shocked by the realisation that these things went on.

On one occasion I attended a launch in his constituency. His wife, my Auntie Sheila, was performing what must be one of the most exciting pieces of theatre imaginable – that huge yard, total silence, terror, will something go wrong; then, smash, the bottle breaks, the cheers, the banging, the whole yard erupts with noise and whooping as the great hull gathers speed down the slipway and slowly turns into the river. I thought it was wonderful.

By this time my Aunt Lizzie was dead, but we still went up to Rogart on holidays, often with our cousins. I learnt to fish for trout with my dad, and to worm the rock pool with my mother, who was a dab hand at it, and to collect wild rasps, and chanterelles, and seashells. She taught me the names of the wild flowers which abound in East Sutherland and about the history of my Highland forebears, and about the clearances, and the diaspora of which the MacLennans had been a part – from Ullapool to Aberdeen, and then with my grandfather to Glasgow, although members of his family also went to Australia and South Africa; a familiar pattern.

By this time, two younger brothers had arrived. Kenneth, known at this stage as 'Libby's shadow' because he followed me everywhere, and David, the baby. I adored them both, and spent all my spare time 'looking after them' and thinking up diversions. . . .

From that time on, small children have played a very important part in my life, and coloured most of my decisions.

For better or for worse, I joined the older generation – in my head – at about eleven, with a strong sense of responsibility for my parents, the 'wee boys', my family and friends and, increasingly, for the world around me and its future.

When I was eleven, my mother took my brother and me on a trip to France and Italy and I became aware of Europe as something we were part of. We stayed in London with our friends the McNeils, and went with them to galleries and to the House of Commons. My twelve-year-old diary records:

> London is magnificent. Lovely snug theatres. The people are gay and lively. I noticed markedly the difference between middle-aged women. They are so much more smart and sprightly than in Glasgow.
> New Year resolutions: Leave a happy atmosphere in the house. Work hard, play hard (piano).
> Wishes: to be in a film. Get scholarship.

And, on my thirteenth birthday, I did – win a scholarship – to an expensive girls' boarding school in the south-east of England. There follows a memo on 18 March 'not to get swanky . . .'

Although I had been to France and Italy, this was far more of a cultural shock. Sheila McNeil took me to the station which was on the other side of London from where they lived. I had worked my way through *Mallory Towers* and the *Chalet Girls*, but this was for real: an indescribable feeling of doom with no escape. What could I have been thinking of? Sheila waited until I had made my first contact on the platform, a name, a 'house', a friendly smile, and then turned to go, smiling encouragement. See you at Christmas.

It was quite clear to me as I stood there that I had grown up. I was thirteen and a half.

I discovered on the train that I would make friends, but that they were very, very different from me, and that they would have a quite different frame of reference. People tended to be called Leonora, Camilla, Georgina, Phyllida . . . they tended to have brothers at Marlborough and to be confirmed in the Church of England (I declined). Some of the older ones had been to 'coming out' dances in the holidays. In the school mock elections the socialists were wiped out.

There was only one other Scots girl there when I arrived, and she was the daughter of a large landowner in Inverness-shire. People found my accent strange. I told some of them I had been adopted as a Polish refugee.

In the bleak second winter term, my Granny Mac died, and it must have been 'decided' that I should not go home for the funeral. I was miserable. My new piano teacher reminded me of her, physically, which added to the misery but was impossible to explain. The quite remarkable woman who was my house mistress tried very hard. She was a dedicated pastoral type of Christian, and we became very fond of each other. Strangely enough, she wanted me to become a diplomat, which would surprise one or two people. Soon after that Hector

McNeil died suddenly in New York and that very particular loss and sadness meant nothing to those around me; how could it? I could not communicate it. I thought of his Glasgow streets – none of these girls had ever even seen a shawlie.

Of course I made friends, and had my triumphs and disasters. I acted Caliban in the Junior School play – and Bottom. I directed. And sang in *HMS Pinafore*. And in the choir. My closest friend and confidant wanted to go to Cambridge and read English, but above all she wanted to go home and have privacy.

I thought I would try for Oxford or Cambridge myself. Why not?

My preference was for Oxford where I already had a 'boyfriend', and where my brother Bob was set on going. The boyfriend was at Balliol and a historian too, and wrote to me regularly which was the acid test at boarding school of any relationship. One term in February when it had snowed heavily and he hadn't written for all of TWO WEEKS, I send him a *worm* in a parcel, saying, 'This is what I think of you!' and then 'felt apprehensive'. But he replied by return of post and came to take me out at the weekend, and things were lovely. I read *The Dolls House* that week and wrote two essays – one on Lorenzo di Medici and the other on the Crusading Psychology. . . .

And in the summer we went to an Oxford Ball. . . .

I was taught history at school by D. C. Somervell, a brilliant teacher who had taught at Harrow and looked like an old, shambling tortoise. His approval meant a lot to me. He thought Oxford would suit me and that I would survive it, and should have a go. His own work included a two-volume abridged edition of Toynbee's immense *History of the World*. Clearly after such an exercise it was no great problem to teach fourteen-year-olds how to fillet their set books with precision, and how to come to the point. I am eternally grateful for the help he gave me with the first skill, if not the second, specifically in subsequent 7:84 research. My Latin teacher was also inspiring and, as a result, I enjoyed reading Catullus and even Tacitus, and retained a facility in Latin which – apart from a genuine interest – inclined me later to medieval history as my preferred subject when I was at Oxford.

But already I had decided to go into the theatre – to direct, I told myself. At school I usually played the boys' parts becayse I was tall and ostensibly sure of myself. I wanted to be slim and floaty but school dinners put paid to that. Sometimes I signed my letters to my brother 'Ellen' (Terry). He played Hamlet when he was in the sixth form, at school in Glasgow.

When I got into St Hilda's College, Oxford, I joined the ETC (Experimental Theatre Club) in the first week, acted Isabella in *The Changeling* in my first term, and went on from there, acting at every opportunity, with or without permission, to the irritation of my tutor Beryl Smalley, who had better plans for me, alas, than Regan in *King Lear* and Oxford Theatre Group Reviews.

I enjoyed Oxford, the place, the extraordinary mixture of people, Duke Humphrey's library, the chance to do anything and everything (except have men in your room at certain hours, which was quite a relief). I became happily irresponsible, and enjoyed myself, falling in and out of love, and friendships. For me it was a time of excitement and confidence; Christopher Hill's work influenced me very much, as did some of my tutors, but it was the undergraduates I met who made the lasting impact – Angus Walker, Paul Noyes, Antony Page,

Dudley Moore, Judith and Eddy Mirzeoff. At the beginning of my third and last year I met John McGrath and after auditioning he asked me to play Molly Bloom in his production of James Joyce's *Ulysses*, called *Bloomsday*, at the Oxford Playhouse.

Some time last year Eddie Mirzeoff's researcher rang and asked me if I would consider being in one of Eddie's 'Forty Minutes' programmes which was going to be about 'love at first sight'. 'But we had our eyes shut,' I protested. In fact, John and I met at an improvisation class held by an American, Stephen Aaron. The exercise involved blindness, sensitivity, and communication.

That summer, 1959, Collette King directed me in John's play, *Why The Chicken* at the Edinburgh Festival. It was the first part he wrote for me. The play was very well received, particularly by Harold Hobson (who had a bit of a soft spot for me) and Kenneth Tynan who had already marked John out in a big way from an earlier play, *A Man Has Two Fathers*, written while he was still a student.

In the improvisation exercise we did have our eyes shut. We seemed to communicate however.

Rehearsing as Molly Bloom in *Bloomsday* by James Joyce for the Experimental Theatre Club, Oxford, in 1958. *Left to right*: John McGrath, Michael Simpson, Elizabeth MacLennan.

Five: Beginning to Tour. 1971-1972

Following our run of *Trees in the Wind* in Edinburgh, some students and others came and asked us would we take the play to their theatres. . . .We decided to try to tour. With sympathy and encouragement from Sue Timothy, the Small Scale Touring Officer at the London Arts Council, we even got a little subsidy for the tour: four hundred pounds for two weeks' rehearsal and six weeks' touring. John brought a transit van with the money he had saved from writing a spy thriller for Ken Russell – *Billion Dollar Brain*.

At first there was no geographical logic to our touring. We would hurtle from Lancaster to Devon, to Aberdeen, to Cardiff, wherever they would take us, glad of the bookings, regardless of the mileage and hazards of getting set up in time, let alone a break before the show.

We developed a fast-learning group awareness, which was maintained by a non-hierarchical company structure, regardless of relative age and experience, and by equal pay. Some actors found it a strain, and others, like Selina Lucas from the Liverpool Everyman, formed strong, mutually supportive friendships as she did with Christine Hargreaves, who replaced Gilly. If *shared*, the stresses and strains of touring are far less. In this respect, of course, John and I were lucky; and David and Feri, although it sometimes caused resentment (oh it's all right for you two), and perhaps later feelings of exclusivity.

The majority of 'successful' performers sooner rather than later become reluctant to tour, particularly if they have children. Folk musicians are notable exceptions. The delights of the open road soon begin to pall – damp B and Bs with pink nylon sheets, Alsatians roaming the corridors, cold fried eggs and marble-eyed landladies, mouth-bending coffee, smoke-filled vans, breaking down, the search for cots, washing shirts at two in the morning, company meetings, greasy chips, pies and chips, pies and beans and chips, more company meetings.

I met the actor Stephen Rea at a concert the other day; he toured with us in the company's second year of life in Gavin Richards' revolutionary production of *Ballygombeen Bequest* and in John's adaptation of *Sergeant Musgrave's Dance*. This was set in a Yorkshire village during the Miners' Strike of '72 with Musgrave and his men returning from Derry to have their revenge. It was a killer of a tour, with two superb productions, but they were on the road from August till December. Stephen told me he enjoys touring in the west of Ireland now, once a year, with Field Day. 'It's not like touring to Rotherham,' he said. I knew what he meant.*

In this way the 'working-class audience' was to become less of an abstract and more a lived reality.

It became hard to explain this to a number of other companies in England

---

* Since then, interestingly, some of the English company has developed a totally different relationship with Rotherham. In 1981 they lived there for a while on the Canklow estate and researched and developed a play about young people and unemployment; parts of Rotherham had some of the highest unemployment figures in the country (sixty-seven per cent). I expect the actors still felt much the same about the diet and being away from home, but differently about the people they met and got to know as a community. And to some extent this is what made the difference on later tours; the sense of an extended dialogue or conversation with people you have got to know. There is mutual respect and pleasure in meeting up again.

who were still struggling to FIND this audience, and nowadays, strangely, people like David Edgar are prone to declare that we all failed in this respect. This is nonsense in my actual experience. At the time I am talking about David was a great believer in reaching working-class audiences and was working on a play in Bradford with the General Will company about the history of the Industrial Relations Bill.

Trees in the Wind was the first show we ever took to Aberdeen, and to Stirling University (thanks to Annie Inglis and to Anthony Phillips, who took the risk when few others dared). We went memorably to Cumbernauld New Town, to the Cottage Theatre. It had snowed heavily for two days all over the north and Scotland, and we had to drive from Liverpool, where we subsequently played a great many shows. Because of the terrible conditions, Selina and I only arrived there about five minutes before the show was due to start. The van had arrived about half an hour before with David, Michael and Victor, and Christine Hargreaves. They were frantically setting up. Finding your way anywhere in Cumbernauld New Town for the first time is not easy, and in a Siberian white-out with visions of an irate audience waiting . . . We needn't have worried.

The show normally took place on three stages. Here there could only be one, and a tiny one at that. We had to somehow squash everything somewhere, mostly reversed, which led to some highly comical sudden changes of direction in mid-exit. Dave was set to wing the lights, there being no time to go through the cues. We stumbled into our costumes with frozen fingers, gulping mugfuls of soup. We went on, the audience intrigued and delighted.

A long and friendly dialogue began, with that most warm-hearted of audiences, and individually with the Laurie family, with whom we were accommodated (impossible otherwise), consuming drams till the wee hours, and meeting some of the Cumbernauld folk who have returned again and again to 7:84 shows, and their children, who now have a flourishing and committed new theatre of their own. This was to become the pattern in so many places.

* * *

This is how we came to meet so many communities all over what is known as the Central Belt – what a way to describe the extraordinary diversity of this part of Scotland: East Kilbride, at that time, a place of high employment and union strength and green fields, where we regularly played the Murray Halls, Dumbarton and the Vale of Leven (where we made our first community show in 1974, the company living there all summer and coming up with a show by David and John Bett done in the style of a Victorian music hall, called *Capital Follies*); Stirling with its proud history, not only of Robert the Bruce. Here the students threw eggs at Elizabeth (the First of Scotland) the week before we came, and were 'disciplined'; Stewarton in Ayrshire, staunchly Labour *and* Unionist, where they paid for us happily to come twice a year and packed out; New Lanark, Robert Owen's dream come true, but sadly almost deserted now.

We made our first trades union and trades council contacts on this tour, and then with *Plugged into History* and *Underneath* two years before the Scottish company was invented.

The character McChuckemup, (who re-appeared in *The Cheviot*) appeared first in *Trees in the Wind* to terrorise the social worker Belle and to drive his wife mad in 'The Song of Driving Mad'.

John Bett
encourages the
audience in
Capital Follies,
written by John
Bett and David
MacLennan,
a 7:84 Scotland
community
show in
Dumbarton
in 1975.

'Capitalism is a lot better on the subconscious than Marxism is. What combination of ideas, circumstances and vision might liberate people from the cells inherent in both ideologies? That awareness gained in the theatre would be part of a much bigger dramatic arena. He (McGrath) quotes as illustrative of this process what happened in France in May '68, while pointing to the dangers of the CP/Gaullist repressive deal which followed.'

Bob Tait, writing in *Scottish International*, October 1971

Quite a few years later the English company revived 'Trees' with some fine actors, but I felt it suffered from an attempt to steer it into a more naturalistic mode, when it was never a naturalistic play.

'Naturalism is part of the middle-class theatre's armoury of suppression because naturalistic theatre *contains* arguments. It is very easy for a strong argument – because it is put into the mouth of one character – to be seen as that character's point of view, and nullified by a checks and balances arrangement in the same way that any strong argument in British politics is always nullified by the checks and balances of the system of government. The impetus behind these things is towards greater freedom. And more exactness in what I am trying to say.'

John McGrath in *Scottish International*, October 1971

Plugged into History, 1972

The next step for 7:84 was directly related to the work John was doing simultaneously at the Liverpool Everyman.

He wrote:

'Six short plays I wrote for the Everyman earlier this year contained the possibility of strong and united statements from the stage that are not mediated through the characters, and through the paraphernalia of mediation the audience carries around with it. What finally trickles through is pretty minimal. I've tried to fight against it by using more heightened language than is usual.'

Four of these plays were performed by 7:84 the next spring in Cardiff, Oxford, Manchester, Rochdale, Sheffield and Aberdeen, for between forty and sixty-five pounds per performance, ending in the new Bush Theatre in Shepherds Bush, London. This largely theatre-based tour confirmed our critical status, our eligibility for grant aid, and most important, our desire to carry on as a group.

The plays were titled *Plugged into History*, and included *Angel of the Morning*, about a Liverpool Dad who gets terrorised by a seventeen-year-old girl who is a member of the 'Fazackerley Tupermaros'; *They're Knocking Down the Pie Shop*, about the cruelties of 'progress' in Liverpool; *Hover Through the Fog*, about the complex conscience of the academic called in as independent arbitrator in an industrial dispute; and *Plugged into History*, about the stress involved in responding to world events.

Here is the introduction to *Plugged in*. A Park Keeper talks to the audience:

Oh. Oh. Oh. Fie on dem. Fie. Da ungsters bin dingrateful, lacksed. Bud I godda shock for ya. Am gonna stunnya. Een in a suplex pent-up houses, high, scraping da sky, een in da man-shuns, een in da man-gin erectors bell-ordered homes, der bin un-ruly elemens. Der bin utters, utter been in da nut-ouses, der been Sigh-Gothics, an you-rotics, an Care-a-noids, an, wuss of da lot, der been sky-so-free nicks. Da sky-so-free-nicks been dingrateful, lacka ungsters, – dey been wuss, agos da man-gin erectors an da duplex men and da-shock-exchangers been noddle has-bands, tieing dem up, givum da doe, bash on demand, bash on delivery, and is da dingrateful spouses da been sky-so-free-nik: whoffor? Ah doan no whoffor. Dey muss be utters, daffy and palmy, whyves of da big men, da pig-men da runna cuntry.

Wassamarrawidum?

Da pig-men made-a da piles a doe. Dey buyum up da manshuns, dey buyum da car-pets, dey buyum da boos, dey buyum da fur-knickers, dey buyum da wooms, ta me-and-her about in: Wha' more good a gurl ars efor? An do dey play ball? Do dey luv up da fella, keep da home cuddly an sty for da pig-man? Ook up a din-dins, scoff for da trough, huggim and fuggim an drop a few piglets? Doe doe doe. Ear me doe. Wha' do dey do? Dey go sky-so-free-nik. I ony go' one ques-chun: (SHOUTS) Whadafugginellsda-marrawidum?

I played a schizophrenic woman who is inhabited by the world's disasters. During the tour, we did a live performance of it in a public park in Cardiff, or at least a large chunk of it. The woman is talking aloud, really to herself, and a

34

young man who has had a row with his girlfriend comes and sits beside her, at first intrigued, then sympathetic, then exasperated. Almost the same thing happened when I sat down; a curious passer-by who was trying to pretend he was not really listening came and sat down and listened for a bit, but when the other actor arrived, he moved off, not wanting to intrude or get into too deep waters. There was a lot of work going on at this time examining received notions of 'madness', 'normality', homosexuality, and of course women's roles.

We were joined for this tour by Gavin Richards and Roger Sloman. It was Vari Sylvester's first of many tours with the company and Tony Haygarth was memorable as the Liverpool Dad.

This tour brought another new departure: we played in a factory in Scotland Street, Glasgow, for the workforce who were occupying it. This was the first of many factory occupations we took our shows to, in Scotland and the north of England.

This first special performance was much appreciated. We were invited to perform again on May Day in the Caley Cinema in Edinburgh, by the Edinburgh Trades Council – the first of many such appearances on May Days throughout the country. The plays were very funny, and they dealt with situations which people felt were vital. We continued to gain support and friends in the Labour movement.

Beginning to use music – *Underneath. The Ballygombeen Bequest*

The third tour, starting in April 1972, took us again to Scotland (and to the ill-fated Clyde Fair), and included *Underneath*, by McGrath, and Trevor Griffiths' play *Occupations*. The two plays, and the company presenting them, covered six thousand miles.

Occupations had been performed at the Stables Theatre in Manchester and again in London under the wing of the RSC but Trevor felt it needed a wider audience. We certainly gave it that. John suggested Roland Rees (later of Foco Novo, abolished by the Arts Council in 1988) as director, and he was enthusiastic about both the play and reaching that audience. Gavin Richards played Gramsci in that production. The questions raised by the play were very topical at that time when factory occupations were happening all over the country. Hamish Henderson had recently published his translation of the Gramsci letters in the *New Edinburgh Review*, and the importance of Gramsci's thinking was at last being recognised in Britain.

Underneath was about two families; the family of a successful architect and bridge builder, specifically one who made box-girder bridges such as the one which had recently collapsed at Milford Haven. Gavin played the architect, a benevolent, philanthropic despot. I played his put-upon wife, the slightly batty Lady Merriman who 'had a perfectly normal upbringing'. Tony Haygarth played their slightly ludicrous but ultimately sympathetic drop-out son who befriends the OTHER family, the Smeddles, whose dad actually WORKS on the bridge, and whose mum – Gilly Hanna – puts up with him and a lot else besides.

It was the first 7:84 show in which we used live music, and with very few exceptions we have continued to do so ever since. 'Come on,' John exhorted us, 'you can do it,' as he charged into the nearest music shop in Brighton and started buying instruments, amps, mikes and speakers. Gavin was surprisingly resistant to this, but others were intrigued. John wrote some songs for the show with Norman Smeddles, with whom he had worked in Liverpool. As musical director we had the benefit of Tony Haynes, who put up with us for quite a few tours and musical developments, until he went off to found Red Brass. The play has some beautiful songs and was very interesting in form.

This breakthrough was accomplished by an exhausted bunch of people, most of whom – fortunately not me – were also playing *Occupations* in the evening, on tour. We rehearsed during the day in Brighton for a week, then travelled to Liverpool, opened *Occupations* there, completed our rehearsals during the rest of that week, and opened the week after, still in Liverpool.

I had both the children with me during all this – happily we were able to stay with John's parents during the Liverpool bit. Danny, then four, developed scarlatina and we had to leave him with his grandparents while we went on to open in Sheffield. We drove back over the Pennines to Wallasey, where they then lived, every night after the show to see him and Finn.

I decided not to be in our next production, the Ardens' highly influential and stylistically innovative play, *The Ballygombeen Bequest*, in order to be more with the children, but I worked on the publicity. It was a sensation at the Edinburgh Festival.

A review from *Plays and Players*, November 1972, by Michael Anderson, gives some idea of the general level of support for the company's work at this time:

'It's no coincidence, I think, that the 7:84 Theatre Company is one of the few to combine political commitment with artistic excellence. Led by John McGrath, it has been concerned with politics at the level of human experience, not in the empty phrases of propaganda.

In mounting *The Ballygombeen Bequest*, by John Arden and Margaretta D'Arcy, the 7:84 company has launched a stunning political drama as good as the best of Arden and equal to most of Brecht. The exploitation of a family of Irish tenants over the post-war years serves as a reflecting mirror in which the ancient grievances of England's first and last colony are caught with glittering accuracy and a deep historical sense. The Ardens use the theatre like a chess-board: all the moves are simple, but the strategy behind them reveals the mind of a grand master. Roger Sloman's clear-cut performance as the gruesome Hollidey–Cheype is an object lesson in acting that presents character in social and political, rather than psychological terms.

Arden is notorious for refusing to take an obvious line, and the role of Hagan, played with vicious menace by Gavin Richards, should convince anyone that the play is not a simple anti-British tract. It's this small-time moneygrubber who emerges as the representative of terror, using dynamite where the English would prefer diplomacy; in the brilliant pantomime of the final scene he and Hollidey-Cheype struggle over a horde of banknotes, old rivals bound together in depravity and greed.

The Ballygombeen Bequest is more than a play about Ireland; it conjures up a nightmare image of capitalism, friendless, tottering and ultimately without hope or help, that will linger in my mind for months.'

Throughout these first two years and frequently thereafter, the majority of our construction work was done by Nick Redgrave. A working-class Cornishman

7:84 The Ballygombeen

Theatre Company presents

Bequest

A play by **John Arden** and
Margaretta D'Arcy

'Present day absentee landlords, the IRA
the British army and various individual
hypocrites, both English and Irish, are
the targets of John Arden's new play
The Ballygombeen Bequest'
Belfast Telegraph

With acknowledgements to George Grosz

7 of the population of this country owns 84 % of the wealth

with art college background, Nick Redgrave became a stalwart member of the early 7:84. He'd worked at Nottingham and John had met him at the Liverpool Everyman. Nick was by this time working at the National Theatre as a prop-maker. He also built the set for *Occupations*.

'The back wall of the set was corrugated iron. We were going to cast it in fibreglass but we didn't have the money. It would have been easier to handle on tour. At that time we only had project grants off the Arts Council so we'd do a tour, then stop, everyone would have to sod off and start again. Liz, John and Gavin and Dave were the political power houses of the company.

I remember my overall impression of the time as being totally knackered. I was at a stage in my life where I enjoyed working all night. It's a lot to do with being associated with a very, very fine writer. John. And some of the best actors around. Against incredible odds getting these plays on.

John was, and is, 7:84 to that extent. He has made great strides in making people who are not used to sitting down and concentrating on things, concentrate. I class myself as one of those. He's not against enjoying things, far from it, but John does believe in structure.'

Nick remembers seeing the Ardens' *Ballygombeen Bequest* at the end of its tour at the Bush Theatre.

'The night I saw it there were a lot of Dublin and Kerrymen in there. The reaction that night I'll never forget. They were just crying and shouting. Incredible.'

This was the night before it was taken off in response to a threatened injunction after a thirteen-week tour. An English absentee landlord with whom the Ardens had been having a battle in the west of Ireland took out a case against the Ardens, and 7:84 for presenting their play.

Nick: 'They (John and Margaretta) paid with cash. We paid by being shat on by the Arts Council for the next year and a half.'

Six: Some Thoughts on the Arm's Length Principle and the Arts Council

Towards the end of the tour of *The Ballygombeen Bequest* in October 1972 Hugh Willatt, the Director of the Arts Council of Great Britain, received two very strongly worded letters of complaint about the content of the play and its criticisms of the conduct of the British army in Northern Ireland. One was from General Tuzo, the British Commander in Chief of the forces in Northern Ireland, asking, 'When there is so much work of beauty and real merit in need of help, is it in any way justifiable to devote public funds to a manifestation of this kind?' (He had not seen the play.)

The second, more explicit letter gave the complainant's account of the scene which had prompted his complaint. (He *had* seen it, in Plymouth.)

'About twelve minutes before the end of the second act, the hero, in a contrived situation, is stopped by a British army road block.

Here, in the longest and most explicit action of the play, two Scottish soldiers enter with a stream of abuse: "Stand still you f-in Irishman", "Out! you f-in Fenian", etc, etc, knee him in the crutch, fling him over the bonnet of his vehicle, search him, take down his trousers and pants; as far as we could see a medical officer injects him in the crutch. He is then flung face down, bare bottom upwards and a cane is put into his rectum, lights dim and he screams, each outstretched hand is then stamped on each time he screams. He is brought to the kneeling position, kneed in the face and a soldier sits on his shoulders. (When he says he has no gun and the soldiers find this is correct, one says, "We will soon f-n-g find one for the bastard before he gets to Derry.")

At this point I stood up, appalled by the sickening brutality, and remarked to the audience that I was surprised that they should sit and watch such nonsense. Several left the theatre with me.

I am told that this exhibition continued for another two minutes or so and climaxed with one of the soldiers urinating on the corpse, (I imagine with bulb and tube). Several young people left the theatre.

Can you explain to me how your Council can possibly justify such a thoroughly sick and evil display?

Can you explain to me why public money should be spent on an untalented company whose aim appeared to be the deliberate and dishonest undermining of our army?

Can you explain to me why no mention of this dreadful scene is made in the programme or the hand-out? Why the continued use of shouted four letter words should be tolerated?

Finally, if these Scottish soldiers had made the remarks they did to a coloured man on stage, then there would have been an immediate outcry over race relations.'

It is certainly true that both the Ardens in writing this play, and McGrath in his adaptation of *Serjeant Musgrave's Dance* with which it toured in tandem from August to December 1972, were highly critical of the British army's role in Ireland; after all, the events in Derry the previous summer had not brought international approbation.

What is particularly interesting in the present context is to speculate over the hypothetical response of today's ACGB, under the rule of Lord Mogg or indeed his successor, Peter Palumbo. The response THEN from Sir Hugh Willatt, Director of the ACGB at the time, bears quoting at length:

'I am sure you will understand that a question like this poses for the Council a very considerable dilemma. The essence of our system is that organisations promoting the arts – including, I suppose, the majority of promotions in this country, of which nine-tenths are of performances of the classics and work on traditional lines – are autonomous and independent. The system has elicited the independent effort of thousands of people, both promoting bodies and artists, throughout Great Britain, and this perhaps explains the widening of interest in the arts here in the past twenty-five years. The Arts Council, with other bodies and individuals, contributes subsidy. In this way we differ from the continental system of state and municipal theatres, opera houses and orchestras, and still more from the system in the totalitarian countries where the arts, heavily subsidised, are nevertheless rigidly controlled.

The result, very occasionally, in the limited area of experimental work by small companies, is sometimes shocking and repugnant to many of us. This is the price of freedom of expression and liberty for the artist, so important for our country and its artistic life; but denigration of our soldiers in the present situation raises special problems.

In the case of *The Ballygombeen Bequest*, our normal procedures were followed. They were given a small grant for a short tour, including Edinburgh during the Festival, and to a number of small theatres and halls in different parts of the country. They are one of a number of small companies of this sort which have in recent years done quite valuable experimental work. They were founded eighteen months ago by a playwright and director of some distinction and their first tour, operated to quite a high standard, did not lead to complaint. John Arden, who with his wife wrote *The Ballygombeen Bequest*, is considered to be one of our leading playwrights and has had plays performed by the National Theatre, the Royal Shakespeare Company, and at the Chichester Festival.

It was on these facts that the grant for the present tour was made, with a small additional grant under our scheme for the encouragement of new plays following a reading of the script by a section of our Drama Panel, including a number of important playwrights and critics. Some of them did not approve of the outlook of the play, but felt that it was a work of merit, unrealistic in style, somewhat reminiscent of Sean O'Casey. We received no complaints until the Bury St Edmunds performances.

I have written at length because I do wish to assure you that the questions you raise are being treated very seriously.'

Sir Hugh Willatt clearly believed in the arms length principle, and in fully consulting with his staff and officials, one of whom wrote him the following briefing memo on the subject:

'John Arden is a major dramatist of the post-war period. Most of his plays use their theme to develop a social or moral argument, several of them include scenes of violence, which in the past have been offensive to many people: for example, *Live Like Pigs*, *Serjeant Musgrave's Dance*, *The Workhouse Donkey*, *Armstrong's Last Goodnight*. However, his purpose is always sincere and whatever he does is never for a cheaply sensational effect. One might imagine that a play written by him today about Ireland (where he lives) would illustrate violently some of the violence that is occurring there hourly.

The scene complained of may be too explicit, but whether that was the author's intention or developed by the director, I do not know. It sounds as shocking as it was undoubtedly meant to be – but the real events as we see on television and read in the newspapers are much more horrifying.

From the earliest times, playwrights have illustrated violent aspects of their age in horrifying and theatrically shocking ways, from Sophocles, through Shakespeare to Edward Bond. Together with the abolition of the Lord Chamberlain's censorship and independence of it has come a loosening of restraints as to what might be said on the stage, television, films or in print. The scene described, the language used and the actions depicted are outspoken to an extent that is clearly obnoxious to some people, but not to others. I say this because the company has apparently received letters of praise from some people in Bury St Edmunds.

In considering grants to companies of this kind who work in an experimental way, the Arts Council takes into account the entire range of their work and reviews this annually. It is almost inevitable that certain plays, or parts of them, may not individually meet with the Council's approval, but they are looked at in relation to the whole work. The Arts Council has never acted as a censor.

Short of pre-censorship of a script and the director's handling of it, the Arts Council accepts that subsidy to artists who comment on current affairs

TONIGHT! 8:00,

7:84 THEATRE COMPANY

COMING SOON *ALNESS AVERON COMMUNITY CENTRE*

WITH

THE CHEVIOT, THE STAG AND THE BLACK BLACK OIL.

PLAY / CEILIDH / DANCE / FIDDLER /
GAELIC SONGS / GIANT POP–UP BOOK /
FORCE TEN GAELS / OIL RIGS / TWO VANS /
PIPER / ELECTRIC PIANO / PENNY WHISTLE /
THE LOCH SEAFORTH / GUITARS / DRUMS /
SHEEP / DEER ....

A ONCE IN A LIFETIME CHANCE TO SEE:–
THE WOMEN OF COIGACH REPEL THE BAILLIFS
THE INDIANS MEET THE MEN OF THE HIGHLANDS ON THE RED RIVER
QUEEN VICTORIA SING AT THE CEILIDH
THE RETURN OF TEXAS JIM TO HIS GRANNIES HIELAN' HAME

WATCH OUT FOR POSTERS AND NEWSPAPERS

7% OF THE POPULATION OF THIS COUNTRY OWN 84% OF THE WEALTH.

will inevitably, in a violent world, produce some work depicting violence in a savage way. We think it better that the freedom to express an opinion be allowed, and the public be enabled to judge for itself, than for sincerely held views to be censored.

Ultimately, the answer lies with the public not to support work which they do not like, because our subsidy is only part of company income and without steady public support in terms of box office receipts they could not continue.'

Nevertheless, as a result of this episode, John was carpeted at the Arts Council in its Piccadilly office and the company was put back on 'project' funding. This is a kind of artistic parole system whereby you have to submit and defend scripts and projected tours on a show-to-show basis, which makes it very difficult to retain a group or plan ahead. It was three years before the 7:84 Company were put on revenue grant status, and were able to plan the year's work that included *Lay Off, Yobbo Nowt* and *The Rat Trap* – probably the most productive and outstanding year of 7:84 England's life.*

Seven: Starting 7:84 Scotland. 1973

The Cheviot, the Stag and the Black Black Oil

The company had covered an impressive amount of ground in the first two years. Our critical and artistic standards and standing were high. The plays in which I had been specifically involved had all tackled the subject of sexism and female stereotyping – *Trees in the Wind* was a study of three modes of feminist practice; *Plugged into History* I have written about in this context. With it went the short play *Angel of the Morning* about an eighteen-year-old liberated leader of the Fazakerley Tupermaros whose father is into sexual repression. *Underneath* had dealt with male chauvinism to considerable effect, both in a working-class and in an upper-middle-class family. We had attempted to grasp these nettles and deal with them collectively within the group in rehearsals and in our organisation.

* It is interesting to compare this response of the Arts Council of Great Britain to what was indeniably very heavy pressure from high places, with their response twelve years later to recent controversies in England and in Scotland.

After the English company's notice of withdrawal of grant in 1984 there was direct criticism of the content of its work. The notice of withdrawal of grant was not withdrawn in spite of the company's audiences of thousands around the country, and at the Shaw Theatre in London where it was packed out, and the company's great critical successes with *Six Men of Dorset* and *The Garden of England*.

The Director of the Arts Council met with the artistic director – but only to refuse to discuss any rescue for the company, and to dismiss its appeal; he also made clear that even though two local authorities on Merseyside had offered to take the company in, the Arts Council would not consider even a donation; an application for subsequent project funding was turned down almost instantly, before any committee could have possibly looked at it, and the ACGB clearly felt no need to justify these departures. In a TV interview on 'Newsnight' immediately afterwards, Luke Rittner, Director of the Arts Council in 1984, said in defence of the cut, and all other cuts included in 'The Glory of the Garden', 'We have decided to identify our priorities.'

Thanks to a less authoritarian policy in 1972, 7:84 had made a start, and would be allowed to continue from these beginnings.

When we set out to establish a specifically Scottish company based in Scotland the situation was very different. Here was a theatre in which sexism was – and to a large extent still is – endemic and unashamed. The success of 1972, the most 'progressive' piece of new Scottish theatre was the *Great Northern Welly Boot Show*. It starred Billy Connolly in his most triumphal machismo anti-granny, anti-mammy, anti-wifey mode and our own Bill, Alex and John Bett in small parts enthusiastically within the same tradition. The women were definitely stereotypes and no two ways about it. The audience loved it. So while there was comedy, latent energy and class awareness in abundance, there were also problems that I was going to find hard to handle. Scottish theatre was, and remains in many respects, stubbornly male chauvinist.

Following the tour of *The Ballygombeen Bequest* in Autumn 1972, and after two hard years on the road, there was the inevitable dispersal – people wanted to do different things. Gavin Richards was off to take over the Roadshow from Ken Campbell, at his request, and that seemed like a good thing. It was to become Belt and Braces. Paul Kessel who had been with us for the previous year, and Gilly Hanna, went with him. She broke away to start Monstrous Regiment a year later. John, myself, David and Feri were impatient to start in Scotland with *The Cheviot*. We had become increasingly aware of the cultural and political differences between the situation in the south-east and the north of England and Wales, and between their preoccupations and those of people in Scotland. Scotland is distinguished by its socialist, egalitarian tradition, its Labour history, its cultural cohesion and energetic participation in argument and contemporary issues. Within its separate educational, legal and religious systems is a strong but not chauvinist sense of cultural identity. Culture and politics are not dirty words. We felt our plays there should reflect and celebrate these differences in language, music, political identification and carry on the arguments. This would need a different but related company.

It remained to secure the English 7:84 Company's tour for Spring 1973 and for that we had Adrian Mitchell's play, *Man Friday* – a delightful reversal of the Robinson Crusoe story, with songs, in which Friday takes on the master's role. Adrian wanted Mike Westbrook to do the music, and we were joined by his band, basically Solid Gold Cadillac.

Band-related problems were to recur in 7:84's life, though the advantages far outweighed the difficulties. There is a problem with conflicting disciplines and perennially with sound levels. Some musicians like to get drunk before, during and of course after the show. This is generally less than helpful to actors. (On one occasion during the tour of *Man Friday* a particularly brilliant trumpet solo was rendered at the beginning of the show, whereupon – to resounding applause – the said genius retired to the dressing room and collapsed spreadeagled across the floor for the rest of the show, the strike, the load – which included him – and, as far as history relates, the next twenty-four hours.)

It tends to lead to a separation, at best, between band and actors – with the band rolling up in time for the show, while everyone else has been working for hours. In a well-integrated company everyone gets involved both in the band and in the acting. It doesn't mean that you get what Gavin used to call 'hegemony of the band' – having played Gramsci he was really into hegemony and could spot it when only a gleam in the eye. (He also worried about 'hegemony of the writer' – the Power of the Pen – until he started writing himself. . . .)

Man Friday opened at the Bush Theatre to fine notices, and we now went north to establish 7:84 Scotland. Leaving Sandy and that company to get on with it, we set off, complete with children, cat and the old English company van (just a loan; we kept it till it fell apart three years later), and a sixteen-seater transit which John bought for the new company for £1,720. We went to find the right people. And to talk to village halls and supporters up and down the length and breadth of the seven crofting counties who were the bedrock of the story, then and now.

John had been researching and preparing the subject of *The Cheviot, the Stag and the Black Black Oil* for the fifteen years he had known me. He had the play all mapped out. We knew where we wanted to take it.

We talked to Tom Buchan and Tom McGrath and Dolina Maclennan and Ricki Demarco about people, and to many others besides. And of course we talked to Bob Tait and Annie Inglis who had already supported the company's work. We went to David and Feri's flat in Edinburgh which became our encampment, office, second home.

On 16 March 1973 John wrote to Ricki Demarco at the Scottish International Educational Trust, for money, stating:

'The nucleus of the company are people who have learnt about the problems of touring: budgeting, administration, getting around etc, from two years with 7:84. They are all Scots, who want to start a Scottish company. They are being joined by some Scottish actors currently working in television and theatre in Glasgow and Edinburgh. It will be an ongoing group, forming a tradition of its own, hopefully contributing something useful to the idea of theatre in Scotland.

Our application to the SIET is for help with the costs of transport. The Scottish Arts Council is giving a grant of £2,000 towards production costs, wages, and accommodation. BUT this will not cover everything – particularly as this is our first tour of this kind. We have to carry everything: ten people, scenery, props, costumes, and lighting board, lights, stands, cable, the lot. We have to buy a transit van. We have experience of second-hand vans, and frankly, one old one costs more in the end than two new ones, as well as being unreliable, and with fears of being broken-down on the east coast when we should be playing in Skye.'

At the meeting of the Trust to consider this application, apparently all was going well. Ricki was selling our cause with enthusiasm, when the chairperson asked, 'By the way, what does 7:84 mean?' He was told. There was a short silence. 'I think we'll move on to the next application,' he said.

The process by which we arrived at the first performance of *The Cheviot*, at the 'What Kind of Scotland' conference in April 1973 in Edinburgh and then opened in Aberdeen, has been vividly recounted in John's introduction to the play called 'The Year of The Cheviot' at the beginning of the Methuen edition. It is a very faithful, vivid, highly accurate and typically modest account of what

'These Are My Mountains', the opening number in *The Cheviot, the Stag and the Black, Black Oil*, by John McGrath, 1973. *Left to right*: Alan Ross, Bill Paterson, Dolina MacLennan, Elizabeth MacLennan, John Bett, David MacLennan.

took place; for of course, none of it could have happened without John's own strength of purpose, determination, sense of humour, talent, writing skill, and huge faith in people. That show and all the participants have had a lasting impact on the development of theatre in Scotland, and made a large contribution to the cultural confidence of many Scots people.

Response from the Scottish Arts Council

As far as funding was concerned, in spite of the company's reputation and touring experience – already considerable within Scotland – the first response from the SAC was No. It won't work.

In a letter to John dated 28 February 1973, John Faulkner, Drama Director of the Scottish Arts Council, spelt out their objections:

1. It was not clear what sort of presentation and appeal the idea of the Highland Clearances would have, even in the Highlands.
2. It was felt that the income had been overestimated.
3. It was felt that the subsistence had been underestimated.
4. It was felt that the cost of hiring the halls had been underestimated.
5. Doubts were expressed about the advisability of such an extended itinerary.

John replied with a patient, four-page, detailed account (which proved to be uncannily accurate) of our estimates, budget, who was to be in it and why he knew there would be interest:

'To begin with I'd like to dispel the notion that we are a bunch of Sassenachs come to thrust our ignorance down the throats of the long-suffering people . . . The idea arose out of discussion and argument with many people in Sutherland over the course of several years. The memory of the Clearances is far from dead, even in the east, and I was particularly struck by an incident during the 1970 election campaign when the present factor to the Countess of Sutherland, Captain Scott, got up to speak at a political meeting: there was a chorus of bleats from the back of the hall, and the cry of "Men Not Sheep" was heard and appreciated with much acuity by the audience.'

He agreed that we should reduce the length of the tour, suggested we should play the last two weeks in the Glasgow-Edinburgh area and continued:

'A gloomy-faced recounting of the woes of a long time ago could be very boring for all concerned, and that is by no means our intention. The play starts with the Clearances, goes on for a quick look at the Red River to see what happened to those who went to Canada, then has a section on the Victorian romanticisation of the Highlands, Monarch of the Glen and all, moves on to look at those who settled in Glasgow, and then comes up-to-date with a sequence on the impact the oil is likely to have on the Highland way of life. It all sounds a bit of an epic, but it will be told in short scenes, with a lot of comedy, and music, and our own accordion band which is even now training flat out. We don't intend to bore people, and we know from the great interest we have had everywhere we have gone to book halls and make arrangements that the interest for such a project is definitely there.

We don't want a miserable evening, we want to break through the "lament syndrome" and get people involved in building their own future – and learning from the past. In addition there is the element of the dance to be taken into account. Wherever possible, i.e. almost everywhere, the play will be followed by a dance, for which the company and the fiddler (Allan Ross) will provide the music. This has proved highly popular with everybody we have talked to as we arranged the halls, and accounts for a certain amount of the revenue. It is also an important part of the evening as an "event" in the places we are playing in.

I am sure this play will not only bring an enjoyable and stimulating evening of theatre to places which rarely, if at all, get such a thing, but also the best way to make the play work as a whole thing.

I have always felt that a serious writer today has to reinvent theatre every time he sits down to write a play. That is what 7:84 and I must do with this play if it is to be a new contribution to theatrical form, or at least a new version of a very old tradition. We cannot do it without your help, though we would try.

You ask me if the play has any overt political intention. We certainly are not proselytising for any party or group, openly or secretly. The play is intended, as all our work is, to help people to a greater awareness of their situation and their potential: how they achieve that potential is their affair, not ours. So have no fears, we shan't be canvassing for anybody, merely fulfilling one of the oldest functions of the theatre (cf. Euripides, Aristophanes et al.).

We go into rehearsal full time on Monday 26 March, and play our first date on Tuesday 24 April. The first week will be in the Aberdeen-Inverness area, the second down the west coast from Kinlochbervie to Kyle, the third on Skye, Harris and Lewis, the fourth in the east of Sutherland and Easter Ross. Most of the halls are provisionally booked and the accommodation arranged. I am half way through writing the play and hope to finish in ten days' time, though the final version of the script will be arrived at in rehearsal with the company and after discussion with several Highland experts of all kinds who will be asked to see a rehearsal of the play and comment. Naturally I shall control and be responsible for what finally emerges.

With these dates in mind I would ask your panel to discuss our application as soon as possible. I shall be in Edinburgh on 12 March and available to answer any queries your panel may have in person if they would so desire. I look forward to hearing from you.

Yours sincerely, John McGrath.'

I have quoted this letter at length because it illustrates so well the way in which John constantly tries to redefine theatre as an integral part of his work, and it is a process in which I have been closely involved, as I shall show in my account of several of the plays that followed. Right up until *The Baby and the Bathwater* in 1984 he was redefining, and again in 1988 with *Border Warfare*, the place, the play and the form of presentation are integrally related. He feels strongly that audiences respond not only to the *playtext*, music, setting, but also to the ways in which the evening is organised – for example, seat prices, welcoming, physical surroundings, the kind of programme, immediate rapport with the actors, dancing after, or the chance to join in – or not. All these are essential to the experience.

It was clearly a surprisingly difficult notion for bureaucrats to cope with, although it never presents audiences with a problem – they take you as they find you and are far more open to stylistic innovation and adventure than is generally recognised.

The other main point about the letter is the timescale; a striking contrast with more recent practice in the management of the arts. For, however hesitant Faulkner may have appeared then, his questions were reasonable and legitimate and we were certainly cutting it extremely fine.

Under the strictures that TODAY define the Arts Council's operation, that would of course be the *end* of the story. They would have to have received such a letter about eighteen months before, complete with full estimated income, details of commercial sponsorship, budgets and alternative sources of funding, the full CV of the administrator, the approval of the approved chairman of the board, the approved directors of the board, and its approved finance committee. In the event, with only *days* to spare, we got a £2,000 guarantee against loss, no capital grant towards the van (alas) and went into rehearsals as planned, only three weeks later. . . .

It is interesting to speculate what would have been lost if they had said no, except that of course we would have gone ahead, somehow or other. The show was a success.

I should have kept a fuller diary, and often regretted it, and did on some subsequent tours. But I couldn't fit it in. Apart from the travelling and setting up, the performance itself played with no interval and was physically strenuous. There was loading and unloading; there WERE the dances in which I played accordion; there was the hunt for food which sometimes ended up, predictably, with Doli and myself cooking in the kitchen of the hall for everybody; there was the search for cots for the children, or somewhere for them to stay during the show; there were their diaries to be written to take back to their school; sums and quizzes to write and check; and oh so many, many new faces and friends to talk to, for whom it turned out to be such a special night.

The boys' diaries, which I encouraged them to keep during this period, give a vivid idea of what was happening in our life and work, and how closely the two were related.

Extract from Finn's First Cheviot Diary, Spring 1973 (He is seven)

17 March. We left at five and got there at 1.50 so I went to bed late. Edinburgh.
Sunday. I went to the park and played football. I saw this banana tree in Scotland (picture).
Monday. I went to a new school. It was called Stockbridge. I had a new friend in my new school.
*Thursday 22nd. I saw the 7:84 Band for the first time. I had a very wobbly tooth. My friend (*Chris Martin, I think, who was in the company*) bought a motorbike.*
Tuesday 27th. My tooth came out, and when it came out I saw it first.
*Sunday. (*we were on a recce of halls*) I saw some stags. We went to Rogart. It was a little place.*
Tuesday 24 April. I went to Aberdeen and the play went very well.

48

I went to Stirling for a very sunny day and we climbed two hills.
I went to Inverness and on the way we had a picnic.
Sunday 30th. I went to a croft and sorted the sheep and there were twins, one black and one white.
1 May. I saw a kestrel chasing an eagle.
Lochinver. We went in a friend's boat and sailed half the way to Achiltibuie.
3 May. Achiltibuie. We had a tiny hall.
5 May. We stayed in Dornie with the twins.
7 May. We went over the sea to Skye.

There is a sort of postscript which says*: this is Ben Nevis, the biggest mountain in Britain. I saw it. Danny said he saw the Loch Ness monster. I went on a ferry at Ballachulish.*

Looking at these diaries now, I am reassured. The boys did not suffer – in fact like all of us they learnt a great deal.

During the Highland weeks, scarcely any critics got near the show – except the bold Cordelia Oliver, reviewing for the *Guardian*, who came up to Ullapool. But we spoke at great length to the audiences everywhere, and I managed to write down some of the reactions I heard. Here is what some of them had to say – just as I jotted it down at the time:

Exactly what kind of a riot are you trying to incite?
Edinburgh lady.

What's the answer? Socialism of course.
Cumbernauld.

If I die tonight I'll be a happy man; I'll have seen the history of my people.
The Bard of Melbost – Island of Lewis.

Never forget, never forgive.
83-year-old lady, Stirling.

The Highlander will always fight.
Dornie

If I said what I thought about the landlords I'd lose my job. You have said it for me.
Wester Ross.

You should have done it the night before the meeting with Olsen's not the night after.
Stornaway.

Political dynamite, they'll never show it.
BBC TV technician.

(Steely) Very nice.
American lady, Tain, near Nigg, where they build the oil platforms.

What do you do for a living?
Golspie, and lots of other places.

Far too short!
An 84-year-old lady in Rogart.

A bit biased: still, frightfully nice to be able to laugh at oneself.
Landowner's wife. Broadford.

Poor dears.
Chairman of the HIDB (Highlands and Islands Development Board)

It'll be a great place, Dornie, when all this starts, when the people fight for their
rights.
Fourteen-year-old Dornie schoolboy.

Emotional politics.
Student at Stirling University.

Never been anything like it here, ever.
Orphir, Orkney.

The more people that know about it the better.
Woman in Bonar Bridge, Sutherland.

What's his name, the one with the guitar and the long hair, is he married?
Young girls everywhere.

Great you're doing this – not enough people realise they're being exploited.
Ullapool.

When are you all coming back?
Achiltibuie and Everywhere.

The last question clearly demanded an answer, and a second tour.

The last performance of that first tour was in Oban where we played the SNP conference, and most of them took our criticisms of bourgeois nationalism on the chin. It was packed out and we drove back, triumphant and exhausted, to my brother David's flat in Edinburgh with two weary weans, still taking part manfully, John driving the van and dropping people off at their flats on the 'milk-round' at three in the morning, and finally collapsed into our beds.

At six that morning my father rang from Glasgow to tell us that my mother had died suddenly during the night.

David and I went home. John took care of the boys, and Feri took care of the arrangements for the last three gigs in Irvine (which was immediately after my mother's funeral), in Livingstone, and Cumbernauld. For months afterwards I had nightmares, feeling somehow – as people so often do – responsible for my mother's death, and unable to cope with the suddenness.

She never saw *The Cheviot*, but my father saw it and loved it – in Rogart. I think he loved the free-wheeling style, and the sheer nerve of it, and the comedy of course. My mother had seen *Trees in the Wind*. It irritated her. She told me, 'I was so bored I fell asleep and burnt a hole in my dress.' She smoked a lot.

I was put out by that observation, I must admit, and was glad that Troy Kennedy Martin was there that night to wheel me tactfully up the Royal Mile to let off steam. . . .But later I realised I was quite like her, and not always in ways I'm proud of. Anyway I forgave my mother that one and it is now a sobering reminder that one woman's finest hour is another's biggest switch-off.

Children

Combining theatre with having a family is not simple. With us it was a conscious choice to stay together and take our children with us as much as possible, even if it meant taking them out of school. They and the school agreed. It was quite demanding, but well worth it.

The idea of childcare was not raised for several years, largely because we were the only parents in the first few companies who both had children and both toured, meaning the children toured with us. I was reticent – perhaps wrongly – about raising this; money was so tight. I am aware that companies with a healthy subsidy in other countries can afford to have a policy of providing crèches and childcare for their members. I feel strongly that this is something that we should be aiming for in the theatre in Britain, but recognise that a huge change in attitude and funding would be necessary, not only in the theatre.

Certainly 7:84 at this time could not afford it. And I didn't want any special treatment. So we just worked hard not to impose the children and at the same time to give them all the time and love we had. It didn't leave much time for anything else – going to the pub, or other thespian forms of relaxation – but there were great compensations. Up early when the others were still in bed, off out to see what was going on in the harbour at Aberdeen, to see the lambs at Morness, to collect conkers, to buy toothpaste, to make a snowman, to find bacon sandwiches, and back to do our 'school' or diaries, then drive on to the next place and get ready for the show.

Sweeping the hall was a job the boys liked, but I remember a BBC documentary team trying to film them doing it, and feeling, Oh God, they're going to go on about these crackpots exploiting their children. But they didn't want to sit with their arms folded at the back of the hall; they wanted to help to get ready, to help Feri at the box office or Kate in her turn to help John or Lynn at the bookstall or ticket desk. They learnt a great deal about people, and about life in many different places. They also came with us to Cardiff, to Liverpool, and soon to Ireland, Holland, Belgium and later on to Canada and the Soviet Union.

And between times they went back to school and fitted in fine, played football like mad, had friends to stay, stayed with friends, and did 'homey' things. One or two very special friends like Sue Timothy and Vivien Heilbron were happy to stay for several nights or even a week if neither of us could get back home, and the boys enjoyed these interludes.

The diary Finn made on the second tour of *The Cheviot* starts at the point where John, himself and Danny joined us at Lochmaddy, North Uist, in the Outer Hebrides. There is a growing identification with the company and what we are doing; he is by now much more familiar with the Highlands, and relating to the world around him – and it is only six months later. The university of life works fast. . . .

Finn's Second Cheviot Diary

2 October 1973. I went to a friend's house in Lochmaddy in the Hebrides and saw a live turkey. We went fishing in a boat and only caught a tiddler. *
In Tarbert we went to FINSBAY and had a great view of it. We went on the ferry back to Skye and on the way we saw two seals. In Strathcarron we saw our uncle and auntie and we stayed for a bit of the dance.
6 October. Poolewe. We stayed with a nice lady and on the way we saw a car with lots of children in a car crash and we stopped and got the people out.
This was a grim reminder of how many miles we have travelled unscathed.
Our grandpa heard on the news the people were all right and the old lady had a fractured skull.
*We had a little time in Edinburgh and then we went on the sleeper. (*One at each end.*)*
We went to Brussels on an aeroplane and had a titchy coconut each.

In Brussels we had been invited to perform by the Europalia Festival, one of the few times we were helped by a somewhat bemused British Council. We also played in Ghent, where John saw the work of Dario Fo for the first time. The Nieuwe Scene were doing *Mistero Buffo* directed by Fo. I stayed at the hotel with the boys because the man who ran it had a very scary-looking glass eye and they didn't want to stay there without me.

It was here that we met Ritsaert ten Cate from Amsterdam for the first time. More of Ritsaert later.

The diary goes on:

In the woods we got thousands of conkers and sweet chestnuts. In Ghent which was very smelly we got on this tramcar and went on another aeroplane to London and all the way to Scotland, and on a sleeper to Inverness and then got the day train to Lairg and then had to walk all the way to Lairg Hotel, the van was there and we then drove to Skerray. In Skerray it was snowing and we saw the play.
We drove back to Rogart and on the first day we went to a friend's croft and had a lovely time.
At the dance in Durness we had a bit of a hassle and Chris got hit on the eye but the play went fine.

There is then a map of the British Isles on which are marked the key places – Orkney, Wick, Durness, Lewis, Dornie, Rogart, Wales, Perth, Edinburgh, Ireland, Leeds, for some reason, and London.

On our way to Glasgow we saw some ski-marks and some people ski-ing. In Grandpa's house we got lots of Coca Cola and sweets and lots of fish.
To Tarbert, Loch Fyne and then to Islay on a ferry and stayed in a farmhouse

---

* This was the house of Zadok McLeod, then the doctor in this part of the world, and his wife Julia and daughter Margaret. Their son John, now the doctor in his father's place, took us fishing. Zadok was a great buddy of my dad's – he used to bring him over to see patients and my father often air-ambulanced out his serious ones to his wards in the Victoria Infirmary in Glasgow. They had had some rare times together. Zadok lost the use of his eye playing shinty as a lad, but he made up for it by the breadth of his vision and the size of his huge spirit: a great man. To this day Kate has a dolly called Lochmaddy which Margaret gave her.

*full of children and one of the fathers managed a distillery and the other had
a real gypsy caravan.*

In Glasgow our grandpa gave us lots of quizzes (just checking up on the state
of their education*) and we helped make chips. We got some new Tintin books.
At Halloween we dooked for apples and went out with our cousins, we had my
grandpa's birthday party and I had two bits of cake and three balloons. On
Saturday we sat in the circle and had some ice cream in the interval. (*In the
Citizens Theatre where they had to open the disused upper gallery
rather than turn people away.)

*The last performance at the Lyceum was full and we sat in a box. The next day
we drove to London. Bye bye tour! Hullo school!*

Over the next few years I have schedules which are scrawled all over with
shuttling of children arrangements; to Scotland, to London with John, to Nana
in Merseyside, to Bet in Edinburgh. Occasional babysitters and long-suffering
friends staying for the odd night while John went off to see the English company
on the road, give notes, or go to a company meeting. For, after this, both
companies were going flat out and this peaked in 1975, which I will describe
as the Middle or 'Are We Really Utterly Crazy' Period.

I used to pray that the bar would NOT be kept open after the show so that
we could extricate the company and away home before the exhausted children
passed out, as they frequently did, on my or John's or both knees in the back
of the smoky van, be dropped off at the end of our street, staggering – for they
were getting bigger – each carrying one child, John with his inseparable bag of
books over his shoulder (ripped jacket, frayed collar) and into to bed. But not
before rewrites to be done, or a budget, or yet another letter to the SAC, or an
application for funds. At two am . . .

The impact of *The Cheviot*

Most people in Britain have been taught something of the history of their kings
and queens, or rather of the kings and queens of England. But the show drew
on the Scottish popular history that only appeared fleetingly in the text books
in the early 70s; a backdrop against which more powerful figures played out
their 'destinies'. We used our own research into contemporary accounts of these
events in a way that was exciting, uncommon and immediate. The Highland
audiences and even those in the south could feel that their actions were part of
that ongoing historical process.

While some people in the south and most in the Highlands knew that the
Clearances had taken place, they were taught that they were – albeit regrettably
– almost inevitable, like (according to this view) the Irish potato famine; one of
these unfortunate 'natural' occurrences, almost an Act of God, maybe devastat-
ing, but happening to them then and not us now. The connection between these
events and land ownership today was not widely made. Certainly not between
the continued exploitation of the land as a resource and the exploitation of the
oil today. Nor did people see these events as relating to, say, their own difficulties
in buying a house in Aberdeen.

The play made audiences aware of these connections, and of many others,
in the way Tom Johnston's book *Our Noble Families* had in its day. People felt

after seeing it that it was possible to fight these things and win. It was a very stirring experience. Many came several times and again and again to the dances which followed. I remember one person who came every night for a week! Many people say they will never forget it.

Nowadays, in Glasgow particularly, although so many people have Highland forebears there is a sense of separateness from the Highland culture, perhaps even a slight superiority. The land question seems remote from pressing urban preoccupations. But at that time we were able to arouse a feeling of common identity and struggle.

The style was extraordinarily effective. It swung effortlessly from sadness to merriment.

Nowadays critics and academics refer confidently to 'the ceilidh-play', as though people had been writing them for years. But it was a new form. On the poster we called it 'a ceilidh play with scenes, songs and music of Highland history from the Clearances to the oil strike', but it was not a play in any accepted sense at that time. In the newspaper ads we called it 'a ceilidh entertainment with dance to follow'. But people in the villages described it as a concert which is the usual term for any entertainment. John's writing was brilliant, members of the company were each individual, strong talents, prepared for any amount of experiment and hard work. The set was a giant pop-up book, beautifully painted by John Byrne. It was perhaps the first touring show in which the actors changed in full view of the audience, and sat on the same level as the audience, only jumping on the rostra to act out episodes and songs. People found it fresh, strange, moving, exciting and very, very funny. They stayed behind to talk, argue, dance and enjoy themselves.

The music was very important.

People in Ireland felt a very strong connection. The parallels are obvious. They liked the fact that we spoke in a different voice about many of the same issues they didn't need underlined because of course 'history' has also laid a heavy hand on the Irish people. When we played in the Abbey in Dublin, and in Cork and Sligo and particularly in Galway they knew exactly what we were talking about. The music and the ceilidh form were familiar and loved.

It will always be hard for companies going to the Highlands to live up to this, partly because that particular group was hand-picked for the job. Mainly because most of them now start from the perceived 'centre' – usually Glasgow these days – and work *out*. But John in attempting to write about Scotland *started* with the Highlands, and worked down from there. He came in 1958 to the village where my family came from – Rogart. In Sutherland the Clearances were most brutal. He discovered the strath, that valley which had supported several hundred families, now had about forty. He found out why, who owns the land in Scotland and how they got there. It hasn't changed so much since then. The same top ten landowners in the crofting counties still own millions of acres in spite of Crofting Acts and occasional Labour governments.

The show got everyone talking. That kind of dialogue was continued in our later Highland plays – *Boom, The Catch, There Is a Happy Land*, and *Mairi Mhor*. There was a tangible sense of involvement as well as 'a good night out'. They were, I suppose, part of an ancient story-telling tradition which is an act of sharing with the audience. We were quite aware of this and deeply affected by

54

the confidence played in us. It was a critical challenge to live up to. It gave us a lasting respect for the Highland audience.

Some of these shows were televised. Recently *There is a Happy Land* was repeated. I was struck by the animated, at times rapt attention of the live filmed audience watching their story – seeing it now myself from the outside. It is a far cry from the sporadic single weeks of 'one-off' shows which are now dutifully trundled out by the Arts Council as what they term 'theatre provision'.

In an article in the *Guardian* (24 November '73), Cordelia Oliver wrote:

'Few theatrical tours in Scotland can have penetrated the country so thoroughly or connected so completely with audiences of all ages and types.

The Cheviot is accessible to everyone, whether they love it or hate it. In Ullapool, in the big dining room at the Caledonian Hotel (it doubles as a local dance hall, and very apt too, since *The Cheviot* winds up as a dance wherever possible with the company, alias The Force Ten Gaels, providing the music) discussion was still raging at three in the morning.

Ten years of McGrath's researches into the Clearances lie behind *The Cheviot* – and it shows.

7:84 (Scotland) is a special kind of spin-off from the original 7:84 Company (itself still actively functioning south of the border); special not just because it is an unusually close-knit, democratic, self-disciplined group capable of combining a variety of talents in a common purpose; but because, in addition, it is powered by the right cause at the right time, a sizzling subject of profound concern to actors and audiences alike. This is nothing less than the wholesale destruction of the Highland culture and way of life which began with proscription after 1745, came to a head with the notorious nineteenth-century Clearances in the name of improvement, and under the mounting pressures for development in the wake of oil discoveries, continues today.

The Cheviot, the Stag, and the Black, Black Oil has just played its final week at the Lyceum Theatre, Edinburgh. Tonight will see the ninety-ninth performance (most of them one-night stands) and the BBC TV adaptation planned for a future 'Play for Today' will stand for the hundredth. After which, millions more than could ever have been reached by any tour, however extensive, will have got the message – that the real power lies with those who own the land; that, in Scotland, this is an infinitesimal minority; that this minority has its roots mainly elsewhere and no compunction about continuing to destroy a culture and a way of life in a race for profits euphemised as 'economic development in the national interest'; but that, as happened in the past, resistance will work if enough people do the resisting.'

Working with John McGrath

Most actors tend to find – usually by luck or happy accident – one or two directors with whom they work particularly well. And some will find – or be found by – a writer with those work they have a particular sympathy. In many cases there is an understandable reticence about analysing the alchemy on which their mutual work depends, and I have a great respect for such artistic relationships, and the fruits of their collaboration.

Similarly, in companies where the idea of an ensemble is important, the

55

director will usually develop a team of people she or he will 'use' again and again, and they will develop a shorthand often which is perfectly understood; often too they will anticipate each others' wishes.

The fortunate writer who works regularly with an ensemble will know more about the individual members' potential and range, will feel freer perhaps to try things out, and also to respond to ideas or invention from the actors. Not many are lucky enough to have the benefit of all three situations – a director, an ensemble, and a writer – with all of whom they have a strong artistic and political sympathy, as I was. Of course there was a choice, and a continuous reassessment involved, and attendant stress. But I have been able to take great risks and flying leaps – and make the necessary prat-falls – from a position of mutual trust, respect, criticism and commitment which has overridden the considerable stresses involved in keeping an oppositional theatre company going with inadequate funds for seventeen years.

Every McGrath play has a formidable and at times quite complex structure, up which the actors must climb, finding footholds with their character to lead the way. As a director John watches the actors rehearse with an intense quality of concentration – critical, fascinated, yet childlike. Although it is a gentle manner, his outstanding quality as a director is his boldness of concept. He expects actors to be equally daring and to use their brains; to be physically brave; to take responsibility for their material and for building a personal relationship with the audience as individuals and as a group; to use the language; to sing well; not to hector or bully; to be worth watching, inventive, comic, passionate but dispassionate, sensitive to each other and to the minutest response, and never to give up. In effect to love their work as he does. Some times it is an exclusive process, but never at the expense of the *audience*.

Audience

How can you judge the individual response? Well, some people come up to you and tell you what they saw, or felt, or something you don't know, stories, information, mistakes, or what they were reminded of.

Billy Riddoch, 7:84 actor, on the importance of this contact with the audience:

'Our theatre is art too. It depends on your definition. We look for living proof because we ask people. It's the difference between being alive and being dead. Keep theatre live!'

Sometimes the faces tell you, and nobody says anything. Or there is a particular kind of silence, a stillness.

The collective response is more difficult to gauge – unless of course you are talking about Live Aid, or Wembley or Parkhead with the Celts winning. For us it can be measured by the size of the audience, in letters, in collections taken, for the miners, the nurses, the Nicaragua Health Fund, the ANC, the striking civil servants, the occupation, or simply the whip-round for the actress who had her wages nicked. Or in the arguments stimulated, the ideas expressed more confidently.

What do we want?

Collective strength. We have experienced it. We know it exists. Mrs Thatcher has said there is no such thing as society, only people. But people need to form groups if only to protect themselves: to discuss, examine, organise, have a laugh, a cry, a discovery, a shock, make friends, move on, compare, overcome setbacks, rediscover friends, values, solidarity. Internationalism, recognition of other artists, delight in other skills, disciplines, languages, other music – as people we need all these; as people and as artists.

And what do we get?

Backache, exhaustion, agreement, sympathy, scandal, jokes, post-mortem, knives in the back, critics, fighting back, new songs, surprises, students, occupations, meetings, other people's kitchens, our kitchen, dances, pubs, more meetings, the locked hall, the missing key, the janitor rules, the wrong time on the poster, who damaged the curtains, you'll hear more about the ashtrays, Victory in Vietnam, sheep outside the hall, Maoists in Hull, Marxists in Achiltibuie, the Shrewsbury Five, Singers, John Browns, 440 people in Clydebank, 2,000 in the Leisureland Ballroom in Galway, not enough programmes, Betty MacIntyre presiding at Rothesay-O, Chile, Joan Jara's smile, the miners' victory, the STUC conference in Aberdeen, Auchmountain – pies and beans and OUJAMA – Dave Anderson running to catch the boat at Lochmaddy, us shouting from the rails c'mon Davey, drunken requests at the dance – gonna play the Dark Island, g'on, play the Dark Island – the Women's STUC Conference, Stirling – g'on yersel, Bessie – Lee jeans, the Flying Pickets, the Unemployed March, the Unemployed Train, the orange luminous jackets, what do we want? JOBS. When do we want them? NOW! Writing songs in Bob and Irene's kitchen, on the boat to Dublin, programmes to be written – always two in the morning. FACTS – listen to this – Christ, wait till ye hear this – sweeping the hall, moving the chairs, no rostra, no blackout, carrying gear up three flights of stairs, writing verses in the van, students from Norway, Canada, Australia, the strike centres, George Bolton's dad at Fishcross, Janette Husband's kitchen, Soweto, Joe Corrie poems on May Day, Hamish Henderson's backslap. Factory occupations, Newcastle theatre occupied, Archie MacMillan on the box, the Mickery Theatre, Amsterdam, Mike O'Neill singing 'Laid Off', feeding baby Kate in a theatre conference in Brussels, shuttling children, caravans, school in the van, Cape Breton fiddlers, choppy seas, half unpacked suitcases, bills to come home to, full house, standing room only, hecklers at the back . . .

Between tours I have researched, worked on contacts, correspondence with audience, students, arranged meetings, reorganised the office between administrators, arranged foreign tours, read scripts, failed to read scripts. Partly out of interest and commitment but also because at NO time were we getting enough money to pay somebody to do all these things which otherwise would not have been done.

Raising consciousness

Clive Barker interviewed John, myself and David between the first two Cheviot tours. We had now been working together in 7:84 for three years.

CLIVE: As an actress rather than someone as closely connected with John as you are, what was the reason for wanting to do this?

LIZ: Working in our kind of theatre I felt that I would be able to be part of a statement which would carry not only the weight of my artistic experience, such as it is, but also the weight of my political beliefs. I thought it was important to try and do this.

CLIVE: John said you talked to a number of actors. Would you say this feeling is widespread?

LIZ: No, I would say, looking back on the last three years, that it's very difficult to find this kind of actor. It's become almost a joke now; we sit down at the end of each tour to start working on the next, and say, 'Well what do we need? We need an actor who can play an instrument, communicate directly with the audience, talk to them, entertain and have strong left wing political views. Somebody who is prepared to go on the road for very little money for, weeks on end, travelling together, getting on with other people. It's a difficult assignment. It requires a very dedicated kind of actor.

CLIVE: You found them?

LIZ: We found some who had some of these requirements and some who had others and some who became politicised in the course of the work. I think we all did to a large extent.

The original object of the company, to put it broadly, was to raise consciousness. I think we raised our own consciousness as much as we raised the consciousness of the audiences. Actors are accessible to political ideas because they have been repressed for so long. The English company, as a whole, has tended to develop more strongly theoretically, with quite a strong imbalance between those who were politically clued up and those who were struggling.

In the Scottish company the work has always been more practical. The collective discussion has arisen out of the desire to get the play together and it's been more tied up with the rehearsal process. We need to find things as we go along.

Eight: Working in the Towns

With this show we began to get more involved with the trades unions, miners' clubs and working men's clubs in industrial Scotland.

For the first time we used a rock band. Several new faces joined the line-up, notably Dave Anderson. He was a friend of Alex Norton, who had spent several years playing guitar and piano round the States. John had gone to see him play in a pub in Bayswater and felt a great desire to import him back to Scotland. Dave had come up to see the company in *The Cheviot* at Kyleakin while on his honeymoon and fallen in love with it.

He joined in with the band that night after the show as we played the dance, and began the dialogue with John McGrath and David MacLennan and myself that continues to this day. He brought with him a fine singing voice, funky guitar – blues, rock, reggae, you name it – keyboards, and a great ability to communicate with an audience. He had never acted in a play. He began to learn, on the first performances of *The Game's a Bogey* in Aberdeen that spring, the hard way.

It was only a year after Victor Jara the great Chilean singer and songwriter had been murdered by the military junta in Chile. John had given Dave a song of Victor's, 'Every Man's a Maker', and he sang it in the show with guitar. At the dress rehearsal John asked him to introduce it with a short piece he had written about Victor. John told him he could read it, it was just a short piece. When it came to that point in the show (I was in the audience), Dave started to read, and then, quite suddenly, his face changed and you could see him thinking – My God, he was a musician, just like me, and they did this to him; they broke the bones in his hands and tortured him, and he went on singing. And the audience knew what he was thinking. And thought about Victor, and Chile, and it went right home. It was quite a debut. Maybe a baptism of fire – anyway, he went on to become a marvellous all-round performer and actor, a treat to work with. Subsequently he wrote his first show for 7:84, *His Master's Voice* – I suggested the title.

Another new arrival was Terry Neason, she of the molasses-candy-black-velvet-voice, and the comedy timing. She was seventeen. George Lyle, who had joined the company to play bass in the band, suggested this girl from Easterhouse he knew who had spent the last year touring with an all-male show band. She worked with us with an ever increasing range, power and commitment till she left to help start up Wildcat four years later. I taught her a lot about acting and she taught me a lot about showbizz. It was a good combination. She calls me Bizzie Lizzie and we enjoy and respect each other's work.

The other newcomers were Terry Cavers, George Lyle of the eloquent

Ina gets wed, in
The Game's a Bogey
by John McGrath, 1974.
Left to right:
Bill Paterson, Terry Cavers,
Alex Norton.

silences and bass, and Bill Riddoch, who I think has probably continued to appear in more 7:84 shows than anyone to date, except myself, with extraordinary power and commitment.

Dave Anderson and John went to see Bill about playing drums in the band. Dave wasn't sure. Bill rang John up and said if you don't take me you'll be making a very big mistake. Come and see me act (he was first of all an actor) in the panto at Motherwell. It was *Mother Goose*. John went along, watched the entire show – no sign of Bill. He went backstage: where were you? You remember the scene where Mother Goose did the washing? Yes. Remember the washing spinning round? Yes. That was me in the washing machine. . . .He got the job. And stayed.

Geordie Buchan, General Joe Smith, Sandy Gordon – the dad in *Blood Red Roses* – so many fine performances; a fine epic actor of whom there are not so many, even in Scotland.

In 1980 I did an interview with Colin Mortimer, who asked me about the development of *The Game's a Bogey*:

'We approached the Scottish TUC and some trade unions in the course of the *Cheviot* tour. We wanted their support to do a play which dealt with the high level of politicisation of the Scottish working class, which is something which is definitely worth celebrating. Particularly now. In spite of the diaspora of Scots throughout the last hundred years if not before, they've still managed to maintain this high level of political awareness. If you look at any union in Britain, you'll probably find that the active element is very, very often Scots. Or Welsh. We wanted to go into the working men's clubs and play to the working-class audience in the industrial belt. And so we chose a hero of the industrial belt, John MacLean.

And we simultaneously went around trades councils and shop-floors and made our own contacts, arranging where to play. The performers went individually to different areas setting things up. Doli to Fife, Bill and Alex, John and Dave to the trades councils, to Whitburn, Glenrothes and so on. I went to talk to the head of the STUC, Jimmy Jack at that time, about what they thought their relationship should be with 7:84. They were very helpful at *all* those levels, very interested, and placed great importance on our work.

COLIN: More than the English TUC?

LIZ: Oh, far. No comparison. I would say that the English TUC only took a peripheral interest in cultural matters in the 70s. For a time in the 80s they started showing more interest and being more helpful. (Note: *In 1984, when 7:84 England was threatened with cuts, the TUC under Norman Willis were extremely supportive at all levels – more later.*)

We were invited to play *The Game's a Bogey* at the STUC annual conference at Rothesay and it was a tremendous success. It was the first of many performances at their conferences. The importance of that can't be overestimated because an enormous number of delegates came and saw us, got involved in discussion, and supported us when we came to their town. And they put us in touch with other people who have supported us ever since.

COLIN: Did the audience respond to a piece of entertainment or the politics?

60

LIZ: Both. *The Game's a Bogey* is a very entertaining show and there's a lot of great turns in it. It's a variety show. But also it's a very uncompromising show because the politics are hard and straight on and the entertainment is hard and straight on. It was written for clubs. You have to make your impact in a short space of time. There may be bingo in five minutes. There's the noise of people going up and down to the bar and the till ringing up the sales. You have to ride all that. So you really have to have a very stark immediate effect. If you want people to laugh they've got to get it right away.

There are certain basic rules that you have to more or less observe. You've got to be on your feet, facing front, speaking as loud and clear as possible and ready to answer back if necessary.

COLIN: You mean it's all got to be out front, no internalised stuff?

LIZ: No, there can be, but it's better to be thinking on your feet. There may be scenes as there were in *Game's a Bogey* where the wife has been put on tranquillisers and expecting her baby and her husband's been laid off. These are quite recognisable, "naturalistic" situations, but they were handled in a very economical way. For two reasons: one, because of the kind of atmosphere in a club and two because people *know* the situation and they don't need you to lay it on them with a trowel. A couple of quick brush-strokes and they're absolutely with you because it's their own lives you're talking about.

Music is very important. There's a wonderful song of John's in *The Game's a Bogey*, an early example of 7:84 songs about women's roles, which is "She's a Girl". That's a song that Terry Neason has been able to sing all over the country in all kinds of situations and get total hush and attention to what it's saying. It's a very reflective song but it's nonetheless the kind of song you can get up and sing in a club. People listen and love it. And the argument is sustained through the songs as well as the scenes and the jokes.

COLIN: So what you're following is not a plot but a political argument?

LIZ: Yes, and the need for a Scottish Socialist Republic. The need for that IS the argument. Everything else is showing why it is necessary, then and now. I don't think anyone in the audience would leave without realising that's what we were talking about.

COLIN: When you say popular you mean with a wide social spectrum?

LIZ: Yes, but I mean first of all big houses. Almost everywhere we go we can pull in a lot of people. There's a lot of public interest in what we do. This has two effects: one that it gives us a tremendously confident base, the other that it gives us a tremendous responsibility, because ever since the first show, *The Cheviot*, we hurled ourselves into the middle of the political arena and people took us seriously. We weren't saying anything absolutely extraordinary, we were saying what people had been saying privately over years but they'd never all got together and said it in public. So there was an enormous sense of relief.

61

From that moment on they wanted to know what we had to say about the current issues: or rather what John was going to write, because that side of it came from him really.

They identified the performers with a certain conviction about what they were doing. So that's one thing about being "popular".

Another thing is that stylistically I would say we've achieved a very varied but distinctive popular style, in which the content and the form are very closely knit. This is partly due to the fact that performers tradtionally in Scotland don't have such strong internal class divisions between variety theatre, straight theatre, and club entertainment – in the way that in England these things are very much separated. You find actors who can play instruments and sing and singers who can act. We've always tended to have a group who can turn a hand to most things. Even our critics tend to say, "It's marvellous to see the performers leaping around doing all these things."

I think that attitude to performing is very close to the principles behind the company. If you're putting forward ideas which are broadly saying that any amount of change is possible and people can do things that are previously held to be impossible, then the people who are saying this should be able to do as many things as possible.'

Nine: Family, Stress and Work. 1974-1975

Boom was the second play John wrote to tour the Highlands as a follow-up to *The Cheviot*. It toured in the spring and the autumn of 1974 with many of the same company. We felt we owed it to the Highland audiences who'd given us such support the first time not to be a ship that passes in the night. We wanted to go back and talk about the issues that we'd started to raise. *Boom* is much more of a story really; the story of a boy and a girl today, living in the Highlands, and the questions that they are confronted with. It arose out of talking to young people and research into the oil industry and American involvement in Scotland. We talked to people at school, who were just leaving.

We drew up figures of what they were hoping to do: what they were going to work at, whether they were going to stay in the Highlands – the question of depopulation. I remember being very struck at the time by the fact that about seventy-five per cent of the boys actually wanted to stay in the Highland area and work either on the land or in related industry, which obviously wouldn't be possible. But that's what they wanted. And about seventy per cent of the girls wanted to leave.

Some of the girls had notions about the 'bright lights and the big city' for instance. John wrote a song about that. The character I played had gone away to work in the south, and wrote letters to her boyfriend back home. There was a scene which we wrote because I read some rubbish out of *Cosmopolitan* that I thought coincided with the aspirations of some of the girls I spoke to of sixteen or seventeen. It was a ludicrous piece about stocking the fridge with 'bubbly' and tempting morsels, just in case, but at the same time it made quite telling and funny comment about female stereotyping. That's in the play now.

7:84 THEATRE COMPANY

BOOM

A CONCERT PARTY IN THE NATIONAL INTEREST
BY JOHN McGRATH

MUSIC FROM THE FORCE TEN GAELS SCOTTISH COUNTRY DANCE BAND – **& THE NORTONES**

We wanted to use traditional Gaelic music again, but to write new music that would work with it. This was mostly written by Alex Norton who again acted and played guitar in the show. There's a song called 'The Red School Bus', about how the children on the north and west coasts and the islands have to leave home to go to secondary school at the age of eleven, and can only come home for the long holidays. This can cause them to grow away from their parents, and their parents' culture, at a very early age. It's written in Gaelic *and* English: John wrote the English lyrics and Doli wrote the Gaelic. The sentiments it expresses were keenly felt by our audience then, and recognised many years later when we sang the song in the Soviet Union, and on Cape Breton Island in Canada.

Angie, the young man in the play, has a long speech at the end which takes place at a planning meeting when the oil company comes to put a pumping station in the village of——wherever we were that night. We had a map of that village, different in every place, and we'd put the pumping station on top of a crucial place in that village. If it was the pub, that usually worked a treat.

Alex Norton, who played the spokesman from the oil company, would say, 'Now I think we'll put the station right . . .' and he would pause, and he would put the sticker on, '*here!*' The audience would gasp as they could see the pub being demolished or some other feature that was really important in their lives. And he would say, 'Of course, it isn't going to make any difference,' and so on. That sort of public meeting was taking place all over the Highlands at the time; people were genuinely worried about what would happen.

This section of the play used to create an extraordinary tension in the hall. The audience desperately *wanted* someone to speak up for them, and they could see nobody was *going* to, because the opposition were all on the platform.

Bill Riddoch as
Angie, impersonates
Gary Glitter
in *Boom*, 1974.

Then, Bill Riddoch as Angie would get up and speak – about the need for local people to control the development in their area, and for them to unite against exploitation. He used to get the audience practically on their feet. One night in particular, at the end of his speech, there was silence, then one woman shouted from the back of the hall, 'He speaks for all of us.'

That was the motivation behind *Boom*. We also made information available in that play that wasn't widely known about the oil industry; how it works, and how much control it had; and, *most* importantly perhaps, the industry's involvement in other Third World countries where oil and other mineral wealth had been discovered; what it had done to those countries. And what it was likely to do here. At the same time that was considered outrageous, extraordinary, and by theatre cognoscenti it was considered wild. It still is.

But the audience in the Highlands didn't think it was wild. They could absolutely see what we were talking about, when we described to them what happens in the Gulf countries and the various coups and economic manouevres that are negotiated in order to keep the oil in the right hands.

We talked about *other* ways of doing things, other political models. We talked about the Tanzanian example, for instance. We quoted a wonderful speech that Nyerere made. People found that interesting because it was talking about specifics they related to – about cattle and feed and bringing some of the benefits of city life to rural areas.

There were arguments within the company about this; whether or not we should talk about the Chinese 'example'. Some of the more reactionary performers, I remember, said they didn't want to be compared with the Chinese! But I said, when you look at what the Chinese women actually said in village meetings, and when you listen to the words and forget your prejudices about the Chinese and about active women, then it could be any rural community talking. Their anxieties are not so different.

Stress

We decided to tour *Boom* again that autumn. John went with *The Game's a Bogey* company to Ireland to open it in the Dublin Festival. I followed the next week with the boys to rehearse *Boom* there. They had books with them and notebooks in which they would keep a diary of their trip to Ireland.

We rehearsed all day and then stayed to watch the *Bogey* and chat with the audience afterwards. Danny was six, Finn seven. The show was extremely popular. We were staying in digs by the sea. On the way home in the van, we had to stop for Danny to be violently sick. All through that night he was sick. John looked after him and in the morning I got the landlady to call the doctor who came within twenty minutes and pronounced meningitis; within half an hour we were on our way, Danny and I in an ambulance, to the Cherry Tree Hospital on the outskirts of Dublin, a fever hospital, with two cases of typhoid at the end of our corridor.

They immediately did a lumbar puncture – meningitis/encephalitis confirmed. Danny's temperature rose to 105° and he became delirious. I stayed with him all the time and tried to sleep in the chair beside his bed. There's not a great deal to be done with this condition except for nursing. Fortunately the nursing in that hospital was great. They let me stay with Danny constantly. John took Finn to Tom and Mary Murphy's who took them in until we came out of the hospital. Their children, Bennan and Nell, were about the same age.

John arranged for Vari Sylvester from the English 7:84 to come and take over from me in *Boom*. Even if Danny recovered quickly, he would not be fit to be left without me while I toured. Priorities. John had to carry on with rehearsals and visit us with Finn at the hospital after work.

Danny became very, very ill – dangerously ill – but then (He has a hard head! the nurse said) recovered, the crisis over, slowly. Big, huge, brown eyes and fair hair. On the fifth day Bill Paterson came to visit him and was great. He gave him a copy of the *Cor* annual, cherished for years, and they had a good laugh.

Tom Murray, in his eighties at the time, an old comrade who had gone to fight in Spain and was a friend of John MacLean, was over from Glasgow. He came to see the show and heard the McGrath boy was seriously ill – found out where, and trekked out to the hospital to see us, with a bag of toffees (which Danny wasn't well enough to eat). I was very touched.

We returned to the Murphy's flat and after Halloween celebrations there, Finn and I flew to Edinburgh with Dan in a wheelchair to be met by Robin Worrall, who deposited us most carefully and tenderly in Balmoral Place, Stockbridge. This was a two-roomed flat which we had bought very cheaply during the summer. John had gone on ahead, on tour with the company again, urged to continue by me. The danger was over and it was now a case of convalescing properly until Danny was strong again. We had been very lucky.

Many times during the following decade I came near to stopping. The personal stress was exacerbated by increasing political difficulties. Each of us from time to time because dispirited, including the children. But we remained loving, and sure about the value of the work we were doing.

A week later, when Danny was up and about a bit in his dressing gown but still not strong, I myself developed mumps – and Finn, now seven, took charge of us, and took his message list to the corner shop, Kelly's, for tins of tomato soup and our daily needs. We were quite sufficient to ourselves and I told John not to come back and risk getting mumps himself. He rang up all the time to see how we were and let us know the tour was going well.

Danny's Irish diary of these events (aged 6)

Saturday 12 October 1974
Today We Went on a Plane To Dublin and we have got a beautiful room With a bed each and a bed-side lamp.

Monday 14 October 1974
Today we went to Bennan and Nell's and Played on a tricycle. It was nice and he gave us 100 conkers. And we played football.

Tuesday 15 October 1974
We Went to the show it was called the Games of Bogey. It was about John Maclean and i thoutht it went very well.

Wednesday 10 October 1974
We went to rehearsals with Mama and Dada and did school there. I enjoyed it.

And we had mackerel for tea at Terry's. There are palmtrees and they have got dates on them in Dublin. The phone-boxes are white and the Pillarboxes are green.

Saturday 26 October 1974
on friday I was sick 5 times and the doctor came in the morning, And said I was to go to hospiTal for ten days, and I went in an ambulance with mum.

Part two

I was in Ward 7 and the doctors and nurses were very very nice. my bed was on wheels. There were three other boys there. Mum stayed.

Part three

I went to Ward 11 and I went there on a stretcher I had a little room to myself. and I read a great many books. Finn looked through the window. here are the flowers I got (Drawing).

Part four

they took my temperature very much and my friend Billy came to visit me. Benan and Nell gave me books to read.

Part five

I got out of hospital on tuesday 5th and they wrapped me up in a sleeping bag and took me home to the Murphy's. We had a seledration with me in bed beside the peat fire and good things to eat.
next day we went on a aeroplane, to Edinburgh

Wedensday 28 November
We got our of bed today And the docter came he sed that we can go to Rogart for the weekend And Dada could come and fetch us and take us there so we are delighted and mum can go out with us if she wraps up properly and we will see are friends in Rogart and there may be snow there. They have got a hayloft that we play in in the summer time. there are three girls and there mum is having a new baybe this week so we may see him or her and we are going by car so we will have a lovely journey. That is the news today.

Thursday 29 November 1974
yestday mum finisht my nEW sweter which is blue.

Saterday 30th Novenber
We spent a week in Rogart while we were there we got two more friends called Stewart and William.
We went to a croft in the hills and saw a standing stone.
The baby that I was talking about has just come out
the End

Ten: The Middle (or Are We Utterly Crazy?) Years, Part One. 1975-1979

I have called this the 'Are We Utterly Crazy?' period because of the ridiculous number of things we were trying to do. Quite suddenly, John was trying to write and direct and I suppose 'lead' two very busy companies. After four years' touring, I was trying to keep some kind of equilibrium with the boys and their schooling, to make time to hear them sing in the choir, watch them play in football matches, look after tadpoles, feed the cat, and plan ahead for the next year's work in Scotland with *Little Red Hen*.

We were still 'living' in London, and the boys were still going to school there. The tiny flat in Edinburgh was necessary when we were working in Edinburgh, as the company could certainly not have afforded hotel bills, and we couldn't go on sleeping on other people's floors forever.

These were years of endless travel, cheap train tickets bought with tokens from *Corn Flakes* and *Persil* packets, arriving home after midnight and leaving early in the morning, enormous dependence on the goodwill of friends and relations, and the great excitement of breaking new ground, doing good work, and discovering the strengths of a truly popular theatre.

7:84 England Triumphs – *Fish in the Sea, Lay Off, Yobbo Nowt*

In 1975 the English 7:84 Company, led by Mick Campbell, Shane Connaughton, Nick Redgrave and Vari Sylvester, reasserted itself and revived John's play *Fish in the Sea* with huge success.

Nick Redgrave member of the 7:87 England collective on the subject of this revival:

'John had suggested that Sandy Craig should be asked to come back as administrator of the *Ragged Trousered Philanthopist* tour in 1973 because Claire was leaving. He had worked at setting up the company and identified with our practices and ideas.

We saw Sandy sitting there like a stunned doormouse. I thought he was a bit academic and cocky. We put him through hell. Hungary, Suez, the Yemen, Industrial Relations Act. Poor bastard. If they'd put me through that I couldn't ... no one could come through that alive. Subsequently we became great friends. I don't think we even gave him his train fare back. I don't think we had the money.'

Sandy *was* brought back to help put on *Fish in the Sea* and got the money from the Arts Council. John was in Scotland putting on a show. I remember him coming down and saying, 'You haven't even given Sandy a place on the collective. This is disgraceful.' 'Oh yes, I suppose it is.'

I think John felt very pleased that there was a will and ability in the English company to keep going.

Later that same year John researched, wrote and directed *Lay Off*, about the operation of the multi-nationals, with a very strong company who stayed on and expanded, to do *Yobbo Nowt*, which he also wrote and directed, and then followed that up with a show about inflation called *Rat Trap* which the same group performed at the Festival Hall.

That made a total of four new musical touring shows plus revising and writing new material for *Fish in the Sea* in *one* year. All, bar *Fish*, directed by himself.

It was a terrifying workload. He insisted on touring as much as possible with both companies.

Especially exciting for the English 7:84 in 1975 were the community centres they played in the Scotland Road area of Liverpool where they became 'our theatre' – a very moving experience for any company and it was a great company: Vari Sylvester, Sharman Macdonald, then Colm Meaney joined us from the Abbey Theatre, Dublin with Mike O'Neill leading a crack band, directed by Pam Brighton. The production had wonderful notices.

'A wonderful generosity of spirit akin to O'Casey at his best informs the work of John McGrath. His plays rarely reach London: a fault which will surely be rectified when the new National Theatre opens its portals to the regions. *Fish in the Sea* confirms my long-held view that McGrath is one of our major dramatists. His epic vision is allied to an ear for speech rhythms which can establish a character in seconds: his humour and all-embracing sympathy are heartwarming. His failure to be doctrinaire and inability to hate are precisely the reasons why *Fish in the Sea* carried conviction.'

Frank Marcus, *Sunday Telegraph*

Each of these shows was taken on a long tour to largely new and untried audiences. They also toured the Welsh valleys *and* toured in Scotland. The style of McGrath's productions was very fresh and intriguing to these audiences. In *Lay Off* he employed a style crossed somewhere between variety and living newspaper. In *Yobbo* it was a seamless music theatre narrative, with a central

70

woman protagonist played with great gusto by Chrissie Cotterill and a fine comic performance from Harriet Walter.

Meanwhile for 7:84 Scotland John was directing *My Pal and Me* – his Glasgow version of his Liverpool musical *Soft or a Girl*, with Hilton McRae, Vivien Heilbron, Alex Norton, the Band, and Terry Neason, which opened on 7 February in St Andrews and was a hoot. Outrageous performance of randy widow from Ginni Barlow. Gerda Stevenson's first job.

The set was 'designed' by John and Allan Ross, and painted with wit and hard edges by John Byrne, who was soon to become unavailable as a set-painter when he turned into a distinguished writer. John Byrne had painted and made the pop-up book for *The Cheviot*, painted the sets for *Boom* and *The Bogey*, and painted all our posters from when we began in Scotland until 1978. He and John seemed to enjoy working together, communicating instinctively.

During this period Trevor Griffiths' *Comedians* opened at the Nottingham Playhouse. It evoked a lot of our preoccupations with the nature of comedy, progressive and otherwise.

I saw *My Pal and Me* at Paisley Trades Council, at that time a regular gig for us. There were complaints from some of the audience that, although it was fun, it wasn't political *enough* – not like *The Game's a Bogey* which they raved about. My diary for this period is full of notes like Govan/York, Sligo/Rochdale, Paisley/Lancaster – which means that the Scottish company was in Govan, the English company in York etc, and John frequently rushing from one to the other, trying to write, research, give notes and go to company meetings. And always greeted with, 'Aw, ye should've been here *last* night – it was the best yet! Pity you missed it!'

I saw *Fish in the Sea* at the Titchfield Street community centre in Liverpool – organised, along with most of the new gigs on that tour, by Alan Tweedie who was very proud of that company and rightly so.

Lay Off, which opened in Lancaster on 26 May, was another hit – this was in my view the English company's most outstanding and consistent year. A high degree of commitment, musicality, skill, energy and flexibility characterised that particular company – not to mention stamina for a very heavy year's touring.

David MacLennan, John Bett and the Scottish company meanwhile went to a residency in Dumbarton as part of the Quality of Life experiment and were paid by this outfit to research a show about the area; we have been doing community theatre as well as political theatre, for a long time. It opened on Saturday, 21 June, was called *Capital Follies*, and played all over the Dumbarton and the Vale of Leven district.

We celebrated on Sunday, 22 June when both the companies played a football match in the grounds of some shipowner's derelict castle, and felt like a Big Enterprise. We were certainly covering the country in a big way.

In 1985 our administrator (one of a team of three by this time!) was complaining of a heavy workload; '7:84 has grown and developed since those days of one production a year.' In terms of bureaucracy this is clearly true, the SAC has imposed a heavy workload, but in terms of output and priorities, it is perhaps useful to look at how much *theatre* we were *actually doing* in 'those days'.

71

7:84 Scotland, *The Little Red Hen*, 1975

John wrote in the programme for *Little Red Hen*:

'Wherever we go in the industrial areas of Scotland – and Clydeside in particular – we meet up with an older generation of working-class militants who constantly astonish us. Active, articulate, passionate and well-informed, they draw their strength and conviction from the days of the "Red Clyde" – days when the naked greed and ruthlessness of the capitalist system was plain to see; days when John MacLean, Jimmy Maxton, John Wheatley, Willie Gallacher and many other great activists expressed the demand of the Scottish working class for the overthrow of capitalism and the creation of a socialist Scotland.'

John first thought of setting this play in the 30s with the character Henrietta developing from a young girl, and the audience would draw their own conclusions for today. I assumed that I would play a number of parts and be involved in the music. On 11 August, with some of the play written (a welcome surprise) we started to rehearse in the Odeon Cinema in Edinburgh. Lo and behold, Henrietta was now two people: the young girl, played by Wilma Duncan, and myself as her older self – then seventy-five, and still going strong.

Elizabeth MacLennan as the Old Hen, with Dave Anderson on keyboards in *The Little Red Hen* by John McGrath. 'The Moon Belongs to Everyone, the Best Things in Life Are Free . . .'

72

Suddenly I found this character just stepped off the page and started telling me – and everybody else – in no uncertain terms what to do and where to go. I was really not a free agent in this instance. She just arrived – out of the text. I was very pleased that we could afford £60 for a beautiful, real wig for her and the right specs, and took particular care with her costume which cost all of £5 in the Lifeboat Benevolent Shop. She carried a string bag complete with loaf and leaflets.

John Byrne again did the poster. But, funnily enough, when later in the tour – the night we were due to play in the new AUEW club in Clydebank – our costumes were stolen from the van, I went on quite happily with the clothes we managed to rustle up because, after the initial panic, I realised that this old lady was probably one of the strongest characters I've had the good fortune to play and could withstand and adjust to whatever circumstances the tour came up with.

We opened on Tuesday, 16 September at the Lyceum Theatre in Edinburgh, immediately after the Festival, as became our wont at that time, to a full theatre. Immediately the more touchy Nationalists realised they were in for some serious criticism. And here resumed our 'dialogue' with Nationalism, which sharply divided the foxes from the hounds. We lost a lot of nervous literati at this point, and a few chauvinists to boot!

At the Citizens Theatre, Glasgow it was seen by 7,272 people in two weeks, all tickets prices at 50p. Their audience had less problem with its criticisms of Nationalism – they wanted the Red Clyde back – without the poverty, the unemployment, the 'beasts in the heid' – and they let us know.

It was a strong performing company. It was good to have Bill Paterson back playing Ramsay MacDonald in rhyming couplets, and as my brother George, who said nothing at all for the whole of the first act, and went on to rebuild Glasgow in the 50s and 60s with some profit to himself, if not to the inhabitants . . .

The show toured for fifteen weeks to about thirty-four venues excluding the three London weeks at the Shaw Theatre the following spring. A short film version was made at the Murray Hall, East Kilbride – a superb gig for us at that time – by Steve Clark Hall. The tour included, apart from the Lyceum and the Citizens, Cumbria, Ayrshire, Fife, Aberdeen, Greenock, Clydebank, Govan, Paisley, Cumbernauld and Sligo, County Mayo, Galway and Dublin. The company wage was £50 per week (accommodation £3 per night).

The Woodmill Miners' Club, Fife gig fell on Halloween and the children with white-stockinged faces guised us as we were fitting-up the show – it was already dark and I remember them singing:

This is the night of Halloween
When a' the witches can be seen
Some are red and some are green
And some are like a turkey bean!

Clydebank Town Hall. Feri Lean arranged for us to play there with the help of AUEW Convenor Alex Ferry, a 7:84 enthusiast. Blocks of tickets went to

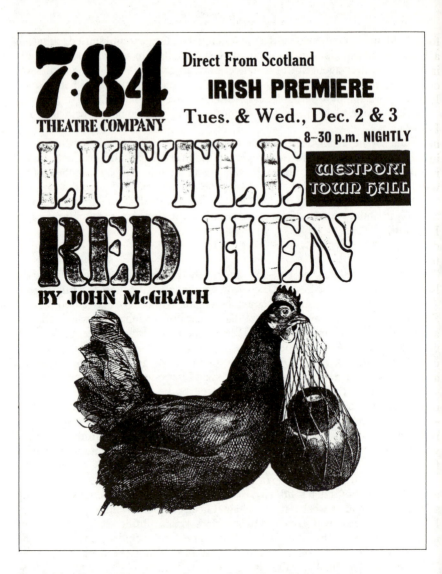

7:84 THEATRE COMPANY

Direct From Scotland
IRISH PREMIERE
Tues. & Wed., Dec. 2 & 3
8–30 p.m. NIGHTLY

WESTPORT TOWN HALL

LITTLE RED HEN

BY JOHN McGRATH

Fairfields, Govan, Linthouse, Singers (all still working) and there were over 400 people in – mostly working. Many of the audience got their tickets direct from the shop stewards committees at these plants. A lot of women, some children. A lot of patter. Great hubbub. In this show I came through the audience from the back of the hall at the beginning and watched my 'grand-daughter' cavorting in the daft Harry Lauder routine opening number – involving the whole company decked in dreadful Japanese tartan – and would usually give out caustic comments on it, and on her performance (mostly scripted).

On this occasion – as on many on that tour – I was offered a seat: 'C'mon hen, sit yersel down – take the weight aff yer feet. Have ye seen the 7:84 before? Ay, they're quite good.' And then, after the show was over: 'Aw ye had me fooled there, I fair enjoyed masel – when are ye coming back?' We raised a huge cheer and quite a bit of money for the Shrewsbury Five who were in prison at the time and John maintains I could have led out the whole crowd straight to George Square to storm the City Chambers there and then. It was a marvellous night.

In Govan I met one of *many* 'old hens' I was to meet as we toured. Janette Husband, 7:84 board member, our supporter over many years, born in Govan, now working in Carlisle, introduced me to her mother. We felt like sisters. And in East Kilbride I met yet another, Isobel Coleman, who had taken part in the rent strikes in Glasgow in the 20s and chalked the streets for the speakers and was still fighting.

East Kilbride was a very different place in 1975 – a strong, employed, working class, very effective trades unions, several successful long-drawn-out strikes to their name. Now, in 1989, sixty per cent of the workforce there is non-union. The new industries are still largely run by women but their industrial power has been systematically destroyed.

Jim Price arranged our week in Ayrshire and Bridget McGeechan, from Stewarton, made sure as always that the hall was full and the chat afterwards as lively as in any place we were likely to visit. Stewarton would support two visits per year. Bridget certainly drummed them up, in spite of work, five children and other major commitments. People like her have made 7:84 possible, and kept us going.

In Aberdeen Bob Tait organised a fine gig at the College of Commerce and of course Annie Inglis at the Arts Centre. We played the trades councils again – Paisley, this time satisfied with the politics, enjoyed the humour hugely. A return visit to Cumbernauld – this time to Greenfaulds School – the new theatre was not yet built; we renewed our friendship with Tom and Jenny Laurie whose hospitality there was legendary.

Perhaps the two weeks in Ireland were the high point. In Westport, Co Mayo, at the University of Galway, at University College in Dublin, and finally at the Christian Brothers College, Colaiste Mhuire in Parnell Square, Dublin. Our hotel was straight opposite the Sinn Fein bookshop, which worried Ginni Barlow and Wilma Duncan.

We renewed our friendship with Tom Murphy the playwright and his family. They were delighted to see Dan looking completely recovered. Tom was now working at the Abbey. Terry Kelleher and Brian Trench, of *Hibernian* magazine, were a great help to us. The Company thrived on Dublin Guinness, hospitality and lively chat.

I was amazed by the number of newspapers, the extent of the argument and intensity of interest that prevails in Ireland about the arts as well as political life. People seem to care about writers and theatre in a way that makes Scottish restraint seem bleak by comparison. Inside the theatre there is an enthusiasm and quickness and emotionalism of response – perhaps the nearest I've found to it was in Georgia in the USSR where people also love theatre.

Glasgow audiences are felt by many performers to be the best in Scotland – and for comedy I think this is likely true. They love to laugh, and they're quite

75

partial to a good cry. But lately I've felt that argument, irony and wit – unless heavily clothed in defensive patter – are not appreciated quite like they were in Glasgow. Is there too much appetite for patter? For the familiar? What about the unfamiliar? The taboo?

Highland audiences love good music, a story and the *skit*. And taking the piss – especially out of the landowners. They like the heart-strings, but the audiences I've come across that can laugh uncontrollably are in the Highlands. Doing *The Cheviot* in Bonar Bridge: at the end of the song 'Awfully Frightfully Naice' which John Bett and I had as Lord Crask and Lady Phosphate, normally Doli followed it with a sad Gaelic song from Mary Macpherson, dressed as a 'domestic' in Glasgow. On this occasion it was impossible. They were laughing too much. She was laughing too. She simply could not follow. We cut straight to the next part of the story. The audience's feelings had taken control of the play for a moment, and that can happen in the Highlands like nowhere else. Although a similar thing happened when we played *The Cheviot* in Galway.

Again when we played *Blood Red Roses* to the Women's STUC Conference in Stirling in 1980; they took the play over and made it their own. We were just telling their story. It's a marvellous feeling.

During the central belt touring I was staying in our flat in Stockbridge mostly by myself while the boys continued school in London with John, and hurtled up whenever they could. I would be dropped off by the van at the end of the street at one or so in the morning to get my tea. I would wash and hang out *eight* pairs of identical kilt socks for the Harry Lauder scene on the line in the darkness while the street slept. In the morning I wondered what my curious neighbour made of it – she certainly gave me some odd looks.

At this stage we divided jobs between us within the company and, as there were a lot of costumes in *Red Hen*, Ginni, Wilma and I undertook their maintenance. Thereafter I went on to rigging and de-rigging lights with whoever was doing lighting, on grounds of (a) sexism and (b) the chance to talk to the audience at the end. I found that if I stayed too long talking to people one or two folk would get cross about being left to pack costumes. So doing the lights and cabling meant I could do both.

Nowadays crews tend to get to the hall several hours before the cast and often even strike as well, although that is still usually shared. Notwithstanding the back-ache, elbow ache and belly-aches, I think it makes a great difference to the way companies relate to each other, to the management and to the audience. Allan Ross was outstanding in this regard. He drove the van, unloaded, set-up, played the fiddle, acted, did the strike, loaded the van again, drove home. He never missed a show or a get-out – phenomenal.

The next spring, from May 31st *Little Red Hen* played to full houses at the Shaw Theatre in the Euston Road in London. There was a lot of curiosity about events in Scotland since the oil 'boom', and Nationalism seemed to be on the agenda. We had a very lively, mixed audience.

76

The main problem with the Shaw Theatre is that it doesn't *feel* like a theatre. The approach is deadly municipal. No pzazz. No neon signs. You have to *search* for the publicity. It feels like a library – which it is. When you get in, you feel as if there might be a lecture on the distribution of maize in the Third World going on, not a show.

There is no doubt that during this period, 1973–1979, there was a great upsurge in Nationalist feeling in Scotland. But, apart from the vague phrases about 'It's Scotland's oil', it didn't have a very strong economic basis. There was a realisation that the country was about to be ripped off. This was something that we wanted to tackle.

The Cheviot is highly critical of bourgeois Nationalism, and of specific figures in the Scottish scene who were part of that process. There is a statement in *The Cheviot* about power being in the hands of the people who own the land – and very many of them are Scottish. But there were quite a lot of National-ists who wanted to claim it, because it was getting a lot of support. I like to think we gave some support to the radical elements in the Nationalist party. I also like to think we have had an effect on the broader agitation for a Scottish parliament. It's very hard to say how far these things were effective, but certainly notions that were quite heretical when we first put them forward became almost common parlance. Phrases out of the first two or three plays became knitted into public policy statements of both the Labour Party and the Nationalist.

In *Little Red Hen*, we absolutely clarified our relationship with the Nationalist Party, and this incurred a lot of wrath from some of them, including Doli. She went off and didn't work with us for a while. People shouted out from the audience. We had three Nationalist MPs in the play who were very closely observed strands of their particular brand of Toryism and arguments – or lack of arguments. They're very funny characters and it's a cruel piece of satirical observation. It was deliberate because we wanted to make it clear that we didn't stand for that. The Old Hen explains the relationship between the socialism of the thirties when she grew up and people like Maxton and Gallacher and Wheatley, who are the heroes in the play, and these puppets at the end. Now this was not very 'nice' as far as a lot of people who were mostly Nationalists were concerned. A certain amount of our more interesting battles since then have stemmed from that play.

So many people have said to me since then, 'Like my granny, where did you find her?' And I say, 'You don't need to *look* for her, if you've got your eyes open.' Of course the Edinburgh trendies didn't want to know because, for one thing, she's a Glasgow granny! Vulgar creature, whose language left some-thing to be desired and whose politics left a great deal more as far as they were concerned. What's more, here was a strong outspoken woman with a mind of her own. She went down very big in Ireland though. They knew about that.

You have to adjust when you play in another country. There's this speech where the Old Hen is talking about the General Strike and how she ran into a blackleg on her bicycle, to send him flying. It's a very funny speech; she describes how she sees him coming and in the play originally she says, 'Right, ya wee bastard, and I went straight at him.' Martin, the guy that was putting us on in County Mayo, said, 'You'd better not say "ya wee bastard", that won't go down at all here. Alienate the audience.' So I said, what should I say then? To get that feel? And he said, after a bit of thought, 'Gobshite. Say gobshite.' I thought this unlikely to be an improvement, but, sure enough, when I came to it and I said, 'Right, ya wee gobshite,' the audience fell about. Just shows you.

The play has got a strong narrative which is interesting, because if you're telling a story it has to be different every night . . . it's like if you tell a story to a child. If you do it properly it never comes out the same, except when you come to the bit that they like to hear – 'And the wolf said "I'm going to gobble you up."'

1975 was a very interesting year. I think it was the peak of public involvement. I was getting quite a few people copies of Lenin on 'the National Question' that year.

When we were researching I went to ask a pensioners' club (in Govan) about how they 'got by' in the 1930s. Someone had mistakenly told them I was going to come and talk to *them* about 7:84. I said, 'No, I'm not going to come and talk to you at all. *You're* going to talk to *me*. And the men can all shut up. I want to hear from the women.' There was an absolute uproar and you couldn't get a word in for the next two hours. All the women over seventy came out with what it was like living then. A very specific period – 1928–1932. If you had two kids or six kids or whatever, how much money you got from the National Assistance and how much it cost to buy bread and pay rent . . . That grew into bits of the play. I spilled it all to John when I got back home, and he wrote the 'Bone Soup' speech in the play directly from that experience.

There's a song in *The Red Hen* that my mother sang to me. She heard it sung on the pier in Stonehaven in about 1918 when she was a child. And it's called 'The Shimmy'. I don't remember singing it to John. I must at one stage have sung it to one of our children. He put it in. When we came to do a read-through of that section, I opened the script and I said, 'Oh no! Oh, you haven't put that in,' because it was almost embarrassing. A lot of what we do is so vulnerable. You do things that are so personal. It takes a lot of nerve. You have not to mind making a fool of yourself, which eventually of course you do because there's lots of affection in the audience towards us, and vice versa.

Eleven: Out of Our Heads. 1976-7

By this time 7:84 Scotland had developed a comradely and loving relationship with the audience. By this time, therefore, John felt able to make a play which was, in some ways, critical of the working class – something you can only do from a position of trust. That was on the drink question.

We felt that he couldn't write a play about drink and the Scottish working man's male chauvinism without talking to everybody who was going to be in it about their attitudes to these questions. In other words, you don't want people going round the country touring a play which is critical of drink and at the same time getting plastered every night. Or – at least – if they are, they should know why. So we had a very comical discussion period. The subject sounds very solemn but the result was far from it. I think that's why people liked that show. We could have done a very couthie show about drink and the Scottish working class, in which everybody has their favourite jokes about what happened when people get drunk. We tried to avoid that, but there is a lot of humour in the situation and a lot of sadness. That was the period when there was a slight boom in social work departments. A lot of people who had seen earlier shows wanted to put us on in their community centres.

In some places the hall was a mirror of what was happening on the stage. In most shows at the end, when we're striking the set and lights, the audience – especially in an informal place where there are tables and drinks – tend to sit a bit longer and they'll chat. The play struck a big chord with women.

The question that is put forward in the play of what is 'normal' for a working-class wife to accept or not accept has been retained around the place. When I go back with other shows, people come and say to me, joking, 'I'm not normal.' I remember one mum telling me about a sex education class. The teacher said to her class, 'Now we're going to talk about all the problems you're likely to encounter in the next few years. Not that I'm saying you are necessarily going to have a life of problems. Far from it. I'm sure you're all nice, normal girls.' The class burst out laughing. She said, 'What's the matter?'

And they said, in unison, 'We're not normal.' They'd been to see the play a few nights before. I wouldn't have heard that if the mum hadn't told me.

I really value these contacts with the audience, because they influence what we do next and how we do what we're doing now, and that you can rarely get in the commercial theatre. You don't meet the audience. You go in one door at the back. They come in another door at the front. You disappear into the night. Their concept of you is something separate.

John's programme note for the play:

'Surprisingly little sociological research has been done on exactly why people drink, and almost none at all on why different societies, drinking the same liquor, get "drunk" in different ways, recognise different forms of "drunken" behaviour. And, not surprisingly, very few political thinkers have made connections between the root problem of living in a competitive, manipulated industrial society, and the particular uses to which we put alcohol.

79

Every society, in fact, teaches its young how to "be drunk" – it has built a code of behaviour that is permissible to its members who get drunk, and this code is very clearly defined. In Scotland, for example, wife-beating is fairly tolerated when a man gets drunk. But not among certain groups of Mexican Indians. Again in Scotland, violence flares up easily in a group of drinkers – but not at all on Ifaluk, one of the Caroline Islands, where "a slightly bleary look about the eyes and a tendency to be jovial or sentimentally friendly" are the only effects of a hard night's battering the booze.

Scots know very clearly that although they can sing or dance in the street

Terry Neason as Janice and Elizabeth MacLennan as June in *Out of Our Heads* by John McGrath, 1976. 'Ye cannae get a decent man in yer sannies!'

and be excused, they mustn't throw bricks through windows or strangle cats. So they are not "uncontrollable" or even completely liberated. They are conforming to a code defined by society and passed on, with modifications, from one generation to the next.

The single most striking feature of the life of working people in Scotland today is alienation ... The purpose of their work is generally not for the good of the community, but to create a surplus: profit.

Women are alienated, starting at an early age, from what they might want to feel, by the pressure to conform to a male image of what a girl *should* feel. Likewise boys have to conform to a manly image, or suffer for failing. The relationship between a man and a woman has to struggle through this network of images, and is distorted by it.

All these different kinds of alienation create multiple splits in the personality. So what makes you feel whole, complete and in charge of your destiny? Booze, according to the code: the excuse to feel complete.

But there is more, much more, that we have decided to use drink for in Scotland. To give us a chance to be emotional for example. To give us courage to bewail our human condition: the sober thing is to button up your fears.

The play tells the story of a working man and his wife caught in all this. Their friend Davey, who sees that if you drink because things are wrong you won't change them, because you'll be drunk. And their works manager and his wife who are caught in the same trap.'

A small group got together to do a workshop. For the first time, we were *paid* to do this – two whole weeks. Bill Riddoch, Kris Misslebrook, Terry Neason, Dave Anderson, Dave MacLennan, John and myself. John Bett reluctantly dropped out. He did not want to discuss the subject of booze. That was a pity because these sessions were great fun and we had a trusting, mutually tolerant team.

One day we recalled our first experiences of alcohol. Out of this session and subsequent discussion John wrote the marvellous scene at the beginning of the second half in which the characters we had got to know all came into the pub for the first time – all under age, and with varying degrees of success trying to cover this up. 'One pint of heavy lager' etc. I finished up all of fourteen, slightly batty, singing, 'Take me back to the Black Hills' with my mouth full of crisps, while Terry Neason (also playing fourteen – the confident pal Janice in high heels and tight belt, 'Ye canny get a decent men in yer sannies!') downed vodka and orange and IGNORED the boys at the table on the other side of the stage. Very little dialogue. A lot of acting. The audience had all *been there*, some way or other. They recognised themselves, their relations and friends; that was the joy.

Later as Harry and June's story deteriorated into 'an ordinary story of a looney and an alchy' they could see how and why it happened and what could be done about it.

'I'm not normal. No, really, I'm not. I'm not even normal for a looney. Normal loonies kid on they're Jesus Christ or Napoleon or the Queen o'Sheba, but me, I kid on I'm normal so I get away wi' it.' (June.)

That speech struck deep with many girls and women. I was to hear it again and again from children who'd watched the show. For several years after I was greeted by the group of children on the back steps of the Citizens Theatre with, 'You're no' normal – are ye?'

We toured it all over Scotland from September to December 1976. The company wage now was £60 per week, and subsistence (when we were on the road) £6 per day. There was a lot of fog and snow that winter. The old orange van was getting tired.

We revived the show the next Spring. From 23 March to 9 April 1977 we gave eighteen performances at the Citizens Theatre Glasgow, to 10,054 people. From 12 April we played for a week at the Royal Court (invited by Stuart Burge). Sold out. On the 18 and 19 April we gave two performances at the Scottish Trades Union Conference in Rothesay. Lively discussion, new contacts. 25 April – 7 May: fifteen shows at the Oscar Theatre, Dublin. Sold out. Drank a lot of Guinness in spite of the play. . . .

What stands out, in my mind, from the show *Out of Our Heads*?

James Grant's entrance, demanding, 'Ten whiskies. On a tray.'

Mark Brown's music: fully integrated into the meaning of the show, more sophisticated, more variety, more depth, and highly influential on later developments.

The Grand Opening in Clydebank Town Hall, organised again by Alex Ferry and Ed Kelly of the AUEW. High level involvement, critical response and mobilised working-class audience in Cumbria at The Washington Miners' Social Club and the Gateshead Boilermakers (part of a week of action by NUPE against Cuts).

The contrast between Cleator Moor Community Hall and the reception at the Royal Court in London – an almost anthropological interest in Glasgow working-class people. I wrote about playing in London in the *Guardian*:

> 'The Scottish Company can and do play Cumbria with a lot of understanding, but when we come to southern England, as we infrequently do, I feel almost like part of a world theatre season – I wouldn't be surprised to see simultaneous translators passed round the audience.'

Out of Our Heads secured us a loyal audience. We might have lost the support of the middle-class Nationalist literati of Edinburgh with *Red Hen* and its fierce criticism of mindless Nationalism. We had gained a huge, loyal, working-class audience, capable of self-criticism.

For me the involvement with battered women (for such was June, the character I played, when she grew up) continued after the run of the play. In 1978 when I was too noticeably pregnant to act in *Joe's Drum*, I went to work in a refuge for battered women in London run by one of the most dedicated women in the labour movement I have been lucky enough to know: Madge Cavalla. For many of the women, normally isolated and imprisoned by their isolation, it was their first experience of living together with a lot of others – often widely different in class, background, colour.

With the government's removal of the board and lodgings payments to hostels, many refuges will now be forced to close down altogether.

Meanwhile back in England (1976)

We played this show during the troubled tour of *Our Land Our Lives*, a play about agro-business being staged by the English 7:84 Company. I felt that its stilted, uncomfortable relationship with the audience was in striking contrast.

I was still on the collective planning group of the English company. At this period they were having some trouble with ultra-democracy – Nick Redgrave who was also on their collective recalls:

'The work process had become the focal point of the company. It became very introverted. About democratic working and democratic sweeping up and democratic nose-picking.'

Nick and Alan Tweedie wanted John and myself to go to see *Our Land Our Lives*. They said that the show was not good enough. When I got home to Edinburgh, late after the performance of *Out of Our Heads* in Paisley Technical College, I found John and Terry Dalziel, another member of the 7:84 England Collective, determined to take advantage of a 'day off' the next day to go to see the show. Unfortunately it was on in Coleraine, on the coast of Antrim.

Nevertheless, we went. We got up at six, drove to Stranraer with the boys (nine and ten and sick from the long car ride) took the ferry to Larne, drove to Coleraine, where 7:84 were opening the brand new theatre, and watched it going down badly. We chatted to Reggie Smith who was running the theatre and watched him looking at us anxiously as the audience – staunch Orangemen and their women in long frocks – rose to sing 'God Save the Queen' very lustily. We stayed in a bed and breakfast in a nearby resort, and set off back next morning. Once again the crossing, the long drive; to the Jack Kane Centre in Craigmillar in Edinburgh. We were late for the get-in, were given a hard time for deriliction of duty, and on with another performance of *Out of Our Heads*. And after all that to vote reluctantly at the next English company meeting that the actors should be paid their full contract, but that the play should be taken off.

After the extraordinary success of *Fish in the Sea* and *Yobbo Nowt*, with the new audiences they had built, the collective felt we couldn't carry on with a show that was losing us support everywhere it played, however much the company might defend it and however much I might sympathise with them. These are some of the difficult moments. Fortunately, we only ever had to do this twice in the history of both companies.

The Trembling Giant – 1977 (7:84 England and Scotland)

Trembling Giant was written for and toured by the English company and wasn't meant to be done by the Scottish company. We had another play under commission from a young Dundee writer. But every now and then commissions don't work, for various reasons. It just proves that the stylistic difficulties inherent in this kind of work are enormous. A new writer coming in has a really difficult job if they don't know the audience. They don't know the demands.

David suggested we did *The Trembling Giant* because the tour was already booked and we had no show to do. We felt we couldn't let people down. John did an exercise in adapting it which was partially successful. I played the

83

story-teller. It had a beautiful set by Allan Ross. Visually, one of the best shows we've done and that's important too. It's nice to take things that look magic around. It makes a difference to people's lives. It did look marvellous and we took it to Ireland, and to the Royal Court (our second visit) at Christmas time.

The company in *The Trembling Giant* by John McGrath, 1977.

People liked it because you could take the whole family. It was more of a fairytale but it had strong similarities with panto. They liked drawing their own conclusions from the parallels, because it was a fable.

I enjoyed the music because I got to play Russian accordion music and I wrote two songs for it, – one a children't nursery rhyme, the other a ballad – 'Work' – about people coming from Ireland and the Highlands to work in Glasgow.

Pause for thought

That July between tours 7:84 Scotland met as a group to have three weeks of informal political discussions on Nationalism, the role of music, sexism and male chauvinism, collective organisation and training. We felt that we needed to restate and develop our basic principles both for the benefit of new company members, and in the light of the experience we had gained. Some people found this very useful (others dozed off) but it tended to clarify our *different* perspectives and objectives rather than unite us as a group.

*   *   *

The beginning of Wildcat (1978)

When we revived *The Trembling Giant* to take it to Dublin, we took on a number of new musicians, and the atmopshere in the company changed. We were feeling the stress of all those years of touring, but it wasn't that. The new musicians wanted a different relationship with music. Language became to some of them 'very verbal'. We had very much encouraged the growth of the band. Now the band was ready to take off in its own direction.

The next show, and the last of this period, was – not surprisingly – written by Dave Anderson, a musician, about the music industry: *His Master's Voice*. It began with the whole company on stage playing instruments, and the whole structure was musical. They were evolving something different and exciting. The show was popular, and during the run it became clear that the main people involved should be free to develop their ideas for this 'band theatre'. If they were to stay in 7:84, it would mean that we would have to stop our own development as a company, which again seemed not quite right.

We had used many kinds of music – particularly folk music, but also rock music – but basically we used music to serve the meaning of the scene, to reinforce feelings, to convey ideas. We had to be free to use whatever kind of music was needed. The musicians on the other hand wanted music to lead the story, to shape the narrative, and to have a consistent rock-based style. And they wanted to stick together as a band.

We were very lucky. In a way that could never happen today the band were allowed, with our collusion, to take some of our grant to start themselves up as a new company: Wildcat. Then we were both allowed to continue as separate companies thereafter, and have done so ever since. My brother David, who had directed *His Master's Voice*, went with them, as did Feri, and Dave Anderson and Terry Neason of our long-standing company members. We were sad to see them go, but felt that it was right for them at this point.

David has become one of the best theatre impresarios I have met for sheer tireless energy and 'optimism of the will'. He happily admits he learnt a lot from us in these early days. Sometimes he gave vent to his impatience in fierce attacks on John – he was not the last – often under pressure during the set-up; and the children would watch, puzzled, for they loved him very much. They grew to understand – or at least accept – the pressures of this demanding work on our relationships.

But the best laughs were to be had with Dave and Feri – over the impossibilities of MacBraynes' timetable for the ferries round the Western Isles, the cultural gap between England and Scotland, and the lack of understanding of many politicos in England of the Scottish working class, its institutions and its cultural confidence.

Our shared perspective was to stand us in very good stead throughout the first ten years of Thatcherism, when all kinds of oppositional theatre in England was being stifled and we were determined to hold on, even to expand, feeling the work to be more necessary than ever.

When David went off to start Wildcat, I knew he should, but I knew I would miss him.

85

Twelve: The Middle Years, Part Two. 1979-1983. Onwards and Upwards

England – The net tightens

Flashback. I was on a wall outside the picketed Grunwicks factory with John, waiting in the crowd for the miners to arrive. They did. They were impressive, but they made one mistake. They went off to a rally in the park round the corner and as soon as they left the police let the bus straight in through the gates. The BBC got the pictures they wanted. 'And there's the bus getting through the protesters at the gates.' Peak viewing on the main news slot at six o'clock.

The street outside the factory was quite narrow and the bus drove at speed. People jumped behind walls when the police moved in to clear the road: it was not funny. When a few years later I watched the TV coverage of the police in action at Orgreave during the miners' strike in 1984, I remembered what it felt like.

On 16 July 1979, three days before Kate was born, I took part with several ex-English 7:84 members in a Sunday Night Benefit for Blair Peach's family at the Royal Court Theatre. Blair Peach was a young New Zealand teacher who had taken part in Southall in a demonstration to stop the racist National Front from marching through that predominantly Asian part of London. After the demonstration he was attacked and killed by a group of policemen. The violent repression of the 80s had begun.

That night at the Blair Peach Benefit I began to feel nervous. Kate was actually due to be born the day before. The show itself was fairly confrontational. At the end, a huge effigy of the head of the Metropolitan Police was passed through the audience and taken out into Sloane Square and burnt on a bonfire. The fuel for the fire was kept under my dressing-room table for some reason. In the dressing room, also working in the show, Jenni Barnet (from Belt and Braces) and Jean Hart were both determined I should have a girl, which I did, on the 19th.

Gavin Richards, Colm Meaney, Jean and I did a rehearsed reading of a piece John had written specially for the event: 'If You Want to Know the Time'. In it he created four characters, fairly ordinary, sympathetic people, who all had in fact either a vested interest in or a positive disinterest in preventing the murder of Blair Peach. It was really about the creeping advance of a pre-fascist mentality in England. The most ominous character had analysed the 'anarchy' of the young, and had come to the conclusion that the only way to bring discipline back to the streets was physical violence – to frighten them. One or two of them may even have to be killed, he thought.

Blair Peach was killed during the run-up to the general election that brought in Margaret Thatcher. Everything was about to change. We knew things would get worse, but we didn't realise just how much worse.

* * *

After the hectic activity of the first eight years in both companies, we drew breath for a period of examination. We knew we would have to be tough to survive another eight years at that place. We knew we had widened our audience and our resources. Both 7:84 companies were now on annual grants, however precarious.

John was invited to Cambridge for six weeks in early '79 to lecture and work on his book, to try to make sense of the work we had done. For his pains, when he came back, the Scottish Arts Council sent an alarming letter saying they would not renew our grant because they thought his commitment to 7:84 Scotland was 'perhaps not quite as strong as it had been'. He reassured them, and carried on writing *Joe's Drum*.

This play was a direct response to the 'thunderous apathy of the devolution vote' which had just happened, and left Scotland in a state of deep political depression. In the preface to the play, he wrote:

'In these circumstances *Joe's Drum* was both an expression of anger and frustration, and a tocsin to alert the audience to the full monstrosity of what was going on. In performance it clearly aroused many echoes, and seemed to say what a lot of Scots wanted to hear in 1979. It is to be hoped that the drum will go on beating into the 80s, to waken us from our curious hibernation.'

This show saw the company back on the road with two big tours. There was a lot of discussion. I thought it a very timely intervention. It toured again in the spring, and played to many full houses. It had an enthusiastic critical reception.

But for me, the new start really began with the joyful birth in July 1979 of my daughter. It was a beautiful summer. On a personal level I had had a strong feeling that we were going to need something extra special to see us through the hazards of the 80s. It turned out to be Kate.

How do you manage?

When I first had it confirmed that I was pregnant again I decided not to tell anyone until the results of the amniocentesis test were known. A pregnancy seems longer if everybody keeps asking for nine months, 'When are you due?' before there is even a noticeable bulge.

But at the very first hospital visit they thought I might miscarry, and decided to keep me in overnight. This created a problem. I had not yet told the boys. I telephoned John to ask him to explain without alarming them why I should suddenly be staying the night in hospital. This he did, and they all came to see me after school. They were ten and eleven. It must have been very unexpected.

I was very affected by their response. The boys were instantly 'bonded' to the unborn baby. 'How big is it, then, now? As big as my little finger?' They had a stake in its survival. Looking back I think that threatened miscarriage was almost a good thing. I was out of hospital the next day and home again. I could rely on their support.

We spent that Christmas in John's mum and dad's snow-bound Welsh cottage, up a hillside, very wet. The kitchen was leaking, the rooms were damp, but we had big fires and stockings and lots of love. I knew that if everything went well the baby in the summer would be joyful for us all.

She arrived on Dan's very last day at primary school, just after I had seen

87

him off with his lunch-box. He had been very happy there and was quite apprehensive about leaving. But after the summer he would be joining Finn who would look after him in big school.

They decided firmly on the name Kate, and from that day on she became 'our baby'. The midwife who called round for the next week understood. I told her that I wanted no token sharing, that the baby would be bottle-fed by all of us. That we would *all* change nappies, and dress her, and do what had to be done, from the start. I did not want this small important person excluding me from the others.

The midwife showed Dan how to clean the baby's cord, Finn how to wind her, and they did it, and their pals were queueing up in their leather jackets and jeans to push the pram round the sunny street to get her off to sleep. Practically all of Danny's class came to see the new baby immediately, and they all sent a card with signatures climbing all over it. Soon the boys were trying to send us out so they could babysit – 'If she needs feeding, we'll feed her.' They were wanting to take charge, and who was I to complain?

A year and a half later, when we moved to Edinburgh full time, I had two teenagers and a toddler and a great deal of work. In our two and a half rooms we were falling over football boots, bikes, typewriters and books, hoping it would be dry so they could play outside.

In January 1980 we finally found a bigger flat. It had big rooms, and space, for the first time. It was great, but I missed the community support systems of that district by the waters of Leith known as the Colonies. I relied on swapping children and babysitting friends from there, and still do.

Our neighbour was a retired shepherd from the Ettrick Forest.

When we moved in, there was always a crowd of children in the street in the evening playing hidey-go-seek, kerbie, keepie-uppie, and all the other street games that were very often organised by the girls. And of course football. Some neighbours got beady about footballs landing on their roses, or their washing. But I got to know practically everybody in the street, and at New Year we first-footed each other.

It is a short walk to the Waters of Leith. The bridge that crosses it has a troll fol-de-rol living underneath. From there it is only a step to the Botanic Gardens. This was where Kate sat in her pram while I worked on my scripts, where she learnt to walk and talk, look for elderberries, found slaters, played in puddles, and put down her roots. Here the boys made friends, played football, did wheelies, practised headers, lurked on the corner, and gained their independence.

Nowadays there are fewer children in that street, and people live more detached lives, but people still sit on the steps in the summertime, and cross-gate chats continue.

When we moved, we had all grown up a lot, but we had grown up together. And that was how we managed.

Rehearsals for *Swings and Roundabouts*

So in January 1980, when she was six months old, I was back in rehearsals, with Kate in the carrycot in the corner. At this point I was living with her in Edinburgh. John, who also still had the English company to look after, and the boys who were at a London comprehensive near Victoria, were still based in London except for the tours and holidays. During rehearsals Danny had to have a minor operation in Charing Cross Hospital, and I went to London with Kate to be with him. I put her in a pushchair that would fit on a bus, so at six months she was propped up taking in the world around her. Within a week Dan was recuperating with us in Edinburgh, having travelled up in another wheelchair.

At the end of rehearsals, we all set off to open the show in Aberdeen. Our car broke down definitively after too much hard work, on a Sunday night near Laurencekirk. We finally arrived on top of an AA relay truck, the entire family, baby, bottle and me still clutching the script. The boys thought it was a great laugh.

Swings and Roundabouts went well. It was quite a short six week tour, including two happy weeks at the Citizens. Giles Havergal was very enthusiastic about it. It was a rather surprising show, in structure a kind of ironical, inverted version of *Private Lives* – certainly just as funny. The audience were intrigued by it.

McGrath's Programme Note:
'There are some moments in all our lives when we become acutely aware of ourselves – wedding days, twenty-first birthdays, days when a friend or a parent dies, or just days when everything goes wrong; times when we become conscious of ourselves as suddenly *defined*, as no longer a mass of possibilities, but a human fact. It is at one of these moments that Andy and Ginny, Freddie and Rosemary find themselves thrown together in our play. In spite of their similarities as "people", there are social forces that enter their most private thoughts – the forces that have helped to define them: as women and men, as working or ruling class.

Class is thought to have been abolished in this country because it is possible for a miner's son to become Prime Minister. Similarly women are said to have achieved equality because a woman has actually become Prime Minister. We know that in fact most miners' sons become unemployed miners, and most women remain dominated by the needs of men. But one of the greatest weapons of capitalism is its ability to confuse.'

A different story, a different style.
Notes in my script of *Swings and Roundabouts* on the character Rosemary I played, who was rather a hopeless, privately-educated, reluctant second wife:

'I'm terrified of stuffing a turkey let alone a pressure cooker.'
'These men in raincoats in the public library make me feel it's all *my* fault.'
'I don't know how to work the launderette and I feel it's stupid to ask. People like me are relics of another time when we could manage. Now we can't even ask for a doctor without panicking. What is going to happen to us?'

I enjoyed doing this play and would like to do it again. Freddie, my husband in the play, was a model Thatcherite, a systems man. People at the time found him hilarious, a grotesque. If we were to do the play again now, he would appear as the model to which we must all aspire – perfectly reasonable and understated. It is a very witty play, and predicted what was to come in the 80s all too clearly.

Meanwhile, the English company were touring Barrie Keefe's play *Sus*.

Boards and Management (1979-1980)

A glance at the minutes of the board meetings of 7:84 Scotland around this time remind us of one or two salient features and differences that mark the period.

John McGrath was still Chairman of the Board – the SAC had not yet insisted on his standing down. Bill Speirs of the STUC was a member, as were Lord McCluskey, elevated by Labour when they needed a Lord Advocate; Mabel Skinner, indomitable fighter and councillor from Inverness; Bob Tait, writer and education college lecturer from Aberdeen; Tom Laurie, our old friend and promoter from Cumbernauld; Isobel Murray, lecturer in Aberdeen University English Department and a distinguished literary critic; Dolina MacLennan, from Lewis, Gaelic singer and company member since we began; Jeanette Husband, politically active in Carlisle, working in the voluntary services there; Norman Buchan, Labour MP and Labour's Shadow Spokesman for the Arts; Jane Mackay, always busy as Glasgow Trades Council Secretary; Janey Buchan, even busier and further away as a voluble Member of the European Parliament; Margaret MacPherson from Skye, writer and doughty fighter for the crofters on the Crofters Commission; Annie Inglis from Aberdeen, lecturer but also moving spirit for the arts in Aberdeen; Kris Misselbrook, representing the technicians in the company; David MacLennan, myself, and Feri Lean, our ex-administrator.

These board members were chosen to represent our scattered audience, the working company, and our political and labour movement support, and not to favour, as now, the interests of the urban west, and Glasgow in particular. I made board meetings very interesting. People spoke up for the demands of their particular area, and kept us in close touch with developments there, quite apart from reactions to the shows. It was the kind of practical expertise which Arts Council people fail to appreciate, being firmly rooted themselves in the Edinburgh/Glasgow cultural consensus.

Christine Hamilton was our new administrator – Annie Rubienska had just moved from administration to publicity and publications.

At the 1980 AGM, the board noted that there was a surplus of £71 after touring *Joe's Drum* for ten weeks and *Swings and Roundabouts* for six weeks, at a cost of £30,000 and £20,000 respectively. The company put £600 into a reserve for replacement of fixed assets. Mary Picken, at this time Drama Officer of the Scottish Arts Council, noted her pleasure.

Joe's Drum had been published by the Aberdeen People's Press (now defunct). We planned a brochure to coincide with the following year's tenth anniversary.

The meeting was attended by two company reps – Bill Riddoch and Joanna Keddie – a regular practice which now seems to have been dropped completely. The company wage would rise from £90 to £100 when the company went on tour, and to £120 in January.

Mary Picken advised the board that Strathclyde University were holding a conference about sponsorship in the arts which we should attend. . . .

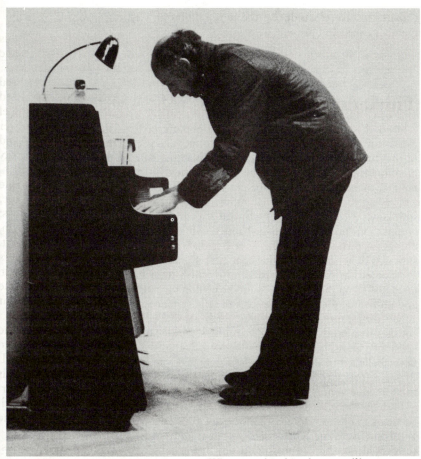

Dave Anderson checks the piano on tour. 'When was this thing last tuned?'

Sponsorship (1980)

It was agreed that the recently formed finance committee would be re-named the appeals committee, to be chaired by Lord McCluskey. A letter was circulated the following month from this appeals committee describing the company and asking for support from a list of 100 companies not considered beyond the pale. It concluded: 'I ask you to give this request your most serious consideration. If the private sector will not support the arts, or confines its help to prestige productions presented to largely middle-class audiences then community groups like ourselves will be forced to draw dismal conclusions about the value of government utterances. In an informed democracy dissident theatre has a vital role. I hope you will support it.'

This letter produced a grand total response of £100 – from the *Daily Record*.

Meanwhile we were planning the Glasgow Play season which John and I christened *Clydebuilt*. Linda McKenney, not long out of Cambridge, was doing some very exciting research for it. We also were planning a tenth Anniversary

Cabaret to take place during the next Edinburgh Festival, involving as many members, past and present, as possible.

Thirteen: *Blood Red Roses.* 1980-1981

I loved this play. Bessie Gordon, the heroine, a fictitious character, is an extraordinary role to play. I developed a marvellous closeness with the women in the audience which afforded me a great freedom in performance; not to mention friendships made. The play touched on problems that were quite familiar to myself and John, albeit in a slightly different context. Like me, Bessie was trying to support an active public life and fulfil the demands of a family simultaneously. In that story Bessie was trying to take on a multinational corporation 'pretty near single-handed' while bringing up two energetic girls, doing her own work, looking after her dad, and being the convenor of shop-stewards in her factory. At the same time she was living with a busy, committed and somewhat handless-in-the-house trades unionist, Alex, who tried not to need his tea on the table but found he couldn't manage without it. Most women end up feeling guilty in these sorts of circumstances.

My own experience of dealing with these kinds of conflicting demands consists of periods of sustained tiredness, never finishing anything properly, a sense of failure, but almost simultaneously a great sense of fulfilment. I have never believed in the 'ideal mother' notion or the 'ideal father', come to that. As far as pressure goes, what was true for me was also true for John, and we tried to cope with it equally.

Perhaps the only thing I suffer from during rehearsals is the lack of privacy. So many things to be done when you get home, people wanting attention which I want to give. An actress friend with young children working on a six-part series told me she had to go and stay in a hotel for the weekend just to learn her lines. I learnt a lot of mine on the train journeys to and from Glasgow – forty-five minutes alone, unless you meet any of that half of the theatre workers of Scotland who travel on it daily.

As my children get older I value the contact with all kinds of different young people that they bring. As they begin to need space and freedom themselves, I may begin to miss the constant proximity, perhaps even their demands. I certainly want their approval and advice, probably more than they do mine. I tried to teach my children to think for themselves, to cook, clear up, to look after each other and others. They try to teach me to be cool, not to panic, to be tolerant, to laugh a bit and not to take things too seriously. We make progress, we make mistakes. As Bessie says, 'I'm still fighting, and I'm going to carry on fighting till they count me out.'

There is a comical scene in *Blood Red Roses* in which Bessie is on the phone to fellow trades unionists in Spain, and around the country, trying to organise a strike, while her children argue over homework, demand food, refuse to go to bed, fight, and generally get on with their own lives. It is very funny and got a big reaction most nights. Finally, exasperated, Bessie says, 'Alex, would you stop *negotiating* and get these two to their beds.' But it is Grandpa who succeeds.

This scene clearly struck a chord with many women in the audience, and many men too. When we shot it in the film, the crew applauded. They must have recognised the melody. . . .

This was one aspect of the play. The other was an epic struggle against a 'rationalising' multi-national corporation. As in life, however, the two didn't slot neatly into separate compartments.

Very, very few rewrites. The play, in the writing and in the rehearsal, seemed to come out very securely. And it was frighteningly prophetic.

In the programme note John wrote:

'Fashion can perform a valuable role for the capitalist state. For it can effectively safeguard the status quo by seeing every form of opposition to the status quo as a flash in the pan; the seven-days-wonder of the burning bra, the passing of the Winter of Our Discontent – even monetarism, and Milton Friedman, they too will pass on as fashions come and go. . . .The struggles of the working class to protect the advances made in their standards of life go on. But they are suffering serious setbacks. And militancy in those struggles – particularly industrial militancy – is now distinctly out of fashion . . . a series of vicious campaigns against 'The Wreckers' has undermined the already shaky morale of the shop-floor organiser.

In this situation, it seemed important – if a little unfashionable – to take a longer look at one of these militants, and at the whole question of what "fighting" means in the age of multiple warhead. And to try to see where exactly the battlefields are, and who is on whose side . . .'

And a speech from the old soldier, Sandy, in the play:

'Of whose empire are we now the colonial people? Look around: we see no soldiers, no military parade with drums and fifes, bugles or bagpipes. No gunboats, no show of strength . . . and yet there is fear – I can smell it . . . long black hulks glide underwater out of the Holy Loch, full of terrible destruction, quiet as the grave. A factory closes in East Kilbride, and a whole town discovers it is dependent on the will of the imperial power.'

This play opened on Monday, 18 August in the Edinburgh Festival at the Churchill Theatre (for one week at eighty-three per cent attendance), two nights in the Brunton, Musselburgh (seventy-three per cent) and in the last week at the George Square Theatre it played to ninety-two per cent capacity.

The notices were excellent. Cordelia Oliver in the *Guardian*: 'Elizabeth MacLennan used all her mimetic skill and truly theatrical presence to make "Battling Bessie" both believable and larger than life, magnificent but vulnerable, from the first gawky schoolgirl to the final, deceptively mellow, middle-aged grass widow and mother of the next generation of fighting women.'

The English company had brought Barry Keefe's *Sus* to Edinburgh, up the road at St Columba's by the castle. It was also very well received, a well-timed intervention in the campaign against the racist SUS laws which allowed the police to summarily arrest any person on mere suspicion.

Blood Red Roses touring schedule, August – November 1980

August

Mon 18-Sat 23	Churchill Theatre, Edinburgh
Fri 29-Sat 30	Brunton Theatre, Musselburgh

September

Mon 1-Sat 6	George Square Theatre, Edinburgh
Tues 9-Sat 13	Cumbernauld Theatre
Tues 16	Duthac Centre, Tain
Wed 17	School, Brora
Thur 18	Assembly Halls, Wick
Fri 19	Thurso Town Hall
Sat 20	Rogart Village Hall
Mon 22	Ullapool Community Centre
Wed 24	Stornoway Town Hall
Thur 25	Tarbert Harris Village Hall
Sat 27	Kyleakin Village Hall

October

Wed 1-Fri 3	Eden Court, Inverness
Sat 4	Glasgow University
Fri 10	East Kilbride Village Theatre
Sat 11	Bathgate Community Centre
Tues 21	Star Club, Glasgow
Wed 22	Clydebank Town Hall
Fri 24	Ratho Station, Norwood School
Sat 25	Webster Theatre, Arbroath
Tues 28	New Lanark
Wed 29	Golden Lion Hotel, Stirling
Thur 30	Shotts
Fri 31	Park Mains Theatre, Erskine

November

Sat 1	Livingstone, Lanthorne
Tues 4-Thur 6	Aberdeen Arts Centre
Sat 8	Third Eye Centre, Glasgow

On the first night John introduced me for the first time to Cathy Macdonald from East Kilbride, one of several remarkable women whose story the play reflected in part. I was relieved to get her approval, and we had a lot to talk about.

During this tour we all decided to settle properly in Edinburgh, where the boys would start at a new school in the autumn. They were pleased with this arrangement.

Like all the best productions *Blood Red Roses* grew with time on the road. Billy Riddoch was on top form; Laurie Ruddic – Citizens-bred – played my husband Alex. He was intrigued by our audiences and some of the places we played, and touched by the standing ovation in Whitfield Club in Dundee. He settled down there to a long conversation with the shop stewards. Missing home.

94

a pale and touching Phyllis Logan as Catriona; and – on the second tour – my real friend to be, Mary Ann Coburn joined us; Joanna Keddie, in her guide's costume as the child. We were a family on stage and off – complete with rows, ganging up and reconciliations.

We played one week in the Highlands as an experiment – interesting. The audience mostly identified with the characters Sandy and Bessie who had come from the Highlands. In Wick, Thurso, Tain, Brora, Ullapool and in Stornaway, it worked. They loved it. But in Rogart, my home village, and one of the more rural places, they thought it was, as Iain Sutherland said, 'Helluva good, but helluva political.' If it had dealt with the *land* question that would have been okay. But *industrial* militancy – the language of confrontation, that hard, bitter scene at the beginning of act II – they found alienating. We learnt from that. We had always respected the cultural differences in our various audiences – this was proof. Nevertheless in the *other* Highland gigs it was thoroughly enjoyed, particularly in Thurso and Stornaway.

To some extent the more militant bits of the play *were* difficult because already by 1981 a huge amount of adverse publicity had been poured on activists such as Red Robbo, after the Winter of Discontent. Nonetheless, the audience was big, very mixed and mainly highly enthusiastic. Eighty-eight per cent in Brora, one hundred and two per cent Thurso, Ullapool ninety-nine per cent, Stornaway ninety-seven per cent, Kyleakin ninety-five per cent, Livingston Lanthorne Centre had one hundred and twenty per cent and had to put in forty extra chairs and the Community Education Centre in Shotts had one hundred per cent.

During the run at the Churchill Theatre in Edinburgh I was asked to do a speech of Bessie's for an item about facing up to redundancy on the Scottish television news when the unemployment topped one million:

'The next six months were very bad.

We did the lot, short of occupying the factory. We had meetings with the management, meetings with the unions, meetings with the government, the Scottish Office, the district council, the regional council, the local MPs, the Provost, the Church of Scotland and every trades council in the area. And we had mass meetings, aye – but as the months went by and we were just keeping the gates open by pure willpower, the meetings got smaller, and quieter, and sadder.

Because it was just a routine: the ritual struggle against closure as seen in factories throughout the land. We gained a certain amount of time, but we knew we couldnae win. And *that* is terrible tae bear. To fight knowing you are gonnae lose – it takes away the dignity of the combat – it turns fighting words into speechifying, and worst of all, it induces cynicism, and if I hate anything, I hate cynicism.'

We were certainly reflecting the lives of many people which would otherwise have been ignored. The opposition to our doing this was bound to grow. This period contained the seeds of a number of problems that would not go away. Mostly they were due to the arrival of an increasingly punitive Tory administration.

We reopened for two busy weeks at the Citizens Theatre, Glasgow on 17 February the following spring, in 1981. By now John was rehearsing his new play *Night Class* with the English company, and dashing up and down at weekends. On to Stirling and Dundee, and we finished up with a week at the Theatre Royal, Stratford East – our first visit there.

While we were in London, 7:84 Scotland was also mounting a five-week tour with the *One Big Blow* company from 7:84 England. So we had three shows on the go.

In his note in the programme, John wrote:

'The Tory government's cynical plan to dismantle the power of the miners by dismantling the entire industry, has been defeated by a massive show of solidarity from the miners themselves. A play about the continuing hazards of this work, about the pits, about the need for solidarity, should be seen by as many people as possible.

We hope you enjoy it.'

They did.

Night Class opened at the Battersea Arts Centre on 20 March. It went to Corby, Nottingham, Stoke, Solihull, and thirty-six other places, inaugurating 7:84 England's new policy of building a circuit of regular dates, which they would visit at least twice a year, to try to establish more continuity with those communities.

I saw it in Mansfield, just outside Nottingham, in a huge Miners Welfare. Fred Molina was spectacular, the music by Rick Lloyd was excellent, with some wonderful pastiche, and songs that clearly moved the audience. Later I saw it in Edinburgh, and the audience seemed surprisingly resistant to being affected by the struggles and feelings of ordinary English people. In Mansfield the audience loved the sly verbal humour, and responded with a lot of heart.

At the beginning of May the boys left their London school. We went for two weeks' holiday, then they started school in Edinburgh, and settled in quickly.

There was a CND March in Glasgow, a march against the cuts, visits to John's family in Merseyside, and plans for a Highland tour. We built some bunk-beds to make more space in the little flat, Kate had her second birthday party, and I seemed to make a lot of chips.

Although I knew we would still be travelling up and down a great deal it was a relief to feel that for the most part we were all together under one roof.

* * *

At this time, the Tory Arts minister was Paul Channon. Teddy Taylor, a right-wing extremist MP who had been thrown out of his seat in Scotland by Labour's John Maxton, had got himself a new seat in Southend. On 28 May 1981, *The Stage* carried a lead article reporting that Teddy Taylor had demanded the axing of grants to nearly thirty theatre companies, and that he had 'recently met funding body chiefs to discuss his case for sweeping cuts'.

The article went on: 'Taylor maintains the groups he wants to see deprived of their grants exist solely for political reasons, and are arts organisations only in the sense that they use theatre to push home their message.'

The list of course included 7:84. Amongst the others were CAST, Belt and Braces, Monstrous Regiment, Women's Theatre Group, Gay Sweatshop, Avon Touring, Wakefield Tricycle, Joint Stock, Pip Simmonds Theatre Group, The Combination, Inter Action and Beryl and the Perils. At the time this gesture provoked derision and disbelief. By the end of the decade, perhaps three of the thirty still existed as 'clients' of the Arts Council.

During 1984/5 *Blood Red Roses* was filmed by Freeway Films, John's company, for Channel 4. We were strongly supported in this by Jeremy Isaacs and David Rose (commissioning editor). By then Thatcher had definitely started winning the ideology battle and it was a very brave film: fear of speaking out had become widespread, even in Scotland.

Elizabeth MacLennan as Bessie, filming *Blood Red Roses* by John McGrath with Freeway Films in 1984.

Diary 1988

Wednesday, 16 March
My birthday. John in Auckland, Kate to play with Kirsten, Finn has a university exam, Danny working for the ski school at Carrbridge.

I decide to try and analyse the onset of the cultural ice age – spreading from the south, with the growth of Thatcherism. My brother David comes over from Glasgow where he is working with Wildcat on the Celtic Show *to take Kate and me out to the Chinese restaurant and, like all our family, she loves rituals.*

We talk about funding. David thinks Wildcat will be okay for three-year funding, largely I suppose because of their financial and critical success last year with The Steamie, *and because they have attracted a big sponsorship package from the Celtic Football Club to write this show commemorating their hundredth anniversary. But he feels the indications are, from reading the entrails, and given our admin problems last year, that we in 7:84 may not. In spite of our exciting Three-Year Plan. But things should work out, given perhaps a hiccough this year. And of course, three-year funding has its own drawbacks. . . .*

I feel sure that we are going to be cut. A chill. I change the subject. Three years ago we had been through it all with the English company, just after the miners' strike. I felt then I needed to prepare for the battle.

Friday, 18 March
Still no notice from the Arts Council, although it was promised today. The other companies too must be awaiting their sentence or reprieve – who needs the Borgias?

Borderline say they too have heard nothing. John Haswell (our acting administrator), Liz Smith (publicity) and myself in the office. I ask them to keep ringing the Council.

Sir Alan Peacock (of the Peacock report on television) was appointed last year to head the SAC, presumably to bring it into line with Rees Mogg, his counterpart in the Arts Council of Great Britain, and with the requirements of Downing Street.

I heard Peacock speak in symposium at the Edinburgh Festival in 1987. He struck a slightly punitive note. His priorities did not seem to include reflecting the joys, preoccupations and struggles of ordinary people. The gap between our lived experience of popular theatre and the dominant perception of what constitutes a 'good' cost effective piece of theatre has never been wider.

When the TV script of The Cheviot *was submitted to the BBC in 1973, the Head of Plays told the producer: 'The second half of the script is totally unacceptable for broadcasting.'*

The Controller of BBC 1, who was then Alistair Milne (later considered a real threat and dismissed), issued a list of cuts and changes, without which he would not transmit it. Both, however, were prepared to discuss the matter, and a few months later the play was transmitted more or less intact, and the response was so great that they repeated it within a few months without any hesitation.

Those were still years of 'liberal' consensus. We have indeed 'moved on' since then. It is a frightening Orwellian state that the present government would have us move into, hands tied, with no dissent allowed.

Fourteen: *The Catch, or Red Herrings in the Minch.* 1982.

The Catch was our tenth anniversary show. For me it was the most co-operative and fulfilling of all the Highland tours including *The Cheviot*, and contained within it both lessons we had learnt over ten years, and some seeds which are still to flower in the 90s.

It was also the *last* 7:84 show to date, apart from *Baby and the Bathwater* in which the preparation, research, discussion, writing, re-writing, rehearsal, performance and the development of the performance throughout the tour bore the particular imprint of John McGrath's style, his way of working, and our joint experience as part of the group.

7% OF THE POPULATION OF THIS COUNTRY OWN 84% OF THE WEALTH

As on a number of previous occasions the experience – both theatrical and political – of the individuals within the group varied considerably, but this was not a cause of suspicion or distrust. On the contrary, we learnt a great deal out of respect for each other's differences and experience, and the results were a striking example of collective strength. It was also a lot of fun.

The company consisted of Mary Ann Coburn, actress and singer – with five years' experience of touring in Scotland in at least three companies, and four pantomimes to her name, she did a neat line in principal girls. She had joined us to play three parts in *Blood Red Roses* and continued after *The Catch* with leading parts in *Johnny Noble*, *In Time of Strife*, *Men Should Weep*, and *Women in Power*. We became close friends and developed a strong working relationship which sustained us throughout two years of mammoth touring.

Rehearsing *The Catch or Red Herrings in the Minch* by John McGrath in 1982. *From left to right*: Catherine Anne McPhee, Alan Hulse, Mary-Ann Coburn.

Mary Ann is a perfectionist, a lovely singer and mover. Of *The Catch* and her performance in it, Harold Hobson said:

'McGrath's technique is based on the music hall and this gives him wonderful chances, with a few strips of painted cardboard, to summon up visions of a coach party, an aeroplane, and a dinghy rocking on a stormy sea, as well as a darkling glen backed by the sun setting over the quiet, misty coast. It is here that his heroine, played rather beautifully by Mary Ann Coburn as a girl who has just come over from Blackpool, wistfully has a vision and a longing not very different from, not much less magical than, Mary Rose's; and Simon Mackenzie, piloting the girl and her husband across the waters, sings a threnody on the decline of the herring industry that floods the heart with sadness and a melancholy joy, which spills over into a mournful dignity in the antiphony of Mr McGrath's lamentation on the effects of germ warfare. If you miss seeing *The Catch* your life will be the poorer for it ever afterwards.'

In *Blood Red Roses*, Mary Ann made people cry every night. Her speech as the daughter who's fed up with politics always brought the house down:

'I think they're gonna argue about politics again. Well I'm no' interested in politics, I never have been and I never will be – it's boring and pointless, and it makes people look all prim round the mouth and it kills people. And it puts people out of work. And it drives away your dad . . .

I want a nice house – of my own – and a nice man, with enough money to keep me at home all day playing cards with Grandpa.'

Alan Hulse, co-founder of the General Will, joined us. He had been working in popular theatre with Foco Novo, Hull Truck and Monstrous Regiment. He'd been at it since 1971, like me. He had recently completed the tour of *Nightclass* for the English 7:84. Alan is a very funny, accomplished actor whose commitment to the project was great. We got on really well.

The other two performers who made up our tiny group were Gaels – Simon Mackenzie and Cathy Ann McPhee from the islands Harris and Barra respectively. Both are now my dear friends.

Simon trained at the Bristol Old Vic as a late starter in theatre, bringing with him a great deal of life experience. He is a clever, sensitive, extremely widely read and knowledgeable person and feels passionately about popular culture, young people, education and the survival of the Gaelic culture in particular. He is a fine, if somewhat eccentric Gaelic singer, and 'a native speaker' as they say. He has been with 7:84 ever since, remains on the board and his commitment is unwavering. He learnt a lot too on *The Catch*.

Cathy Ann had been with him at the beginning of Fir Chlis (the Northern Lights), the Gaelic theatre company based on Harris for three years. She is arguably our finest Gaelic singer, an instinctive commedienne and a great favourite with the children, including my Kate. Perhaps the best thing she does is chatting up the audience – being a very outgoing chatty person anyway, it seems to be just an extension of her enormously friendly open approach to people and her good nature.

Simon, Cathy Ann and I were to travel all over Scotland together, to the USSR and to Canada later with *The Albannach*, and *Baby and the Bathwater, The Happy Land* and *Mhairi Mhor*, our last Highland show, in autumn 1987.

Our stage manager was Sue Rumball, who had been working in more conventional theatre at the Lyceum, and was finding out a bit about how our sort of theatre worked; shy, hard-working. Alan Woolfe, an experienced and committed 7:84 hand, strong on company democracy and impossible get-ins, was production manager. Bill Winter was DSM, ready for almost anything, and Ali McArthur 7:84 lighting designer of great distinction and imagination – now touring with the Proclaimers.

Annie Rubienska (publicity) had joined us in 1979 for *Joe's Drum*, not quite sure where exactly the Minch* was, but very sure of her politics and her heart,

* *the sea surrounding the Inner Hebrides*

and wanting to work for 7:84 since seeing *Ballygombeen Bequest* as a student. 'That was the road to Damascus,' she said later. 'I wanted to work with them after that but I had to wait for a while.' When Feri Lean, 7:84 Scotland's first administrator, left to help start Wildcat in 1978, Annie took over. She had seen all the shows and was, above all, concerned about what we were saying and how effectively. She liked *Game's a Bogey* best, but thought *Joe's Drum* was something to be proud of: 'It created a lot of discussion, an important role of the company.' She would drop in on the workshops in Logie Green Road and take part when her tour booking allowed time, between wrestling with Mac-Brayne's timetables.

Christine Hamilton, Glasgow University drama graduate, fresh from the Citizens front of house, was our administrator having joined us for *Blood Red Roses* of which she was immensely proud. It portrayed a fighting woman with whom she could well identify – on most things. (She was cross with John for making Bessie have another baby at the end.) She was to stay with us until the end of the *Clydebuilt* season which was a major commitment and for which she badly needed more money and more staff. But her enthusiasm for the specific politics of our work was – and still is – boundless and a central factor in her approach to administration.

Unlike many of the new breed of administrators who now run our arts 'institutions', she never struck me as somebody who could just as easily administer a bacon-packing plant. We came to value her first class intelligence, energy and rapport with people, particularly with potential supporters. She could even be diplomatic with 'hostile elements' – perhaps her experience in the front of house at the Citizens prepared her for that. Her work now as arts officer for the Scottish TUC must benefit from a close working knowledge of the needs of both artists and audience on the ground, gained with 7:84.

That was the group on the road – plus myself on keyboards (as the entire band), as narrator and as many characters including Chuck Eagleburger, a US Marine. And John McGrath of course, writer and director, and Kate McGrath aged two.

Linda MacKenney, who had joined us to research for the planned *Clydebuilt*, season would pop into rehearsals to get to know and encourage us during this period.

For two of the Highland touring weeks Fiona Macmillan, recent Edinburgh history graduate and friend, babysat and ran the ticket desk/bookstall when Finn or Danny were not doing it, and it was the start of a long association. I had to pay her wages, and hers, the boys' and Kate's fares, ferries and accommodation.

This was our extended family, and most definitely Kate's. Just as the company who performed *The Cheviot* over the course of one tumultous year and thousands of miles had become Finn and Danny's extended family, so here was Kate's, nearly ten years on: sitting on their knees in the van; Simon telling her stories in the corner of the pub in Achiltibuie; used to waiting in rehearsals, sleeping in vans, halls, late nights, meetings, ferry crossings, looking out for seals. John added to the play as we went along, as things changed.

Mark Brown wrote the music that wasn't traditional, Jenny Tiramani designed the ingenious set painted by Alistair Brotchie. John Knowles on attachment from Nottingham Theatre Design School worked as a student assistant. Albert

(John Tinlin) aged eighteen learned fast about operating the lights, and about the pros and cons of Southern Comfort in his spare time. . . .

We opened at the Edinburgh Festival on Saturday 15 August 1982 at the Moray House Theatre and played to full houses for two weeks. The reviews were terrific.

John Fowler of the *Glasgow Herald* wrote:

'The gift of 7:84 Company Scotland is to make political theatre fun, a rare combination . . . the audience was soon happily singing along in rebellious chorus. If it goes with a swing in Edinburgh, what a hit it will be in the West Highlands.

The acting is good. Elizabeth MacLennan excelled in her portrait of a US army sergeant with padded shoulders, steel helmet, and psychotic fear behind the eyes. Catherine Ann MacPhee lectured her (imaginary) hens beautifully in Gaelic.'

The *Guardian* thought it was the show which 'best expresses John McGrath's real, searing anger for Scotland.'

During this time the English company were presenting *One Big Blow*, written and directed by John Burrows, at the Bus Depot in Annandale Street – also to full houses and great acclaim. This was the company which turned into the Flying Pickets, and rose the next Christmas to the top of the Hit Parade. They started singing *a capella* in the show, carried on in the van, and ended up touring to huge audiences everywhere. We had enthusiastic accounts from Finn who worked on the front of house (for peanuts) and Dan who worked on *The Catch* (ditto), during their school holidays.

Simultaneously we played our Tenth Anniversary Cabaret to 200 per night at the Edinburgh Trades Council Club in Picardy Place – many past and present 7:84 performers took part, including Terry Neason, the Flying Pickets, Anne Louise Ross, Dave Anderson, the 7:84 England Band and Mike O'Neill, Rachel Bell, Dennis Charles, and Hilton MacRae. Hilton and I took turns at compering. Bill Paterson held up the song sheet one night.

It was a busy festival and we transferred *The Catch* to George Square Theatre and continued to large houses. And on 7 September we set off on a tour which lasted through till November.

John meanwhile set up a four-week tour of Clare Luckham's *Trafford Tanzi* for the English company and worked on his adaptation of *The Knights* by Aristophanes.

As with *The Cheviot*, the issues raised in *The Catch* became more and more current as the tour went on: the NATO presence in Scotland, the ineffectual position of the newly formed SDP, the Anthrax on Gruinard island, the need for fishing quotas, concern over nuclear waste dumping – all issues dealt with in the play and in the songs, sometimes with comedy, sometimes as unadorned, plain facts.

I decided to keep a detailed log book of the entire tour, and began immediately. It is by far the fullest existing account of the impact of any 7:84 tour. It records the company's and the audiences' day-to-day reactions and their interaction. By and by, I think every member of the company wrote in it at some point, recording their ups and downs, tiredness, exhilaration, good meals, bad sea crossings, hazardous van journeys. It illustrates the essentially co-operative essence of this kind of work, and how it depends on goodwill, mutual tolerance, non-competitive creativity and subsidy.

The tour went all over the Highlands and islands but also to Stirling, Glasgow, Cumbernauld, Dundee, Aberdeen, Arbroath, Buckie, Peterhead, Dumfries and Shotts – a very wide cultural spread. As it moved, the involvement of the audience with their more particular areas of concern was noticeable. In the ports, for example, worries about the fishing quotas, and the EEC directives, elsewhere – especially if there was a strong nuclear presence – defence issues. And some unpredictable responses; the surprises, the arguments, which go on and have been picked up and continued in subsequent Highland shows.

John Fowler who flew to Lewis in the Outer Hebrides to see the show, wrote in the *Glasgow Herald*: 'Four hundred people came in out of the rain, and in spite of the apocalyptic message, laughed immoderately. Seeing *The Catch* in Stornoway was for me a remarkable vindication of the argument that John McGrath puts forward in his book, just published, called *A Good Night Out*.'

A letter from one of our audience in the *Stornoway Gazette* the following week said:

'Last week I was privileged to attend one of the most exhilarating performances I have ever seen. I left the town hall feeling buoyant and uplifted, grateful to have heard feelings which I know I share with many young people being expressed on stage.

Throughout 7:84's production of *The Catch* I was aware of many different emotions within myself: at one point I felt despair; at another humiliation; and at another utter helplessness. By the end of the evening that despair had been countered by hope; the humiliation by the realisation that we are beginning to resist; and the helplessness by the awareness that we in the Western Isles are not fighting single-handed against militaristic and bureaucratic tyranny.

My eventual hope was not merely inspired by the magnificence of the play and the conviction of the actresses and actors. The reaction of the audience itself – especially that of the many young people present – was enough to give me a great deal of confidence in the continuation of our own struggles against the advent of the NATO base. This play undoubtedly touched a chord in the souls of all who are aware of the issues at stake.'

Tour to Moscow, Tbilisi, Leningrad – December 1982

Our visit to the USSR in December 1982 was in many ways an extension of *The Catch* tour. Out of that company the group included John, myself, Mary Ann, Cathy Ann, Simon, Kate (three) and Danny (fourteen). Kris Misselbrook came and we were joined by Allan Ross and Dick Gaughan.

We rehearsed for three weeks for no money, did a benefit to raise money for our fares to London, and thereafter we were the guests of the Soviet Friendship Houses who looked after our expenses within the USSR. We took the children at our own expense.

We called the show *Napoleon's Revenge*. It was a collection of songs and sketches from several shows and perhaps the centrepiece was the 'Bonnie

Scotland meets NATO' sketch from *The Catch* with the American GI's farcical account of the NATO Icelandic Gap defence theory. I persuaded Allan Ross to pick up his fiddle again. He and Kris didn't mind being directed by me while John was directing the English company in his new play *Rejoice*. We concocted a show which gave a fairly vivid idea of our style, music and general approach to the audience.

We set off with lots of thermals and very little idea of what to expect. The Russian audiences, and our hosts everywhere, were wonderfully friendly. This was five years pre-*glasnost* but in theatre and intellectual circles things were already on the move – Andropov was in power, preparing the way a bit.

Moscow

Our arrival at the House of Friendship in Moscow closely resembled the Marx Brothers in some kind of Pan Soviet *Night at the Opera* or *Hellzapoppin*.

Our visit coincided with the sixtieth anniversary (every year in Moscow is an anniversary celebration of something) of the unification of the Soviet Republics. In the same building were troupes of artists and performers, musicians and singers from *all* the republics. ALL trying to do a technical rehearsal – apparently *simultaneously*. Terrifying fur-clad visions in boots with huge drums, multi-coloured costumes and swirling swords leapt around us, like Mongol hordes bursting out of tiny cubicles, speaking in at least seven languages.

Nobody was able to understand that we needed a base amp and speaker for Dick's bass guitar. It nearly caused a major diplomatic incident with the poor official, who thought he was looking after us so well. I wondered if we would be asked back. But the show went on that evening – tense, not knowing what reaction to expect.

In the event we got a very warm reception, and the show was televised coast to coast, with special interest being paid to the anti-nuclear position, nationwide TV cameras pointing right up our noses throughout.

We were introduced to many people in the peace movement and to many other artists. We were superbly looked after and explored the city freely in our time off, going off in small groups to different theatres, art galleries, to the ballet, to eat ice cream at the circus and to talk and sing through the night. Walking round Moscow in the snow, and travelling on the subway, people took turns to carry Kate, in her red and blue boots, because she was so warm. She became known as the Hot Water Bottle, and gained us instant friends across all the language barriers, as children so often do. She and Dan went off in the bus to see the Czar's Summer Palace while we were rehearsing. The bus broke down, but they told us it was Brilliant.

We were invited to the drama school, and watched the students give an impeccable performance of *Oklahoma!* in Russian, with the dance sequences heavily influenced by Russian folk dancing and athleticism. The standard of the singing was very high indeed. Actors train for five years in Soviet theatre, and hardly experience any unemployment thereafter. They found it *inconceivable* that over seventy per cent of our profession here are unemployed. Beyond belief.

We pointed out to the students our connections with their own Soviet *Blue*

Blouse groups of the twenties and they were amazed. I don't think that was part of their syllabus, any more than it is (or was) in the British drama schools at that time. This was pre-*glasnost* of course. . . .

The *Oklahoma!* episode reminded me of the time in 1974 when John was introduced to a Chinese delegate at the STUC conference at Rothesay, after the performance of *The Game's a Bogey*. John was at the time wearing a Mao jacket, probably bought in the Charing Cross Road. The Chinese delegate was in an immaculate Saville Row suit. He smiled widely as they shook hands, pointing to John's long arms sticking out: 'Far too short!' he said as they looked each other over and laughed.

We saw the Taganka Theatre company playing Liubimov's production of Bulgakov's *Master and Marguerite* to an audience crammed in like sardines, and John and Kris saw an adaptation of Barry Keefe's play *Gotcha* in a fringe basement theatre. Then on to Tblisi, Georgia.

Impossible to describe the warmth and friendliness and crazy fun of the group who were our Georgian hosts – the Cinema Actors' Theatre Company. We played in their theatre to a beautiful reception – I had foolhardily decided to do the story of Fionn McCuill in Russian for the tour, never having spoken a word so far. This was fine in Moscow, but in Tblisi, given Georgia's independent character, it would surely be better to try and do it in Georgian I thought gaily. So we asked our translator to arrange for someone to meet us off the plane and help me make a transcript into Georgian *for that evening*. No such person materialised.

We were taken on a beautiful drive into the hills to see the old churches, to hear about Georgia's independent history, to sample the local wine and tea (which reputedly explains Georgian longevity – the wine or the tea, depending on your ideological position). But not until *6.30 pm* (we were to go up at 8.00) did our translator appear. When he did, beaming hugely, I couldn't understand a word of what he had written – not one word. 'Just say it to me, slowly please.' And I wrote down in fumbling phonetics. The show was on and I went on with my fingers and toes (and tongue) crossed.

Cathy Ann and Dick were in fine voice – both among the finest folk singers in Scotland today within their quite distinct Lowlands and Highland traditions. Dick did 'The Maclean March', 'The Battle of the Braes' and 'The Demon of the Crooked Cross', John's song about the rise of Hitler. Cathy Ann gave a mixture of Gaelic songs from the Clearances and mouth music. Mary Ann sang 'What can't be done by one and one and one can perhaps be done by three', which is John's gentle song about the victory in Vietnam. She sang too about the overthrow of 'The Giant of the Frozen East' (their Czar Giant) which has a very catchy Russian tune they enjoyed. And lots more besides. Allan Ross, very comical as the Trembling Giant, tickled them greatly, and they loved his fiddle playing.

Then came my Fionn McCuill speech. I stepped forward and said slowly the first two lines, trying to keep smiling. And when, very soon, I ground to a halt I just had to ask the audience when I came to a difficult word. They said it *for* me, smiling encouragement. Unforgettable. We were in a 'behind you' situation. They were delighted and so were we. The Georgian language seems to jostle with consonants.

Here is an excerpt from the piece of paper I clutched in my wobbly hand:

'Legenda Gveubneba rom ertchel fin chakuli (McCuill) tavis mebrdzolebtan
ertad nadir obna . . . chven chven kveknebshi, ma dzraobisa da achali tschovre-
bisatvis brdzolis mussika.'

The last phrase meant something like, 'The music of what is happening.
That is the finest music in the world.' They seemed to agree wholeheartedly.
Perhaps it was the relief that I'd finished. . . .

That night was the first of our exchanges with that exciting, talented company,
the Film Actors' Studio of Tbilisi, or, as they are known in the Soviet Union,
after their revered director, the Tumanashvili Company. After the show – there
and then – they leapt up, cleared the stage and spread it with a feast and
flowers, and the celebrations began: speeches, songs, those wonderful seven-part
harmonies, and Kate at three, already the object of long romantic toasts. We
went on celebrating till two or three in the morning.

Our bus had long since gone home, but nothing daunted we sat outside the
theatre in the clear starry winter night on the skip (our only prop/costume
luggage thanks to lack of money and Kris's clever organisation). The administrator of the theatre called, or more accurately hi-jacked, a passing trolley bus.
The driver obliged by turning round and going the *completely* opposite way to
his destination – to our hotel. The company, our escorts and the few late night
passengers already on the bus had a ceilidh all the way back home.

Next day (after a huge Russian breakfast with meat and eggs and endless tea)
we held a public rehearsal in the drama school. During the official reception
afterwards we were lured away to a props room, where an informal ceilidh had
been going on for a week. More songs, vodka, toasts – the great Georgian
art-form – and a real sense of internationalism.

That evening the Tumanashvili company performed *Baku and his Pigs* for us,
a Georgian play about the idiocies of bureaucracy and very funny indeed –
especially Amiran Amitanashvili, who is a wonderful comic actor.

We cried to leave Georgia and promised to do all we could to bring them
here.

As soon as we got back we urged Feri Lean who was at this time dreaming
up and organising the very first Mayfest, to get them over. Glasgow would love
them. She tried very hard, but technical and bureaucratic difficulties prevented
it. After he had made two further visits to the USSR as a guest of the newly
formed post-*glasnost* Theatre Workers' Union, John was able to encourage Bill
Burdett Coutts to bring them to the Edinburgh Festival. They were the hit of
the 1988 Festival with their production of Molière's *Don Juan*.

But on that sunny December day in 1982, clutching our presents, flowers
and our vivid memories, we wondered if we would see them again.

Then to Leningrad – perhaps the most beautiful and exhilarating city I've
been in. The Hermitage, the museums, Nevsky Prospect, the Kirov. I took Kate
to her first ballet. We sat in a parterre box in that glorious imperial theatre –
packed out, as seemed to be all the theatres we visited – £2 for a ticket, and 5p
for the subway ride home. We saw *Petroushka* in their version of the original
production and costumes. It was wonderful.

Our own performance in Leningrad was the best of the six we gave. Perhaps
we had got used to the new sensations and the extraordinary variety, colour and
contradictions of that vast country. Many of that particular audience understood

English. Many distinguished actors who were extremely friendly stayed behind to talk.

It was at that time only the second visit by *any* company from Britain for nine years, the last being by Richard Crane and Faynia Williams who did a Gogol piece the previous year. Post-*glasnost* there is a lot of exchange, and we can learn so much from each other as artists and as people. Particularly now when 'The National Question' is again high on the agenda in both our countries.

The summer after that visit, in 1983, while we were playing *Men Should Weep* at the Theatre Royal, Stratford East in London, we did a fund raising benefit for Equity's International Committee for Artists' Freedom, and raised £737 that night. I spoke about the committee's work and the importance of internationalism:

> 'Perhaps you would like to know something about the organisation you are supporting. It is active at the moment in supporting artists who are experiencing political opposition in Turkey, Iran, Argentina, Poland and South Africa, amongst others. Just today, for instance, the committee received thanks from Chile for money raised for children's theatre by a company disbanded by the fascist regime.
>
> Currently they are defending a Turkish artist imprisoned for reading her poems in Paris. Written twenty years ago, they have suddenly crossed the line between being acceptable and being subversive. Amazing what a change of government can do for you! The actors' union in Turkey has been silenced for twelve months – something is also being done about this.
>
> Most recently the committee has come to the defence of a group of distinguished actors in Egypt who have been threatened with prison for the sin of IMPROVISING. That could put *most* of us entertainers behind bars!
>
> No performer who has been lucky enough to play abroad or watch visiting companies work here would deny the benefits of such international exchange. Some of us in 7:84 were lucky enough to play last year in the Soviet Union. We learnt so much for ourselves.
>
> Would those who declare "Bomb the Russians" exempt the Soviet comic artists and clowns? In today's acrobatic world, if one country tumbles, we all fall down.
>
> Let us exchange the language of laughter and joy which cross barriers more effectively than such threats. We will need them in the next few years. We will need this committee ourselves if the demagogues so near to this government are in charge of our policy for the arts.'

As with all visits, especially working visits to other countries, I found myself examining our *own* situation when we returned much more clearly. With a bit of distance, it becomes harder to accept things as they have become in Britain lately. At the TV conference in the 1988 Edinburgh Festival, one Russian TV director put this very well: 'Look in the mirror first, before you find the wrinkles and spots on *our* face.'

Out of that experience of Leningrad with 7:84, Dick Gaughan wrote his song, 'Do You Think That the Russians Want War?' and later John wrote *The Baby and the Bathwater* about the impact of Orwellism and anti-communism on the rest of the world and Central America in particular.

But the show we took there, that started the chain reaction really, was *The Catch*. A small stone can cause a big ripple. At the end of that tour began the mammoth work that became the *Clydebuilt* season.

Fifteen: The *Clydebuilt* Season. 1982

January 1982. Everything was frozen. On 6 January we moved into a bigger flat, during the coldest winter in ten years. John borrowed the company truck and he and the boys went to London and brought up the furniture and more books. They carried it all up two flights of stairs. That week, people were ski-ing down Dundas Street. I took Kate to nursery on a sledge. In Rogart they were building a new hall. Danny stayed with friends in Cumbernauld. Finn had 'O' grades coming up, and a school play. While fixing up the flat I was reading all Ewan MacColl's plays. John began rehearsal for the first play of the *Clydebuilt* season.

This was an attempt to broaden our artistic base, to pay tribute to our popular theatre antecedents such as the Unity Theatre, the Bowhill Players, the Theatre Workshop and the Workers' Theatre Movement and to resurrect some of the then neglected socialist writers of the 20s, 30s and 40s, to reaffirm that oppositional and popular theatre is a worldwide and ongoing phenomenon and not an aberration of the 70s to be easily cast aside.

Linda McKenney had done the research well and produced an impressive document, with outlines of over fifty plays, from which we struggled to choose the four best, finances dictating a season of four major productions. We decided to hold in addition four other sessions of public readings and discussions from the other plays that we were excited about, one of which I was to direct and arrange at the Third Eye, on Theatre Workshop and the plays of Ewan MacColl.

The others were: on the work of Joe Corrie, the miner playwright and poet; on Glasgow Unity Theatre; on the rest of Ena Lamont Stewart's work. These would give a fuller idea of the *range* of working-class plays in Scotland during the twentieth century. We hoped some of the plays would be picked up by other companies, and indeed they were.

We have since then published editions of Joe Corrie's plays, poems and theatre writing, *Men Should Weep* and *The Gorbals Story*. Several of the plays are definitely back in their right place in Scottish theatre history, being taught in schools and colleges and being produced again. I still have hopes that McColl's extraordinary and innovative *Uranium 235* will at some point receive the revival it deserves.

These Sunday readings and discussions were lively and well attended. At the Joe Corrie readings we also sang a lot of his delightful ballads, like 'Tumble and Go'. Jan Wilson did a very strong line drawing of *Martha*, his one-act play. On each occasion we had people who were around at the time and closely involved come along and take part in the discussion. A number of the original Unity Players came; Ewan McColl and Ena Lamont Stewart both talked about the way their plays grew. Ewan took part in a concert of his songs we arranged for the Sunday evening. Recordings of these occasions and copies of a number of the plays were put in the Scottish Theatre Archive at Glasgow University Library, by Linda McKenney.

All this took place – we were pretty busy – *during* the rehearsals and run of the four plays which were in full production. Everyone enjoyed John's production of George Munro's *Gold in His Boots*. It was a novelty; large, stylish, ebullient, comic, with plenty to say for today. It had a strong cast of several 7:84 stalwarts, and some newcomers, including Elaine C. Smith. She had admired the company since she was at school. 'That's my kind of theatre,' she had thought. This was her first job as a professional actor.

In Time of Strife was given a beautiful, naturalistic production by Sandy Neilson who had played my comical husband in the tour of *Swings and Roundabouts* and was brilliant as Nicky Fairbum in *Joe's Drum*. Aplomb is a word that might have been specially coined for Sandy. To my mind his production of Joe Corrie's *In Time of Strife* would have justified the whole season alone, and with the oncoming miners' struggle it was prophetic. It was of course written about and immediately after the General Strike and miners' lockout in 1926/27. Corrie wrote it after himself refusing to return to work on the terms offered by the Fife coal owners. It still has great power.

Johnny Noble by Ewan MacColl, the third play, was directed by David Scase

Elizabeth MacLennan as Maggie, Judy Sweeney as Isa and Martin Muchan as Alec in Ena Lamont Stewart's *Men Should Weep*, 1982.

from Manchester, a member of the early Theatre Workshop company. He himself had played Johnny in the original Littlewood production and was delighted to be asked to recreate it now. He was very impressed with and proud of the quality of the performers John had assembled. Dick Gaughan played his first acting part – the story-teller, Ewan McColl's own part. A startling black presence, he was very compelling. And Martin Muchan, Jonathan Watson, Linda Muchan, Judith Sweeney, Mary Ann Coburn, Ginni Barlow and Finlay Welsh formed a striking ensemble. The production had a dream-like black and white cinematic quality.

They were less comfortable in the more agit-prop style of *UAB Scotland*, a short play by Harry Trott, first performed in 1940, though it was an important piece. One of the few pieces of actual AGIT-PROP theatre in its proper definition that we have done, contrary to some supposition. It dealt with unemployment, and had considerable resonance for today.

The last play in the season, and the only one in which I appeared, was subsequently revived three times – *Men Should Weep* by Ena Lamont Stewart. Written for the Glasgow Unity Theatre and first produced by them in January 1947, it placed a group of working-class women firmly centre stage.

It particularly centred around Maggie Morrison, working mother of seven children, who also maintained an unemployed husband, his old mother, and a child with TB. In spite of extreme poverty, Maggie struggles to keep her children fed and out of trouble: 'Once they've been laid in yer airms, they're in your heart tae the end o' yer days, no matter how they turn oot.'

Her husband despairs: 'I've had nae prime. I got married. Nae trainin'. Nae skill. Just a labourer when there wis labourin' needed, and when there's nane . . . the Burroo. And there's nae escape that ah can see.' Nevertheless Maggie manages. She relies on the help of her fiercely independent sister Lily – scornful of all men, and of her neighbours with their death-defying black humour, to maintain a sense of dignity, a sense of humour, even, finally, a fiercely independent spirit. The women's world of the play, the acutely observed dialogue and theatricality, made it irresistible, and for me deeply affecting to work on, as I did for the next year and a half.

Both Linda and John thought it was the best play they had read and should come last in the series, though Linda always had a particular liking for Joe Corrie's *In Time of Strife*.

We wanted to do it because:

1. Ena was still very much around and had been shamefully neglected by the theatre establishment for thirty years.
2. The story was largely told from the women's point of view and their perspective was critical, even assertive, and very humorous.
3. John wanted a non-naturalistic production. The combination of Ena's play, its feminist relevance and Giles Havergal's interest in directing it for 7:84 audience and actors was exciting. It would also involve a strong company of seven women and two men, a number of whom were in the other plays. We hoped it would be the culmination of an interesting season. It was.

The style turned out to be very much related to all these factors, and was therefore very striking. In his review in the *Daily Mail* Jack Tinker described it as, 'A long neglected masterpiece . . . Ena Lamont Stewart is still alive today. From her warm compassionate observation of human nature in the Gorbals slums during the Depression, I would guess she is a forgiving soul. I hope so. Less kindly mortals would have every right to feel bitter that the acclaim given to the school of Angry Young Men in the fifties had actually been pre-empted by the writings of this gentle, middle-aged woman ten years previously.'

Ena herself took a slightly different view: 'Of cours it hurt, let's not mince our words. Men select the plays that are put on. They are more likely to put on a play by a man than a woman. Male chauvinism is rife in Scottish theatres. Scotsmen are the last to come out of their stys.' Then she added quietly, with amusement: 'I daresay some people are surprised that I am still alive.'

Programme note from the author, Ena Lamont Stewart

In 1947 Robert Mitchell of Glasgow Unity Theatre invited me to write a play about a Glasgow family trying to survive the Depression of the thirties. I had spent the early thirties behind the counter of Aberdeen's Central Library; I remembered the crowds of grey-faced men in cloth caps, some just looking for 'a good murder, miss', many others reading anything that might help them to understand what was happening to their crumbling world.

The late thirties found me behind a different kind of counter in Glasgow's Royal Hospital for Sick Children; its admission hall afforded me a splendid, if often harrowing, opportunity to indulge in blatant eavesdropping. I have always loved the speech of the Glasgow people. It is marvellously rhythmic; it lends itself to pathos and to humour. 'Aw *naw*!' on high doh can be a cry of despair, an octave lower, a keen of deepest sympathy. Writers, so it is said, are given to hoarding sights and sounds from early childhood, and this may well have been the foundation of what went, all unknowingly, to the making of the play. In my early years the Sunday morning air of Glasgow was loud with the sound of church bells and thick with the yellow smoke from thousands of chimneys as we followed my father to his church in Anderston.

The streets were crowded with youths punting footballs; ragged children with the curved tibias of rickets played in the gutters; babies, barely visible above thick, fringed shawls mewed feebly and fruitlessly. I stuck close to my mother and didn't know why I felt frightened of these people so noisy and dirty on the Sabbath day. My last opportunity to watch and hoard came in the early war years with visits to Molly Urquhart's Rutherglen Rep where Paul Vincent Carroll's Glasgow plays were staged in all their verbal richness. Out of all this mixed experience and observation came Maggie and John Morrison walking on to the paper as if I had known them both, long before they knew each other.

Ena Lamont Stewart

For me personally the show was a big challenge. Coming as it did, last in the *Clydebuilt* series, the expectations were high.

All four shows had built the audience. People were interested in the idea of the season. We knew a lot was expected from *Men Should Weep*. Feri Lean frantically arranging Mayfest on a shoestring met me during rehearsals at the Citizens

Theatre. 'I hear it's going to be wonderful' – always very unnerving. And I was playing the lead. This time directed by Giles Havergal at his best.

I made a conscious decision to stop feeling responsible for *everything* – as I tend to do – and to concentrate solely on Maggie, my very demanding part. We had a superb cast, with that special feeling that we were involved in something bigger than any of us. Ena came to the first read-through and got quietly pleased. But she refused to come to any more rehearsals, saying she'd die if she had to . . . and as she already felt 'exhumed' we didn't feel like taking the risk . . . but, 'I'll be here if you need me.' She smiled her wicked, twinkly smile.

We wanted her to love it when she came again at the end of the first week. And with one or two caustic reservations, she did.

We opened on 4 May 1982 for two weeks at the Mitchell Theatre, Glasgow, and we were into a hit. Colossal. Wonderful reviews for the play, the production, the whole cast. John for thinking of it, 7:84 for doing it, and (thankfully) me as Maggie. In some ways for me it was professionally the highest point of the story so far. Because that show grew and developed and the company stayed very strong through three tours.

The Times said it was 'brilliant in every aspect' and it was highly praised in the local and the national press.

I became very fond of Jan Wilson who played my sister Lily the first time round with her beautiful, caustic wit. She was great to work with. Ginni Barlow came back to play Lizzie. Ann Myatt and Andrea Miller joined us in the second tour – all powerful actresses. We were quite a team. Jo Cameron Brown's bird-like Granny; her mother became almost a fixture, sitting in the dressing room – our staunchest fan. Mary Ann as Mrs Harris – 'Veloury hat? Oh ye mean yon scabby aul' felt bunnet wi' the moultin' bird on tap? If yon wis veloury, I'm a wally dug.' Judy Sweeney was Isa, bitter and bold with a great sexy laugh. Linda Muchan pulled everybody's heart-strings as my daughter Jenny. Laurie Ruddic, again with us, as Ernie the fourteen-year-old terror, and as pampered Alec the favourite, no-good, son. My three husbands: Dave Anderson – touching and bewildered; Roy Hanlon – his quiet authority, dignified and beaten; and Pat Hannaway, from the Citz, coming late into the production, surrounded by all these *powerful* women. Instead of being the paycock, the cock o' the walk, suddenly he was at the receiving end of Andrea Miller, Ann Myatt and all the rest of us. . . .

The same August we re-opened it at the Churchill Theatre during the Edinburgh Festival, and then at the Moray House Theatre. Michael Billington called me the Madonna of the Gorbals: 'One of the finest dramatic offerings I have seen in twenty years of coming to Edinburgh . . . Popularity and high-definition skill go hand-in-hand . . . Working-class content marries with skilled artifice and the results are sensational . . . all I can say is that if this does not come to London, the metropolis will have missed a great production that not only honours a Scots classic, but that opens up a whole new way of presenting working-class drama.'

The next spring we played it again at the Citizens Theatre, Dundee Rep, His Majesty's Aberdeen, and we went on to fill the Theatre Royal, Stratford East at the end of the final tour for five weeks. The theatre was packed out for the entire run.

The *Wall Street Journal* thought it was 'a remarkably mature piece of feminist writing, with much of the humor and emotional power of Clifford Odets at his best.' The *New York Village Voice* said 'the audience for *Men Should Weep* is not the West End crowd: they are younger and scruffier, with even an occasional punk here and there. They are clearly moved by the play; more surprisingly, many British critics on not-very-left-wing papers admire it too: a play about unemployment in Glasgow fifty years ago has new meaning at the moment of Margaret Thatcher's re-election.'

There was talk of doing it in Milan and on Broadway. Ian Albery wanted to discuss a limited run at the Wyndhams Theatre.

In our different ways it meant a great deal to us all. We never lost faith in that play or that production. We had our differences, but the discipline and commitment on stage from company and crew was quite exceptional. There were three long tours. In many ways I felt it got better and stronger all the time.

Here is what Ena said on the *last* night.

'To John McGrath, the begetter, to Linda MacKenney, to all the splendid 7:84 Scotland Company on and off stage, and to Giles Havergal who waved his wizard's wand over these people who so mysteriously walked on to my scribbling pad thirty-six years ago and exhumed them (and me!) I send my warmest thanks for all the hard work that has brought so much pleasure to me and to so many others in Scotland and at Stratford East.

'With much love to you all, and my good wishes for health, happiness and good luck in the future.'

We were very pleased for Ena's sake. Every national paper had acclaimed her from the *Wall Street Journal* to the *Aberdeen Evening Express*. I was grateful for the success and the fulfilment of one of the most marvellous parts I'm ever likely to play.

Men Should Weep marked a transition both for the company and for me. Whether people realised it or not it was the start of something different. We had now become a management and people were cast to play. Get-ins were done largely by the crew. Company meetings became more formal, more for airing grievances, exchanging information and instructions. This change was several times noted in company minutes but as no one was prepared to commit beyond the run of the tour, there was no alternative. The board were quite clear that for people who came into the company for one show only to decide the company's future plans (which they were not prepared to commit to themselves) would be power without responsibility.

But, equally, people who hadn't toured with us before began to want to work for the company and others to come back.

The money and press coverage were good, the prestige high. We played in big theatres. Simultaneously Thatcher had started winning and it was at the end of our third tour of *Men Should Weep* that she was comfortably re-elected for a second term. So although *Men Should Weep* was a peak, from the peak came a descent and growing opposition.

Meanwhile wherever possible we remained involved with the movement.

While *Men Should Weep* was on tour some of the company were also touring a street theatre show called *On the Pig's Back*, written by John McGrath and Dave MacLennan, funded by NALGO – I think their first venture of this kind as part of a NALGO campaign against the Cuts. It was very much enjoyed by audiences throughout the country and Kate Craik was largely responsible for organising a tour from Orkney and Shetland to Alexandra Palace which did a fine job; NALGO were delighted. We felt their example could well be followed by other unions in similar circumstances. Wildcat collaborated on the show, and have worked again with NALGO on their big success *The Steamie*. The combination of these two shows was the kind of spread we were after; most of us were delighted, although it meant our resources were at full stretch.

During the run of *Men Should Weep* at the Citizens Theatre we did an extra benefit show for the health workers – after a big demonstration in Glasgow in June '83. At the end I said:

> 'Today, on this Day of Action, it is as well to remember that the advances in Health and Welfare – albeit inadequate – that have been achieved since the Thirties were due to the unremitting and successful struggle of the Labour Movement, not to a handful of Japanese investors. Today's vicious Tory government is intent on dismantling all that – health and a decent life belong to the seven per cent in their dreadful ideology. We will not accept this. Half a million people in Scotland have demonstrated that today. We will not go back to the 1930s. We support the health workers. Today we've raised about £1,000 – let's double it now!'

Curtain Speeches

I'm sure the parallels were clear to most of the audiences from that show. The audience realise it's not easy to come out, particularly after a long, emotionally taxing role, and put yourself on the line. But then it's not easy to stand on a picket line at six in the morning before taking the kids to school. Or to be on strike for weeks on end. So some things are worth making an effort about.

Similarly there are times when you know instinctively – no speech; not tonight. These things are hard to analyse, but in a company that know each other and their audience, tacit agreement is often reached on this.

Over the years many 7:84 shows have raised money – notably for the miners during the Strike and for Nicaragua. But some actors and directors are strongly against curtain speeches even in 7:84. It relates to their overall perception of the performer's role. If, as we tried to achieve in 7:84, the performers are on the *same level*, in a dialogue with the audience, then it is *not* jarring or intrusive for an appeal to be made, or thanks to be expressed, or a raffle drawn, or a dance to begin. If it's done gently.

If you want to hypnotise the audience, then to shake them out of their 'state' would be a rude awakening, would 'spoil the illusion'. In some kinds of theatre that would be so. But if a heightened awareness, or a sense of shared joy, laughter or sadness is the desired result, then we should be able to share our wider concerns. It is a difficult area, and has to be handled sensitively.

Whatever the pros and cons, the habit of saying thank you to the audience at the end of the show has now been discontinued. Another move away from the popular/variety tradition in which you are greeted, made welcome, thanked for participating at the end. A friendly tradition displayed by aspirations to 'high' art.

The theatre is a very public place. In it we may experience extremes of joy and sorrow but we experience them in public. Actors, by definition, speak out. We are heard, and accepted or rejected. No theatre can be truly popular without taking such risks.

Style

Men Should Weep employed a new and to some extent 'expressionistic' acting style which has since been copied widely with varying degrees of success. In many of the more exuberant 7:84 shows I have developed – from *Trees in the Wind* to the *Baby and the Bathwater* – a bold, but not exclusively cartoon style, useful for polemic and for comedy. Although the play called for a high level of emotional energy, Maggie needed something else – quieter, contained. I had to pare everything away. My notes on the script were all about that. I told Giles after one particularly exhausting rehearsal that I felt like a big bag of icing sugar being forced to write my name out of a tiny nozzle. At one opening night in my good luck card he sent me one in an envelope: Use it, Lizzie!

Equally, Giles was influenced and excited by some of our 7:84 techniques. The 'Hing' in Glasgow is an exchange of comments, usually caustic, on the passing scene, always between two or more women, conducted from one tenement window to another. Giles of course, a Glaswegian, was familiar with this, and would use it regularly in his famous pantos. We suggested a 7:84-style development of this in which the comments are delivered straight out to the audience. This led to a way of doing a number of duologues, not always comic, which raised them out of naturalism. It also led to the way we did the bigger choruses of all the neighbours, which has since been widely used.

Jan Wilson is very experienced in traditional popular comedy techniques, and brought her sure timing and precision. Most of the company, like almost all 7:84 companies, were experienced in pantomime. So the style really was a composite of 7:84 rapport with the audience and familiarity with using and developing variety forms, and Giles' 'expressionism', visual flair and staging boldness.

Here I had the luxury of undertaking no quick changes, having only one part (!); to be able to *grow into* a great play, over a year at least, to be able to refine and distill, to trust each other as an ensemble on stage was a great experience.

We did a particularly good show in Cumbernauld where, because of the curious shape of that theatre, it was impossible to have the setting as planned; once again we had to more or less improvise the staging. Jan and I led the way and we all were sure enough of what we were doing, crew and performers, to adapt; some things worked better than at any other time.

That kind of trust and flexibility is precious. It also reinforced my wish that we could afford to play more in repertoire in 7:84. So often a play finished with life in it yet, but the economics dictate the end of the contract, and a new show. When a show is revived – and this has been the case with many of our most successful shows – it almost always gets better the second time round. Frequently a play becomes even *more* relevant. It is wonderful to be able to pull out the play for the moment – not *necessarily* always a new one. We should have the flexibility, both organisational and financial, to do this. Nowadays all Arts Council 'clients' are forced to schedule and budget far too far ahead.

The role of the executive producer

Men Should Weep did not suffer from being re-rehearsed and performed, a lot due to the dedication and interest maintained in the project by Giles – he really enjoyed working with 7:84 as management, with John as producer. He said he felt liberated by having it all organised by somebody else.

But it was also due to the months of planning the whole season and sustained interest in promoting the life of the productions by John as executive producer. All the *Clydebuilt* directors had the benefit of this kind of care and attention which let them get on with the job of directing the show. John undertook, with the help of the people working in the office, the setting up of the finance, the budget, the tour, crewing up, the rights in the play, relationships with theatres on the tour, press, publicity and poster material, distribution of these, company structures and internal relations, consultations on casting and script, and planning ahead. It was very time-consuming, particularly when there was writing to be done.

Giles recognised the need for this kind of support, and welcomed and appreciated it. He offered to produce John's next show, but, sadly, it was only a lighthearted offer. His other commitments would have made it impossible. So when it came to *Women in Power* – which suffered as a consequence – John was on his own: no producer to back him and an overstretched office for whom everything became rather too much. As usual it came down to money. And there was always the feeling that John could manage.

Meanwhile in England

Immediately after the season, John went to London to write and direct a new play for 7:84 England – *Rejoice!*, a response to the ending of the Falklands war, and a lot else that was going on in Britain as well.

It opened at the Liverpool Everyman on Tuesday 7 August, then came up to the Assembly Rooms in Edinburgh, while *Men Should Weep* was playing in Moray House. It won an award at the Festival.

In the *Scotsman*, John Clifford, the playwright, reviewed it:

'I'd never have guessed John McGrath would have wanted to write a Broadway musical. True it belongs to a post-Tebbit Drury Lane – with a cast of four and a piano – but otherwise it's got all it takes. A socialist pastiche of *My Fair Lady*, in some ways it's a great improvement on the original. A highly perceptive look at what's happening in post-Falklands Britain, it's also enormously entertaining.'

It toured on the English company's new circuit through September, October and November – Yorkshire, the Midlands, Wales, Merseyside, Lancashire, Cumbria, and parts of East Anglia.

Elizabeth MacLennan thanks Councillor Jean McFadden for the support of Glasgow District Council during the *Clydebuilt* season.

Clydebuilt Ends

The *Clydebuilt* Season was a great success. Four expensive, beautiful productions, well-crewed and well-toured. A series of associated readings, discussions, concerts and events which generated a lot of long-lasting interest. Money raised for the health workers. It was an elaborate, ambitious project for a company operating from a small office and no theatre, with a very small office staff and a derisory grant. In spite of packed houses, we ended up with an alarming deficit and the start of our administrative troubles, but our artistic standing was never higher.

Diary 1988

The Cut

Sunday 20 March
Our recently appointed chairman of the 7:84 board (considered to be a 'suitable'
figure by the Scottish Arts Council) rings to tell me he has received a letter from the
SAC the day before – didn't he know we were anxiously waiting? – saying we
are assured of ONE year's funding, and how he is to be congratulated for that.
And thereafter? I ask. Withdrawal of revenue, he says. You mean a complete
CUT? Well, yes. Why didn't you say that in the first place? Because I suppose he
did not fully realise the implications of the announcement, or at worst agreed with

it. Either way, from the company's point of view he can be said to have failed.

(The full hostility with which the SAC intended to implement this was not yet apparent to any of us, but on the Monday morning the letter was there in the office, with a warning not to divulge the contents until after their press conference two days later. That seemed a bit suspicious – did they think such a cut could be slipped in unnoticed?

Monday 21 March
Apparently so, for there was no mention of it in the SAC press release which arrived this morning. Just a bland account of where this year's money is going, not where it is NOT. I had the joyful task of breaking the news to John at one am in Auckland on the long-distance telephone as soon as we had read the contents of the letter.)

Tuesday 22 March
Resisted the temptation to leak the proposed cut at the Mayfest press conference – our next production (No Mean City at the Kings Theatre) is to be the cornerstone. The press were full of the show this morning. I felt however that both the press and our public had a right to know that we were under serious threat, and that it could be the last *7:84 Scotland production. John agreed that I should leaflet the SAC press conference held to announce their three-year plan tomorrow.*

Wednesday 23 March
I found myself conducting an impromptu press conference on the steps of the Arts Council building in Charlotte Square, with the support of Linda McKenney, who was on our board, and her little boy George in his pushchair, happily unaware of the crisis.

We handed out leaflets to startled press and television journalists as they went into the meeting.

7:84 SHOCK CUT
SCOTLAND'S BEST LOVED AND INTERNATIONALLY ADMIRED
TOURING THEATRE COMPANY RECEIVE NOTICE OF COMPLETE
FUNDING CUT FROM ARTS COUNCIL
NO VALID REASON
APPEAL MOUNTED
FOR FURTHER INFORMATION RING 7:84 OFFICE

The press were understandably shocked, not only by the cut but by the SAC's secrecy. They were not satisfied with the evasive answers given at the official conference by the flustered officials. I was immediately interviewed by several television, magazine and news programmes, and the Arts Council's cut, and attempt to cover it up, were headlines in the Scottish papers and on all the national news programmes the next day.

The Arts Council, having made no reference whatever to appeals, were forced to commit themselves publicly to some kind of appeal situation, not wishing to exacerbate the public concern. It was our wedding anniversary . . .

Friday 25 March

John flew home, having broken off his engagements in New York which he had planned on the return journey, with messages of support from the New Zealand Writers' Guild and Congress of New Zealand Trades Unions.

He was of course greeted with a battery of questions and said that he was sure there was some mistake, that the Arts Council would change their mind if we cleared up misunderstandings. (Indeed, it was not until he read some of their anonymous reports which have such heavy bearing on their deliberations that he fully realised how hostile is the theatre arts establishment, not only to what he is trying to do, but to the style of the presentations and, perhaps most alarmingly, to the enthusiasm with which it is greeted by our audience.)

Tuesday 29 March

John met the SAC drama officer – discussed appeal procedures. An emergency 7:84 board meeting discussed action. Bill Speirs, Deputy General Secretary of the Scottish TUC, agreed to resume his role as chairman. He had been chairman before, until his appointment as Chairman of the Labour Party in Scotland, but had stayed on our board. Now he was free to come back. An action committee was appointed, with every member taking on areas of responsibility for the appeal.

We recognised the need to interview and appoint a new administrator, probably for a higher wage than the rest of the company. Until now we have resisted pressure to erode our equal pay policy, an integral part of 7:84 to date. How many more compromises will be demanded?

Wednesday 30 March

I had warned Councillor Jean McFadden of Glasgow District Council, Chair of the Mayfest Board, about the cuts before the Mayfest press conference in case the story should be leaked, and herself embarrassed. She has always supported us strongly, specifically with our Clydebuilt *season, and I knew we would need that support now even more. She came with her husband to all the* Clydebuilt *shows and stayed behind to many discussions.*

We were planning to move the company's base to Glasgow; John's suggestion which had met with enthusiastic support from the board at our last meeting.

Jean met John for lunch and promised to help us find a base in Glasgow, and to investigate the possibility of further financial support from the district council. Glasgow is in many ways already our spiritual home, indeed quite a few people already think we are based there.

Drove to London in the evening. Stayed the night in Yorkshire on the way, with Tervor Griffiths and Gill. Our friendship goes back to Trevor's days with the BBC Education Department. I remember him, very moved, coming backstage after Plugged In *when he saw it at the Oxford Playhouse in Spring 1972.*

We performed his short plays, Apricots *and* Thermidor, *as a late-night show after* Trees in the Wind *at the Festival in '71. When he is feeling extravagantly generous McGrath has been known to say that he only wrote* Trees *to provide something to precede Trevor's play; Trevor's enthusiastic involvement in that was a great encouragement, and has been since, on a number of occasions.*

He and Gill live almost exactly half way between Edinburgh and London, and we frequently fetch up there for tea and sympathy and a dialectical pit-stop. This time we needed it more than most.

Friday 1 April

Good Friday. All Fools' Day. Nobody rang before twelve to say, April Fool, you've got 100 per cent grant increase. . . . Spent the weekend in London tidying John's room, prior to sending more archive material to the Cambridge University Library, which is likely to be one of the last to be abolished; with any luck.

Last spring Linda McKenney helped us to sort out the contents of the English company office and send it to Cambridge, who have agreed to house it. So much theatre history has vanished. I was anxious that it should not happen to us, and thereby parts of the work be eradicated forever.

In 1984, aware of mounting pressure, I had started to assemble some sort of personal 7:84 archive. John and I have kept quite a bit.

He is trying to get on with writing Border Warfare. *It is difficult.*

We spend the evening with Mark and Sue Brown. She is an artist and a Labour councillor in Fulham (which went Tory at the last election). She is angry and active. Mark makes me laugh. He has had a long association with John and the English 7:84: he wrote the music for Fish in the Sea, Yobbo Nowt, *much of the* Trembling Giant, Joe of England *and, more recently,* Rejoice! *For the Scottish company he wrote the music for* Out of Our Heads, The Catch, *and is now involved in the early music for* Border Warfare. *He is philosophical about what is happening to us. He knows they won't stop John writing.*

Tuesday 5 April

We finished clearing up John's papers and went for supper with the Mitchell family in a Polish restaurant. It is good to see friends, especially at a time like this.

Wednesday 6 April

I am compiling a list of books to send to Catalyst Theatre in Edmonton, Canada for the research on their 'Food' project. John goes to a meeting of the committee of the Edinburgh TV Festival to discuss the projected visit of Soviet film makers this summer.

I pick him up at Michael Kustow's office at Channel 4. Michael is ebullient about Border Warfare. *He is already committed to it in principle and wants to see a full script. He says he'll do it with or without 7:84 – it's John's work he's interested in. It's good to hear that. Why do you have to be so nice, I wail, and start crying; he is very handy with the Kleenex – clearly there have been tears before in this office, I say, and we laugh and I begin to feel better.*

I have known Michael since he was seventeen and he played stately, plump Buck Mulligan in Bloomsday. *Kate leaves him a drawing of a surprised dog.*

Thursday, 7 April

7:84 Action Committee meeting at the STUC offices in Glasgow. Bill Spiers is there. We agree to let the SAC know we are putting right our admin. difficulties immediately, and taking steps to reduce the deficit which is anyway less than they think. Everyone agrees to stand by our artistic policy and plans for the next three years or what is left of them. And to beef-up the board. I volunteer to send out letters, especially to our support abroad who have no way of knowing this has happened.

No Mean City, *our next production, to be directed by David Hayman, will have a high profile at Mayfest, and if we follow up with* Border Warfare, *timed to coincide with lodging of the appeal, we should be in a strong position.*

The drama officer indicated to John at the meeting last week that they will only make a final decision after seeing two more shows. We should have mounted both of these shows by November; we will time our appeal for support to coincide with that. The plan is to open Border Warfare *at the end of October. Financially it will only require a small commitment from 7:84 as Freeway Films will pay for a lot of it.*

Thursday 14 April
Harry McShane, a great socialist fighter, died: the end of an era. I first met him when we were researching the John MacLean Show, The Game's a Bogey *and he came to talk to the company about Maclean whom he knew well.* He told us of the hundreds who attended Maclean's economics lectures at the corner of Bath Street in Glasgow, about his imprisonment and hardships. He introduced us to MacLean's daughter, Nan Milton, whose book on the life of MacLean we sold at performances of the play. He told us too about his gestures and mannerisms – Bill Paterson, who was to play him, listening intently. He said he had a white rubber collar, which could be wiped and worn again.*

Friday 15 April
I am writing letters, letters, letters – no money, of course. I declined to tour with the Traverse, and a job in Belfast. With John trying to write under this fearful pressure, and the appeal to keep going, I do not feel I can be away for long.

I still hope to be able to go to the Catalyst Theatre workshops in Canada next month, but it is looking increasingly problematic for the same reasons. We have already advised them of our crisis and they wrote a great letter of support to the SAC.

Saturday 16 April
Michael Kustow is staying with us in Edinburgh. We go together to the Modern Art Gallery. There we find a fascinating exhibition by Goebbels of the so-called 'decadent' artists of the 20s and 30s in Germany, including the sculptor Ernest Barlach whose work reminds me of Kathe Kollwitz, and is very moving. We wondered how long before the 'decadent' label would reappear here. With Clause 28 under way, not long.

Sunday 17 April
Seeing The Mahabharata *in Glasgow*
In 1985 John, Kate and myself had sat enthralled by Ariane Mnouchkine's production of Henry IV, *performed against the spectacular setting of the Palais des Papes in Avignon. We are great admirers of her work which was first seen in this country at the Round House in London when she brought over her production of* 1789, *an epic treatment of the French Revolution. John has kept in touch with her since Oxford, where she assisted him in his open-air production of Aristophanes'* The Birds.

Her Henry IV *was about four hours long and in French, but Kate, who was only six then, was riveted by it all the way. We had no problems taking her to the Peter Brook production of* Mahabharata. *I assumed that in such a piece of story-telling theatre, of which it is a triumphant example, the audience would*

---

* *When, in 1982, we played in Leningrad we saw the street named 'John MacLean Street'.*

have the right to move, sleep, eat or take a break if necessary. In the event, for her, and for everyone there as far as I could see, it was pretty spell-binding.

We were still smarting from having read some of the Arts Council assessors' views of our work: 'Story-telling is not theatre,' one had declared confidently. What would he (for surely it was a man speaking), what would he feel about this? For all its visual splendour, and the magnificence of its setting, The Mahabharata *was first and foremost a large exercise in story-telling. Indeed, a guided tour of the story-telling techniques of several continents: those employed by the Hindu elephant-god, Krishna, half-comical, half vengeful; those of the desert African tribesman; the Japanese warrior; the Hindu dance-story; even the Polish actor-seer. They were all story-tellers. How could anyone say that story-telling is not theatre?*

The problem only arises if they do not want to hear your particular *stories. . . .*

Ariane Mnouchkine's most recent production which I saw this January also had an Indian subject. L'Indiade ou l'Inde de Leurs Rêves *by Helene Cixous was performed by her company, Theatre du Soleil, in their homebase theatre, the Cartoucherie, in Paris. It is an account of the tragic events surrounding the partition of India, and I found the contrast of approach interesting.*

As in the Mahabharata, *the production began by engaging the audience on a specifically intimate, personal level. At the beginning of the* Mahabharata *the Hindu elephant-god (played by the actor Bruce Myers) sat cross-legged on the dirt, took us metaphorically by the hand and quietly began to tell the story. It was 'Once upon a time' acting.*

In L'Indiade *Ariane, on the other hand, tried something curious, at first apparently comic, that coloured our whole understanding of the events subsequently played out on the epic scale. While the audience were taking their seats, a number of the actors, as the lowest 'caste', were sweeping and cleaning the huge acting area. Meanwhile an older actress was among the audience – at first it was not clear if she was an odd-ball, or an actor or both – asking people in the audience, 'Where are you from, lady? Mister you come from where, which place? Excuse me, lady, how many children, you have a husband, is he from your country?' and then turning to the rest of us and announcing with a big toothless smile, 'She is from America! From the prairie, two children? You are from the mountains? It is cold? Do you have enough clothes? Is your mother with you? From the city! This gentleman is from the city, from Lyons. His wife is in Africa! Will she come with you? Where do you come from? Is there food there?' and so on.*

She moved among us, establishing a world of LOCALITY, of where people start from; that was the context *for the idea of partition, separation and the huge movements of people that followed in the play, even as the larger-than-life in impact, but miniscule figure of Ghandi appeared, and then Pandit Nehru. They too had their own sense of locality, so often denied to political figures in plays, indeed by the media altogether.*

It was a highly successful way of doing something with a particularly cosmopolitan audience – because her theatre is now rightly famous – which we in 7:84 have often experienced at an intense local *level. Ariane could awaken that 'village' response on a big, impressive scale, and perhaps it is THAT as much as her production values and the physical beauty of her shows which appeals to John and me so much.*

*Peter Brook has long been engaged in a similar quest but from a different
starting point. When I read his book I thought: Wait! We found the very
qualities you are looking for in our own backyard, or more specifically in the old
Sutherland crofters telling (or singing) of the Clearances, or the pensioners'
club in Govan where the women told their story of how they survived with no
money in the 30s. Most of the theatre audience in Scotland has a rare awareness
and lack of inhibition about its cultural roots. Perhaps that has sustained us in
the face of so much opposition. Certainly Peter Brook felt it most tangibly in Glasgow,
indeed the entire company who appeared in* The Mahabharata *were overwhelmed
by this level of involvement.*

NOTES ON THE PLAY:
Draupadi, the perfect woman. How difficult this is to play.
*The actress, Mallika Sarabhai, who played Draupadi, is a wonderful dancer
as well. Her performance is no male projection, but rooted in her femaleness,
her womanliness. She is always* apart *from these men, who are therefore infatuated
with her and try to possess her. She is intact whatever happens to her, but still
vulnerable.*
*The blind king, calling his wife without whom he cannot live, makes her name
sound like a gaping wound – Ghandhari.*
*Abhimanyu, the beautiful boy, half-man half-child, we see our own sons in
him, his name is a caress; Abhimanyu.*
*Kate's favourite, the imposing, stick-like figure of the ancient, the wise old
man, inscrutible Bhishma. She loves the name.*
*Around 1964 I was passing through the Israeli town of Bersheva, on the edge
of the Negev desert. Our friends who lived in the new part of the town, where
the roads were not yet made up, took us proudly to see the huge, new, modern
hospital on the edge of the town, all glittering glass and concrete. To our left
the tall figure of an Arab appeared striding across the desert, as if from nowhere,
with a child slung over his shoulder, and he swung noiselessly through the glass
doors into the gleaming hospital.*
When Bhishma appeared I remembered him.
*All the next day I thought about the story: all these fearful wars fought by men
who were not the fathers of their 'own' sons, who had been 'fathered' by the Sun,
the Wind, by Dharma. Perhaps this is why they went on fighting. . . . I
remembered Aurelia, the character I played in* Trees in the Wind, *who keeps thirty
hours of evidence on tape of 'what men do to each other in the name of history,
and what they do to the earth in the name of improving it, and what they do to
women in the name of love.'*
She tells Joe, the Marxist cat burglar:

'Women are not responsible for history. Men are. Women don't
believe in it. Men invented it. If you don't believe in history you don't
fight wars, you don't struggle for power, you don't compete. You don't
have nations, commonwealths, empires – men's games.'
    Is it not brave to be a king, Techelles.
Usumcasane and Theridamas.
Is it not passing brave to be a king
And ride in triumph through Persepolis?

I believe in the women of Persopolis. Women move among the realities: hunger, shelter, clothing, love, birth, death, children, shit, pain, anger, beauty. Men inhabit a world of destructive fantasy: wars, torture, cruelty, rat races, boots in faces, stabs in the back, control, domination, rape, self-adoration. But the Age of Tamburlaine the Great is over. The pill and the razor blade have cut him down. . . .

Of course the women of Persepolis might one day let Tamburlaine back in – on foot, in plain clothes, filled with cowardice and humility to take his place with the children; who will be playing among the ruins of the temples, palaces, jails, supermarkets, custom-sheds, rocket-silos and museums which will have fallen into decay, being no longer needed . . .'

Both Mnouchkine and Brook are highly subsidised. The French government spends about three or four times as much on the arts as we do in this benighted country, and are proud of it.

If Border Warfare *happens it will only be by brilliant planning, nerve and enough people attempting the impossible together. There will never be enough money, and certainly not enough time. Five weeks' preparation for an epic. No one will know how hard the design team will have to work into the small hours to achieve the impossible. I expect we will have to fight for the right to have a SINGLE preview, let alone several, let alone a grant at all. And then we will be subjected to an already knife-sharpening press, who would throw stones at the poet Sweeney if he flew into their backyard.*

Sixteen: The Joys of Touring

Playing in Holland

Actors in Holland and Belgium are accustomed to play in several languages. Could *we* do that as a company? The Nieuw Scene, a company of Flemish actors, for example, play in French and Flemish. I saw the remarkable Dutch company, Werkteater, perform a play about death at the Mermaid Theatre in London – in English. I understand they also played it in Flemish or French when required. The performance was deeply affecting – the English perfect.

The Dutch audience watching us in *Honour Your Partners* (in 1976) enjoyed the Marx Brothers sequence which was how we told the story of the growth of the American corporations, and of the cotton workers. That show began and ended with the Declaration of Independence, a magnificent piece which had a particular resonance for us at that time, coming up to the Devolution Referendum – 'We hold these truths to be self-evident . . .' I enjoyed doing it. Recently I read that it forms the basis of the new constitution of Vietnam which seems quite extraordinary.

We discovered the Van Gogh Museum during that tour to Amsterdam. If you went to the gallery for the last forty minutes before it shut, you could get

The McGrath family.
Elizabeth MacLennan and
John McGrath on 7:84's
Dutch tour, in 1976;
Danny and Finn McGrath
in Holland in 1976;
Kate McGrath, home again
after a tour.

in cheap, so we went nearly every day and gorged ourselves on sunflowers, and sun-baked colour. Danny felt he'd discovered an old friend since *he* had been painting sunflowers from the age of three with great devotion. And islands with fences round them.

Children's paintings are not afraid to proclaim the world as they see it. I take their signals seriously.

The boys enjoyed Amsterdam. The best chips. Gargantuan breakfasts. We became friends with the theatre critic Jac Heyer who has a wicked smile when he chooses. He told them about what it was like living in an occupied country as a child.

Danny McGrath – A Diary of Holland, 1976 (aged 8)

Sunday 21 March
We all went to the station to meet the company. arfter that they all got into the van. Afentually we arrived at Hull and we got on the boat then we had our dinner it was 4 course menu then we went to our cabin it had bunk beds and oranges I was on the top bed

Monday 22 March
In Holland the postboxes are blue. the theatre has got three machines for playing games with, one is called the bally Wizerd and the other is called the Bally champ and the third one is called cric-o-chet.

in holland the cars drive on the right side of the road and there are trams which drive in the middle of the road and go fast. on the way to the shop we saw some children playing there own kind of hopskoch it was lots of squares made into one big square. The children didn't have a playground they play in the street

Friday 16 March
Today we brought some Dutch playing-cards with pictures of holland on the aces. we went to the Rijks Musium with Vermeres paintings and Rembrants paintings. there is one vermeres painting which was a girl and her mother looking for nits in her hair. On the way back we saw houndreds of crockuses there were yellow and white ones and purple ones. it was like a maze Because I got stuck in them and I didn't want to step on eny of them

Saturday 27 March
Today we saw barges with glass roofs on them. We planed to go on one on Monday.

In the afternoon we went to the theatre for a meating it started at 3 and it finished at 5 then we had a game of pinball. I came second

Sunday 28 March
Today we went to Delft. I had sole with chips arfter we went and played at the beach. we played catch mum and Dad had to try and carch us. then we went to Delft It is famouse for makeing blue and white patens. we saw lots of Delft pottery shops and in Delft the canals are smaller than in Amsterdam.

Monday 29 March
We drove to the north of holland threw a place called Volendamm were we saw clogs being made and I brought some small ones to bring home as a souvenir. we went past lots of dykes polders and windmills of all sizes. then we played in the sand dunes

Tuesday 30 March
Today in the Morning I found a laDy Bird then we went to one of the biggist street marklet It is called Waterloo Plein we saw swords and a ball and chain and we saw clothes made of carpets We saw lots of leather coats with fur at the end and the colars Dad was going to buy one But they were too expenseve Then in the afternoon we went to the theatre museam where there are models of the scenesthe first one we saw was a cave and the second was on the sea.
    The next room we saw was the Harlequin room.
    This is the ticket to the museum.
    children get in free

Thursday 1 April
We saw lots of barrol organs big ones little ones and Medium size ones. in the fish store we saw squids and langoustine and we brought some red mullet and some langoustine Then we went out to a restaurant with a Dutch friend and he is a Journalist.
    In the arfternoon we went on a roundvart which is the Dutch word for round trip of the canals

Friday 2 April
We had armond cakes and sandwiches and lemonade. then we went to a theatre shop. I brought a sword and a ponocio nose.

Halls and theatres

I like theatres that proclaim themselves, the traditional kind – the Theatre Royal, Stratford East, the Citizens Theatre, Glasgow, and the Berliner Ensemble's Theatre am Schiffbaurdamm, whose sign you can see streets away. We played *There is a Happy Land* there in 1987. The backstage area is organised for the benefit of the show, not the architect. It is the company's home. Dressing room cubicles are small and pokey but practical, with showers. Old costumes and props everywhere. The food in the canteen is grand – Mama's best, complete with dumplings, lots of hot stews, closely rivalled by Rose's famous fare at the Citizens' canteen. The Berliner Ensemble clearly marches on its belly.

The Citizens Theatre, Glasgow has many magics. Firstly the fact that it is there at all, a beautiful, elaborate traditional theatre, now fully refurbished, formerly a proud but faded beauty, standing in the midst of so much devastation in the flattened and now high-risen Gorbals. Her partner, the old variety theatre nextdoor, is no longer. What was likely to happen could only happen in a theatre. The staff were very welcoming. This has a lot to do with the personality of the host-director, Giles Havergal, who so often greets his audience and his visiting companies in person. You feel you have been invited to a great party. Most important, it was associated with very brave, bold and innovative work, in the face of quite a lot of 'worthy' opposition. The audience knew it. They turned out.

For us too, a loyal and rather different audience came: children, young people, working-class people who wouldn't otherwise flock to the 'straight' theatre. For many years they fought to keep the seat prices low. It worked. Touring to many theatres as a guest company, you grow to appreciate the friendly ones. This has always been a home-from-home to 7:84, accepting our different conventions most gracefully: the queen bee of Scottish theatres.

The Abbey Theatre, Dublin, is full of ghosts. The new building itself is not glamorous, but the sense of that company's stormy past is very strong. When we played there, the front stalls were serried ranks of blue-rinse Americans in diamanté glasses, who had come on organised tours, which included tickets to the 'historic Abbey Theatre'. But it is the Dublin audience which makes that theatre a great place to work in.

The Theatre Royal, Dumfries is a beautiful eighteenth-century theatre in which Robert Burns caused a riot by singing 'Ça Ira' during the French Revolution. Our attempt to revive that tradition went down a storm with the audience, if not the management. . . .

The Theatre Royal, Stratford East – a Victorian playhouse. You feel you could lean out and shake hands with the people in the circle. The heart of this building is the bar – all glittering glass and mirrors and chat. Another courageous, imaginative and welcoming director – Philip Hedley.

The Cinema Actors' Theatre in Tblisi where we played *Napoleon's Revenge* in 1981 is not much to look at from the outside (they have a new one now) but, backstage, baboushka reigns. There is a kind of green room with old squashy sofas and hangings, a big samovar constantly on the go, and food; it's dark and comforting and there are cubicles off it for changing, so you can communicate without leaving the dressing room. There is plenty of light where you need it. The warmth and musicality and talent of the company assembled around their much-loved director Tumanashvili spreads through the whole building.

Of course in the village hall you are looking for something rather different.

Village and community halls

Highland village halls of the old kind are now fast disappearing. With the help of Sports Council grants new high-ceilinged, concrete boxes are going up all over the region.

The buildings they are replacing were largely made of wood, often clad with panelling, not too high, but high enough to get a set in with a squeeze. The acoustics of the old halls are lovely – made for singing, for fiddles and voices.

The access to and from the audience is good. When it is quiet, it is really quiet. There is no sound or buzz of air conditioning. The approach to such a hall gives an air of expectancy, even excitement. You will definitely see friends, hear news, experience something a bit different. Afterwards there may be a dance. Or a walk to the pub, and back to the dance later.

In these old halls – like the ones that used to be in Rogart, Tarbert Harris, and still exist in Achiltibuie, Arisaig, Shinness – there is rarely a dressing room as such, but nearly always a quite well equipped kitchen. Often only one toilet – for both audience and performers.

The new village halls – like Acharacle and Corpach – are bigger, boomier, with lots of concrete, often hard stacking chairs and a high ceiling suitable for badminton, but not so good for shows. The acoustics will be tricky, but the audience may be bigger and have come from further afield *because* it's a fine new hall. There will be enough toilets and a good kitchen.

The need to traverse the stage from one side to the other at the back is often not catered for and you may end up running round the back of the building hoping nobody's put their chairs in front of the side door entrance – nightmare!

There are no showers, and not a lot of hot water, as you would expect in a city theatre, and nine times out of ten in 7:84 we change in one room. Often this helps to work out whatever changes there might be in the script for that night, while ironing costumes or checking props.

In many of the new civic theatres and school hall stages the stage is high and smallish. The smell of Lysol militates against magic, as does noisy air conditioning.

Among small Highland halls I'd single out Arisaig on the west coast of Moidart, looking out over the silvery sea and islands, where you can hear the corncrake as you walk back after the show, and in summer it will still be light.

They want to build a new hall in Achiltibuie. But the old one, small, cramped with all the characteristics I described, sits close to the new houses, looking out over the Summer Isles with the distinct outlines of 'cleared' cottages near by. It has seen some experiences and nights to remember. If they do make a new one, they should learn from the old: the wood panelling makes it sound like the inside of a fiddle.

Props – theatrical and personal

When Maggie in *Men Should Weep* comes back from the hospital in act two having left her little son Bertie in the TB Ward, saying, 'They've kep' him in,' as Maggie I used to carry his clothes in a bundle, folded, with his wee boots on top. In reality they would have fitted a four-year-old, while, according to the text, Maggie's son is about eight at that stage in the story. But the shoes were very small and defenceless, and that was what mattered.

Perhaps my favourite prop was the red hat in *Men Should Weep*. In the entire play the costumes were of black and shades of black and grey as was the very impressive set, designed by Geoff Rose. Then, at the beginning of act two it's suddenly Christmas: two thin chains of coloured paper go up. Suddenly John the husband, in work for the first time in years, produces out of a brown paper bag a present – a brilliant red, velvet hat. It is quite startling. The audience used to gasp. Maggie (me), grabbing at it; 'It's a hat! John, yer a daft scone!' The joy, the fun of the next scene – with my po-faced sister Lily looking on and Granny and the neighbours giving their verdict. That prop, made by Morna Baxter, played a very special role with its sudden explosion of colour, and hope.

The large teddy bear that David Anderson carried as Stanley Baldwin, Danny (aged seven) coveted for a whole thirteen-week tour of *Little Red Hen*, and was awarded on the last night. The lamp post Nick Redgrave built for *Game's a Bogey* with Bath Street on it, beneath which John Maclean made his speeches. Sometimes a simple single prop can summon up a whole town.

In *Blood Red Roses* I had a basket for Bessie with a pair of gloves on a string dangling round one of the handles. I often think mothers in plays appear without any of the paraphernalia that they usually carry about their person. My own touring bag is full of bits of drawing paper, hair clasps, sharpeners, crayons, a conker, marbles perhaps, Kleenex, some sweeties with crumbs on – a reading book. Usually something given to me by a child for the journey like a talisman – for years it was a little pencil-monkey which clutched things, a tiny tortoise and a pencil sharpener with a red hen on it which sometimes cut my finger when I was searching for a Kleenex. Then it became a black and white clown. They end up on my dressing-room table now joined by the tiny Guatemalan dolls Jenny Tiramani gave me for the *Baby and the Bathwater* with encouraging notes from Kate. This must be the way it is for many actresses with children.

Finn and Danny too gave me drawings to pin up, like 'The Open Road' with the world's flags. I remember a huge castle with swarming besiegers (Finn) and aircraft bombing it and diving at it while others fired arrows and catapults. And pictures of drawbridges and portcullises, trains, vans and ferryboats . . .

And a picture of the 7:84 Band. And me always with long hair and a big U-shaped smile. And sometimes tomatoes in my tummy, or whole fishes.

No politics, please

Laurie Ruddic is a fine character actor, who played my husband in *Blood Red Roses*. He once said, in an interview about 7:84:

> 'I would not like to make it the be all and end all of my life, politics I mean – as Liz has done – I think it's a mistake to bring it onto the stage. Liz tries very hard because of her background, to a large extent . . .'
> Interviewer, Colin Mortimer: 'Ah, right – it's motivated by guilt?'
> Laurie: 'I don't have to try so hard. I come from a background that's not – well, what would you call it – upper-working-class, middle-class: my father was an educated man, a Glasgow musician. I had a fairly good schooling. I'm not privileged. I never was.'

There are a lot of myths along these lines. Maybe they contain an element of truth. For me the background, if you like, provides a perspective – a context. It is the foreground I am interested in.

When I look at my background, childhood in Glasgow, close contact with a tightly-knit Highland village community, Oxford, LAMDA, Rep, TV, films, West End theatre, rubbing up against the ruling class and living with working-class people, I know I have been lucky. Privileged, yes – to see for myself how things work and to draw my own conclusions.

Monologues

Not always accorded the status of 'proper acting', but central to 7:84's work, and usually delivered direct to the audience. Most 7:84 actors enjoy doing them – hey, my turn now! Watch this!

The play *Little Red Hen* starts and finishes with a series of superb, scurrilous monologues. On a good night the actors would follow each other on like gladiators, the audiences rising with increasing enthusiasm to each onslaught, the rounds building. Our audiences tend to enjoy them too – the more outrageous the better. Examples:

John Bett's Duke of Sutherland in *The Cheviot*
Bill Riddoch in *Joe's Drum* – am extended monologue if ever there was one
David Anderson as the landlord in *Boom*
Allan Ross as King George V in *Little Red Hen*
Bill Paterson as Ramsay MacDonald in same
Terry Cavers as Ina in *Game's a Bogey*
Cathy Ann McPhee in *The Albannach* – recruiting the audience onto her side
Colm Meaney as Fred W. Taylor in *Lay Off*
Gavin Richards – the final monologue in *The Reign of Terror and the Great Money Trick*

Clearly John likes writing them. He says:

'Monologues are important because the extended exposure of one character allows the audience to come close to an understanding of them, and allows them and the actor to lay out a great deal of the relationship between that character and their context – society, community, family, class. It allows them to reveal their history, their motives, and their hopes for the future, to come closer and at the same time to have a distance, a perspective, a self-awareness that is not so easy in naturalistic scenes. Because they have to deal directly with the audience, the audience will judge them as they will judge a person they meet for the first time. The audience's critical faculties will be heightened, even while they're enjoying themselves. That's what we're about.'

Designers

Until the arrival of Jenny Tiramani who was trained at Trent Poly in Nottingham, where they understand these things, 7:84 had a deep suspicion of designers.

Bob Ringwood designed *Trees in the Wind* – I understand he's now big in opera and movies. He was tireless, optimistic and able to concoct magic for no money. It looked beautiful and cost very little: this was usually the first part of the brief. The second part of a touring designer's brief would be to make a set that would fit into one small transit van. And be put up and down daily, both quickly and effectively. Designers often found this restricting. . . . Jenny grew up with that idea and was endlessly ingenious within the terms of the possible.

Given those restrictions, 7:84 has managed to produce some striking, original and even beautiful designs.

Nick Redgrave on the subject of set-building:

'I've got my own workshop now earning a living at telly. I get far more pleasure knocking nails in a simple, or on the face of it, boring set, knowing it's for 7:84, than making lots of interesting rococo work for television. That's what it's done for me, personally.'

Get-Ins and Get-Outs

These are the heavy bit, and sometimes bring about the end of a happy company
– if only for the night. . . .

They are closely related to the above, designers, to how well the van is loaded,
and to whether the stage is beside a ramp (the very occasional Utopia) or on
the edge of a cliff or a five-way traffic island.

Most town halls have three or four double yellow lines all round and the
janny has gone for his tea. After the show most jannies want to get away
immediately to watch the football.

In a *good* get-in there are:

1. No stairs!
2. Direct access to the stage
3. Keys
4. All the set can be transferred from the back of the van to the stage and
   assembled there in its intended order
5. Some sort of dressing room
6. Hot water
7. A working phone
8. A safe, approachable mains power supply

In a *bad* one:

1. None of the first eight
2. Not all the bits fit
3. The lighting operator is hung-over, jilted, sad or mad and is moving slowly
   on the rig
4. The cast arrive too late to tech. properly and the crew miss their tea
5. Everybody complains about everything, especially me
6. Nobody has any 10ps and, if they do, all the phones within a five-mile
   radius have been vandalised
7. An important prop or costume has been left behind at the last gig and it's
   probably my fault!

Talking to the audience

With 7:84 this may take the form of an extended dialogue over years and perhaps
several shows. There is a kind of curve here: at first surprise, enthusiasm,
excitement. Followed by delight to meet again, discover new things together.
Perhaps a new hall. Then perhaps a period of absence, separation. 'Why have
you not been back for ages?' (Not good enough for you now, eh?) 'What
happened to Bill Paterson?' or 'I see he's on the TV now.' 'Don't you ever get
fed up with this sort of thing?'

Actors not accustomed to working with 7:84 before are sometimes surprised
to be nobbled by members of the audience afterwards, wanting to know what
they think about, say, the land question, or the poll tax, or the show that visited
here five or even eight years before – perhaps when they were still at school! A
partisan, critical, but supportive approach, with a sense of continuity.

'Not as good as *The Cheviot*, of course'

I always think of Bill Riddoch when people say this: he played in every 7:84 show for six years, starting *immediately* after *The Cheviot*. He schlepped the country, turning in some quite wonderful and consistently good performances and he must have had to listen to hours of that 'not as good as *The Cheviot*' routine. I wonder he didn't thump someone. Well I suppose he did, but not for saying that. Anyway that's another story. . . .

People who say that divide, to my mind, into:

Those who felt their lives and perceptions were altered by the experience of seeing *The Cheviot*.

Those who have HEARD that their lives and perceptions would have been altered IF they had seen *The Cheviot*.

Those who haven't seen a 7:84 show SINCE *The Cheviot* and have now dropped out of political activism of any sort.

Those who have not seen a 7:84 show since and have joined the other side.

Those who haven't seen any – or very few – 7:84 shows since, and resent being reminded of their earlier youth, enthusiasm, idealism, subsequent cynicism, yuppification.

Those who want to get a rise out of us.

Those who want to get RID of us.

And I suppose there might be *some* people who, having been to *every* show, think *The Cheviot* IS the best thing we ever did.

We were warmly welcomed in Easterhouse with *Little Red Hen*. Some young lads helped us into the hall with the gear, full of jokes and patter and technical questions. They stayed for the show and loved it. 'Don't forget to come back.'

We came back the next year with *Out of Our Heads*, and they were pleased to see us again.

Next time – it was *The Trembling Giant* – a couple of the same lads, who couldn't have been more than fourteen or fifteen, had got hold of a film camera and equipment and were making a film, doing it all themselves – 'Well you said we could do it.' I wished we could have seen the film.

Nearly ten years later we were playing *The Baby and the Bathwater* in a very deprived scheme on the edge of Easterhouse called Barlanark. I understand the Tories have plans to yuppify it. They'll have their work cut out. There was a community council meeting called at the same time in the adjoining room to the hall where we were playing. We had one of those emergency confabs – technicians understandably a bit fed up, having gone through three hours of setting up, janny-baiting etc, to be faced with the prospect of a possible cancellation.

Somebody suggested we should ask the very sparse audience of at this stage maybe twelve or fourteen people, whether they wanted us to go on, or get their money back. In the toilet outside there were kids taking heroin – the blocks outside were semi-derelict – the community council's meeting was obviously more urgently important.

We asked them.

'What d'ye mean? Are we no' good enough for you?' asked a young lad there with his pal.

We did the show; in the back row two kids were sniffing glue out of crisp bags. But the others were very intent, and quite a few more trickled in after the end of the meeting to see what was going on – until there were twenty-one. Not *one* of them said, 'It's not as good as *The Cheviot*.' They were there and we were there. That was what mattered. At the end they stood up and clapped.

Making interventions

In October 1981 when General Haig let slip about the US plans for a limited nuclear war in Europe and the shit hit the fan, we were touring the area which is Scotland's nuclear arsenal with *The Catch*. What we were talking about on the stage was also being discussed for real, in secret, at Gleneagles down the road. The heads of NATO and Casper Weinberger were there, deciding our futures. We were a part of what they had started to call the 'European Theatre of War'. Part of the subject of our show was the NATO presence in Scotland.

A performance in these circumstances is bound to be direct, interventionist, and subject to considerable scrutiny. We wrote new verses, the audience listened intently, they sang along. Alan Hulse rewrote verses in mid-verse – I tried to catch up on the keyboards. The trust on stage in these circumstances has to be hyper-acute and with a small company – in this case of only five performers – it very often is.

The show also drew public attention to the existence of the anthrax-contaminated island called Gruinard, 250 yards from the mainland near Ullapool, which at the time was a fairly well-kept secret. During the tour, a group who called themselves Dark Harvest dumped contaminated soil from Gruinard, first at Porton Down, and then at the Tory Party Conference at Blackpool. Within a week the Ministry of Defence had put their Gruinard clean-up plans under review. While we had no connection with Dark Harvest, I think we had considerable influence on the outcry which brought about the recent decontamination programme.

We also played that show in Thurso near where the atomic energy reactor is stationed at Dounreay. We played to about 400 people in the town hall. In the same hall, to discuss the same questions the week before, David Owen, the leader of the newly-formed SDP, had fifteen in the audience.

In 1981 several of us toured a show, which included some of the same material, to the Soviet Union. It was hardly reported in the British press but the Russians didn't regard it as a fringe activity: peace was high on their agenda. Our intervention was not unnoticed.

Stand and deliver

The epic actor must enjoy the effect and prepare it carefully. It is often necessary to be standing up. In many of our best places this is so that you can be seen by the people at the back, or so that your support, which frequently stand at the back so they can make a quick dive for the bar, can hear what you're saying and they're not too close for a fight. If you're standing, you're in control of all the elements of what is essentially a variety performance. You can get quickly, for example, to a microphone or an instrument, or behind the keyboards, and the audience can see the moment of change from narrator to character or from character to character or from scene to scene. Audiences enjoy this in the same way they appreciate the moment when the high-wire artist steps out onto the wire. If she just appears on it half of the effect is spoiled. A superb example of this kind of performance is the Australian Circus Oz.

The birth of a show

Opening a new show never happens when you are ready for it: it is always a rush. You have not paid the bills, made the packed lunches or found any tights, but somehow or other you get yourself to the dressing room in the theatre. No matter how well you have prepared, events will overtake you, for after all a play, like a new baby, has a life of its own. Indeed the ritual and the excitement of both are quite similar. Going to the theatre for a first performance is a bit like getting yourself to the delivery room in one piece. You pack your case carefully remembering the toothbrush, the face-cloth and the good luck cards, you get there in plenty of time and get ready, taking care to breathe properly and relax.

In the dressing room there is the the company of other women, sympathetic, going through a similar experience. The room is warm, preferably quiet. There is hopefully time to reflect on what you're there for, to make-up slowly – especially if it's the first time – iron a costume, check props, find out how many people are 'in', ring home if the phone works.

Then, always somehow before you're ready, you're in the 'second stage'; it's beginners on stage, a rush, a panic, try not to push too hard, breathe, relax and you're on. The author/director is around, willing you on, sympathetic – it's his/her baby too, but somehow you're on your own, everything else fades into the distance, the voices are heard slightly faintly as if your ears are blocked with water. The noise of the audience on the tannoy suddenly changes to the sound of live people, waiting, expectant. You can hear your heart thumping, or is it the baby's heart? Breathe, relax, you're there, a bit of a splutter, you're on, the play's arrived. You're a bit light-headed, flushed, it's exciting.

Starting a show

How do we begin?
Often in 7:84 by greeting the audience and introducing ourselves:

'Hullo, good evening and welcome to 7:84's new show!'
'A laugh and a song and a dance,
And a heavy political stance!'

Another of my favourites:

'I'd like you to welcome Carlos Arredondo who has come all the way from Chile at great expense in order NOT to be there tonight!'

A feeling of warmth, sharing, adventure, even danger in the air.
Or an opening number – more difficult. Perhaps a slightly forced joviality. 'Come and have fun at the funfare, Roll up and have a nice time.' Tricky.
John is great at beginnings and introductions: 'My name is Harriet Beecher Stowe. I am a lady novelist from Cincinnati, Ohio . . .'

'Good evening. The name is Blair. Eric Blair. But for some reason or other, when I started to write, I called myself George Orwell . . .'

'My name's John Wheatley, from Shettleston, and I'm a Pape . . . don't be deceived by my diffident manner, comrades, I bloody mean it . . .'

'Hullo there, Geordie Buchan here. Just mosied down on the number 9 from Drumchapel and I'm looking for a lumber . . .'

'I'm Mrs Cartwright from the Ministry of Defence and I'm awfully worried about what's happening to our civil service after forty years of socialism in Britain . . . not that my *present* minister is any sort of socialist – Mr Younger – no he's not. The prime minister couldn't find a more loyal servant: if she says "Sit!", there he is, already sat; if she even thinks, "Jump!", there he is in mid-air.'

'I am the Claw of the Eagle! You seen the Eagle, huh? The US Eagle? Well, I am the Claw. I strike like a thunderbolt from the highest dome of the pale blue sky, Zap!'

'I'm not normal, no really I'm not. I'm not even normal for a looney . . . normal loonies kid on they're Napoleon or Jesus Christ or the Queen o' Sheba, but me, I kid on I'm normal. So I get away wi' it.'

The beautiful plain-song of *Trembling Giant. 'Pater noster rex, mater coeli est regina.'* Interrupted by Sean McCarthy as an extraordinary obscene dwarf, soon to grow into a giant by accumulating beans.

The Forest of Scotland in *Border Warfare*, misty, mysterious, full of wild animals, voices and the ghosts of the victims of Scotland's history.

Seventeen: The Squeeze. 1983

Calm before the storm

During the last week of *Men Should Weep* at Stratford East, in June 1983, Margaret Thatcher was re-elected with an even greater majority.

We went on holiday as soon as the show finished. Our friend Vivien Heilbron came with us. I felt as though I'd left a big part of my life behind. It had been hard work, keeping things going at home with both boys in the throes of exams. I had lost over a stone since the last tour began.

It was great to be in the sun. John worked on preparing *Women in Power*.

I wrote this poem on that holiday:

PAUSE IN PROVENCE

This house we stay in has a hidden courtyard
Visitors rarely use the blue door,
Behind a white net curtain.
Outside, mimosa droops its golden trail
Cicadas declare seige in two part harmony,
The ivy wall too high for them.
Only the lizards dare,

Or nonchalant candy-striped butterflies
Escaped from the sweetie jar.

I sit in the sunshine behind the house
Low vineyards beyond my high wall
Rosemary and marguerites in between the vines
Tall bamboo and mulberry trees frame the fields
Beyond them, the dizzy hills, the maquis,
And over my high wall of safety
A thin trail of ants steadily marching
Along the clothes line,
Destination unknown.

1983. A new generation of theatre-goers had grown up who embraced the style, the directness, and the variety offered. New companies had sprung up, like Wildcat. Now more new companies – Borderline, Communicado, United Artists, Cumbernauld Theatre Company, Clyde Unity, and many others – were starting in Scotland. After the success of *Clydebuilt* it seemed important to explore the European popular repertoire, to experiment with different styles, new skills, new music, to retain a company, if possible, on longer contracts, to extend our training programme, and the range of our bigger shows.

John had started to work on *Women in Power*, his adaptation of Aristophanes' 'Thesmophoriadzusiae' with Thanos Mikroutsikos, perhaps at that point Greece's most popular composer after Theodorakis. The new work was to be presented under the name of *General Gathering*, and would not replace but *extend* our existing repertoire. We were optimistic. Our audiences were expanding all the time.

It was a time of huge anti-nuclear demonstrations in Europe; in Germany, in London, Glasgow and Edinburgh. The women at Greenham Common were being very effective. The industrial labour movement was still taking on the government. There were strikes by the nurses, the teachers, and in local government. They had popular support. But at the same time the forces were gathering, both in the country and within the arts establishments and even within the company itself, to undermine our support and to lead to our subsequent marginalisation.

A growing weight of bureaucratic procedure was being demanded ever more coldly by the Arts Council. We had difficulty in attracting imaginative and energetically tireless administrators for such low wages and difficulty in getting good young actors to commit now to even a one-year contract. Strange, in the face of so much unemployment. People were becoming cautious of commitment.

We began to feel the effects of the change in the political climate, the growth of serious unemployment, the impoverishment of community centres, the decline of trades councils, and worst of all from our point of view, the wholesale destruction of touring political theatre in England.

We were faced with the confusion and sense of impotence and disbelief with which the whole population faced the hardening of Thatcher's systematic plan to wipe out not only collective forms of action, and all kinds of communal decision-making, but also the 'liberal consensus' – and to eradicate socialism from Britain forever.

General Gathering

John wrote in the first *General Gathering* programme:

'We shall be looking for the material of popular theatre in many places. The first, and perhaps the greatest, popular comedy-writer was Aristophanes, and his work still retains a boldness and originality which few since his day have managed to attain. But Sophocles and Euripides were also popular playwrights, and we must find the courage and the imagination to bring their works to a popular audience as well.

The outpouring of Elizabethan and Jacobean theatre must be the greatest source of truly popular and great drama. In particular we shall look to Ben Jonson's comedies and Shakespeare's tragedies. Molière wrote many – though not all – of his plays for a mass audience, and they too still have a lot of entertainment for us today.

Brecht, Dario Fo, O'Casey, Odets, Gorki, and many of the greatest writers of the twentieth century have been anxious to make their work accessible to people who would not normally go to the theatre. Their works are only inaccessible to a Scottish audience because of language- or time-barriers. We shall try to break down those barriers.

We hope very much that *General Gathering* will be able to stir people's imagination and their self-confidence.'

And on Aristophanes:

'Never afraid to tackle important contemporary issues head on; always ready to question taboos or satirise the habits of men and women; Aristophanes was a clear first choice: "Living at a time of extreme political turbulence he chose the really big issues of the day as his subject matter; no topic was too big to tackle – politics, war, religion, the arts, judicial systems . . . no public figure immune; Cleon, attacked so vehemently in *Knights*, had already prosecuted Aristophanes for libel. Nothing was sacred. Everything and everybody was fair game."

Not long before Aristophanes died the Greek assembly passed a law banning the presentation on stage of well known figures for public derision . . . if this law had been passed forty years earlier, Aristophanes could not have written his comedies.'

Women in Power

Women in Power had started singing rehearsals during the last week of *Men Should Weep*. While we were in London we worked as a group on singing with Robert Pettigrew who had worked with us so happily on *The Catch*. During the afternoons the six of us who were carrying on as a group had a lot of fun harmonising such standards as 'The Surrey with the Fringe on Top', with Robert on the piano. We began to sound a bit better. It made a change from the evening performance which was very concentrated and exhausting, and, as often happens, the show benefitted. The show was to open at the Assembly Rooms, Edinburgh as part of the official Festival, directed at that time by John Drummond. The rehearsals proper began in July with the full company and the presence of the flamboyant and exuberant Thanos Mikroutsizos, pianist and composer.

The very first Mayfest had put on a Sunday evening performance at the Kings, Glasgow, of Thanos' orchestral cantata, *Makronissos*. It is based on a series of poems by the Greek poet Iannis Ritsos and had been widely performed and recorded in Greece. Maria Dmitriadi, one of Greece's top singers and at that time a regular exponent of Thanos's music, sang. She too was booked for *Women in Power* – to sing Praxagora. I read the English narration and the poems which are set to music. We had one rehearsal with Thanos, and the Scottish musicians whom he found first class, being particularly impressed by the brass players. It was an exciting concert and I found the Ritsos poems – translated for the occasion by Irini Iglesias and John – very moving.

John and Thanos had celebrated the Greek election of a socialist government together with Irini the previous year while we were touring *The Catch*. Now they were working very hard. Thanos had already composed the music for the women's anthem, 'We are Moving', and met some of the company he would be working with after the show. We had a very short rehearsal period for the complexity of the work. The show and staging were demanding and different. Jenny Tiramani had designed a beautiful Greek village with tree and houses, moonlit sky and cobbled street. The men who were to play in *The Knights* – the other half of the bill – were all good comics. Keen to start. Six weeks later that company had dissolved in acrimony and recriminations. The band, mostly new to 7:84, and first-class musicians – were baffled.

Usually such things are passed over quickly and a company with a strong infrastructure and funding might move quickly on to the next project, trying to put the mistakes behind them. Some friendships survive, some meet awkwardly in different circumstances for a few years, and by then things have simmered down. But in this instance the effects of that show failing – for it was taken off quite abruptly after a week's run at the Festival, and the tour was cancelled – were not easily forgotten. They left on John, and to some extent myself, a lasting scar.

How did this come about? I don't suppose the members of that company will ever agree about what went wrong. I wrote down *my* feelings soon after the event, in order to learn from the mistakes and cope with the aftermath, which was decisive for the future funding and confidence of the company. Here is part of the text I wrote at that time.

Women in Power – an analysis. October 1983

John explained to the company in great detail the kind of style he was after, and we read slowly through the first parts of the adaptation, all of which was written, but for the last section due to the forthcoming election (it involved parodies of leading political figures who might change).

Thanos' music on tape was very exciting and original. There was a distinctly nationalist-chauvinistic opposition to the idea of Maria Dimitriadi, the singer, coming from Greece – why can't we get a Scottish singer? As it happened, Maria dropped out (for domestic reasons) and Carol Kidd, the fine jazz singer, took her place. She was perhaps the most responsive and prepared from the start to make a fool of herself if it would achieve something.

The first day Carol missed her train and came two hours late by accident to the read-through – mortified. Later John set an improvisation; he asked several of us to recount what had happened to them on the way to work – a story-telling exercise. Carol, in front of all these 'professionals', told her chapter of accidents with great self-mockery and fun and we were all delighted. She had shown great nerve and communicating skill.

These vital qualities of nerve and communication for this show were both in short supply throughout most of the early rehearsals. What went wrong?

FEAR OF SEEING AGGRESSIVE AND 'UNFEMININE'

An example. Discussing our characters – what kind of people. When I described the circumstances which I felt might have made Kleo, my character, a political leader, I suggested, amongst others: persecution in her family, supporting a child on her own, having got rid of her man.

One of the men said (as if providing the satisfactory explanations) 'I think there's something a bit weird about Kleo – a bit dyke.'

British mainstream theatre is male-dominated. Most fringe. *All* Scottish.

FEAR OF MAKING MISTAKES

The rehearsal process involved telling stories, 'gross' acting, poetry.

This requires an openness and inventiveness that was in short supply.

SOURCES

We had to hand the main, current books on the theatre of Aristophanes – a fascinating read – with many helpful, detailed, practical notes. Only one performer read any of these, let alone John's book on theatre practice, *A Good Night Out*, to which the work directly related.

COMMEDIA DELL ARTE

Broadly, a technique that is not widely taught, seen or practised in Scotland. An Italian touring company, 'Pupe e Fressedde', who do commedia, came to Mayfest on our night off from *Men Should Weep*. None of the company went to see them.

There was resistance to all but naturalistic or 'natural' acting from all but two of the men. The first is a talented, shrewd performer. The other a natural comic. He was frequently mocked in the process, although he really wanted the show to work as McGrath intended.

SEXISM

At the end of the second week a 'stagger' through. The men did their bit, unseen as yet by the actresses who now dutifully fell about loudly, supportively and self-consciously to make sure the men were happy.

The men had previously objected to the amount of time spent in discussion. Particularly on the women's scenes – an unaccustomed imbalance, in the 'normal' theatre! The women's scenes received less vociferous response from the men. They did not feel the need to bolster, more ready to undermine and ridicule the women's efforts.

DANCING

Several had never danced in a show before and found learning a basic routine difficult. High tension created in effort to learn steps, therefore contact on a relaxed level during songs/routines difficult.

SINGING

Some resentment over the amount of solo singing given to Carol – she was getting undermined already by her fellow workers.

John was *most* careful to help her and not overload her. Thanos very much liked the quality of her voice.

NOTES

'The performances must be brilliant and clean-cut to give the audiences confidence in where we are taking them' – this note from John in my rehearsal script, week one. This was never achieved. Generally when notes were given none were taken down or retained by the company.

At the end of week two I asked John and Mary Picken, our latest administrator, to consider letting me go from my contract. I felt undermined by the negativity, by lack of concentration, by exhaustion. The saddest part was not feeling able to discuss these problems collectively, something that had always been part of our practice.

John said he would think about it. I suggested that another of the actresses could play Kleonike – she had the 'bottle'. Jenni Tiramani, the designer, whose long commitment and friendship I cherish, said, 'What about your relationship with the audience? You can't give up. It's important.' So I went on.

CONCLUSIONS

1. We must not open again without a preview
2. I will not do the next show
3. Workshop/training/preparation/reading are essential to develop new styles
4. Sexism is the enemy of women's fulfilment in the theatre as in life
5. The next ten years are going to be *very* interesting!

AFTERTHOUGHTS
On the women's costumes

The designs, based on a study of Greek vases, pictures of Amazonian women etc. Very exciting. The women to look as though they were wearing men's borrowed clothes in the *first* half – comic, gross – not a problem. All enjoyed this.

But in the *second* half John wanted the women to look 'terrific', 'strong', 'healthy' – in their *own* costumes. Jenny's beautiful designs were *adapted* by each actress to become sexy, competing with each other for 'glamour'. Male-appeal. Make-up emphasised this with some even using false eyelashes, glitter, lip gloss; a far cry from the Greenham Common Women, or even the brilliant Amazonian super-women we originally conceived. Jenny and her overworked design student were to some extent victim of the prevailing attitudes, and tried to please everybody while clinging to the design concept as far as possible.

On women in action

1 November. This weekend 187 women were arrested for pulling down miles of perimeter wire at Greenham. Today Michael Hesletine promised to shoot any one who came within the sensitive area. Almost all the press, even Tory, are supportive of the women by now – and many 'ordinary' women were shocked to read this.

But two months ago we had to cut references to such women because it was beyond the scope of that particular group – to deal with or to characterise the kind of women who are prepared to take such action. Lack of support for these ideas undermined John. Had he *insisted* it would have been seen as dictatorial, and even though he suggested and coaxed it was still seen as dictatorial. After all, he was a man. . . . And so the connections between the play and today were not made.

I am grieved that my attempts to make it happen failed. But I would be the first to attempt a similar breakthrough again. It is the corollary of working in a democratic fashion that you may be overruled by the timid.

There is a lot of work to be done.

October to November 1983

Women in Power, by John McGrath, at the Assembly Rooms, Edinburgh in 1985. *Left to right*: Judy Sweeney, Mary-Ann Coburn, Anne Myatt, Elizabeth MacLennan, Andrea Miller, Carol Kidd, Linda Muchan.

The reviews of *Women in Power* were mostly vitriolic. It felt as though we vulgar populists had dared to invade the sacred ground of the high art classic repertoire. We were soundly thrashed and trashed for it. A spectacular critical bashing. Apart from Simon Berry in the *TLS*, who put his finger on it:

'*Women in Power* was to have gone on tour in Scotland after its stormy Edinburgh showing. Perhaps its imagination, wit and vitriol would have been better appreciated elsewhere, but 7:84 last week decided to close the show after their Festival run.'

Maybe we should have opened it in Glasgow . . .

Danny summed up his support by leaving out a picture for us entitled 'Critics'. It is of a Huge boot crushing a coke can, 'Crunch' – we were really touched.

On the afternoon before the last performance John rang me to say that Finn had badly broken his leg saving a goal in a school football match, just before his Highers.

That evening I ground my way through the performance – to an almost full, enthusiastic and supportive house, our friends and fans were now pouring in to hear one of the actors on stage make cynical jokes about McGrath and 7:84, and disown the show in which he was appearing, while ingratiating himself with the audience at the same time: they were a bit baffled. But afterwards in the bar my friends said they admired our bravery and loved the show, and we went home to lick our wounds.

The Scottish Arts Council made it clear that we had had our *one* chance to expand, and were pleased to let us know we had failed. They made it quite clear that we would get no more money for such developments. Within a year John had offered to resign – he felt unable to work in the atmosphere that had been created. But he was prevailed upon to stay, and in order to cope with the new circumstances he set up a new tripartite company structure and took on David Hayman as associate director, and John Haswell as associate artistic director. He also tried to find a company base.

Eighteen: Plans for a 7:84 Centre

For some time several of us had been feeling that 7:84 needed a centre, a building; a place to meet, eat, train, invite people, visiting companies, hold classes, have play-readings and consolidate our position. John drew up a practical, optimistic and imaginative document with production plans, to convert the Little Lyceum in Edinburgh for such a purpose and gained some interest and support in theory from the Edinburgh District Council, and more cautiously from the Lyceum themselves, who couldn't quite decide what to do with the place anyway. Then silence fell. Underwhelming disinterest. Edinburgh District Council fell into their now familiar inability to communicate.

7:84 England – Confrontation. 1983-1984

The English company were by now having their troubles too, recounted by John in his book *The Bone Won't Break*. We were desperately anxious about their future. Pam Brighton's production of *Six Men of Dorset*, largely funded through the TUC by the individual unions, was a call to battle – the audiences flocked, all over England. The company was strong. I saw it at the Sheffield Crucible where it played for a week – in a packed house of miners and their families. They felt the company belonged to them. For by now Thatcher was into what she clearly regarded as the *definitive* confrontation with the miners. All our futures were tied up in this one.

Within the English company at this time there was a very sparky group, including Pip Donaghy and Eve Bland, who now did Peter Cox's play *The Garden of England*, about the Kent miners. It was directed by John Burrows, of

THEATRE COMPANY SCOTLAND
PRESENTS

THE ALBANNACH

A VERSION
BY
JOHN McGRATH

OF THE NOVEL BY
FIONN MacCOLLA

WITH MUSIC BY EDDIE McGUIRE

TARBERT VILLAGE HALL
THURSDAY 30 OCTOBER - 8.00 pm

TICKETS: £3.00, £1.50 CONC. FROM ISLAY FRIGATE HOTEL: TEL: 088-02-210

Subsidised by the Scottish Arts Council

One Big Blow fame. They worked closely with the miners and their families. Again with massive support from the Labour movement they played nightly to audiences in their thousands in Sheffield, Newcastle and Manchester city halls.

7:84 Scotland – Isolation

7:84 Scotland were doing workshops in Edinburgh for a play John wanted to write about George Orwell and *1984* – *for* 1984 – under the working title, *The Imperial Policeman.*

There was some opposition to this project when it grew into a one woman show, not from actors but from our increasingly powerful finance committee. It will be difficult to sell; first you said it would be five, then three, now just her, etc. Although they grudgingly accepted that it would allow more performers on stage for the big spring show which was planned, John's adaptation of *The Albannach* by Fiona McColla, with music by Eddie McGuire, which would require a band.

Nineteen: English 7:84 Axed – The Glory of The Garden. 1984.

In March 1984 while we were in the workshop discussing the role of the Thought Police for the *1984* show, news came through that the English 7:84 Company grant had been cut – completely.

At the English company board meeting only a month before in London I had asked our drama officer, who seemed friendly enough, whether we had any cause for anxiety given the heralded arrival of cuts. No, no, she said, everything seems to be fine at the moment, and smiled. Then came *The Glory of the Garden*, the Arts Council of Great Britain's plan to bring the arts in line with 'market forces'.

In what they described as 'a planning exercise for the decade' and with considerable opposition both within and without the Arts Council, they halved the money for books and withdrew money from thirty-three clients, including five music festivals, two orchestras, fifteen companies and four touring companies, out of which two were clearly politically oppositional – Roland Muldoon's CAST, and 7:84 England. The money thus saved, described misleadingly as 'new money', was redistributed to regional arts associations who would toe the line. It did not represent an increase as it was painted, but robbed Peter to pay Paul. It offered the kind of 'devolution' (the word was used again in the document) which had been 'offered' to Scotland in 1979, and represented a fudging of the issues, frustrating a genuine desire for regional autonomy.

At a public meeting called to protest against the cuts, Jonathan Miller the distinguished theatre director – who had not been attacked himself – put it eloquently:

'We have here at the head of the Arts Council, a group of people who have a highly partial view of the social reality of this country, whose so-called redistribution of funds does not in fact reflect the social reality but reflects a highly partial view of a prosperous upper-middle class. We are not only presiding at the funeral of the English Theatre but at the funeral of the Arts Council.'

John McGrath put it succinctly: 'The Huns and the Visigoths are amongst us. I think the Vandals are at the door. What we say is not what they would like to hear.'

Some time later Richard Luce, Arts Minister, summed up the position to a gathering of the lucky arts officers when he said: 'You must accept the political and economic climate in which we now live. Such an attitude of mind could bring surprisingly good results.'

I recorded the BBC six o'clock news that evening as it carried an item on the cuts: in the same bulletin the government published the bill which was its first move in the abolition of the Greater London Council and six metropolitan councils, thus removing from people at a stroke 150 years of voting rights, and representation.

Nissan set up its first British plant in Washington, Sunderland – with plans for one union and company loyalty, Japanese style.

Bill Sirs declared support for the miners but admitted that the steel industry could be 'crucified'.

Leon Brittain, the Home Secretary, commenting on the miners' strike, declared, 'To hear our critics you would think it was the police and not the pickets who were responsible for the violence.'

A spokesman for the Thatcher government accused the Queen of political interference on her visit to Jordan.

1984 was certainly living up to Orwell's predictions, but with the totalitarian boot on the other foot.

We immediately stopped the workshop and went into emergency action. We drew up lists of supporters, institutions, MPs, trades unions, colleges, etc, who would help. Only a few people in the Scottish company fully realised the seriousness of the situation and its implications for the future of the company in Scotland. Bill Speirs of the STUC was quite clear what problems lay ahead.

Both Neil Kinnock and Ken Livingstone gave us strong practical support, as did Normal Willis and his colleagues at the TUC. At a press conference called in the House of Commons to launch *Six Men of Dorset*, one of our responses to the crisis, Neil Kinnock made a major statement on Labour Party arts policy and priorities. It was not covered by one single national newspaper. Most of them didn't bother to turn up.

Neil Kinnock's support for 7:84 went back some years. We had played *Trembling Giant* at the Royal Court Theatre in London over Christmas 1977. It was a family show, a fable. Neil Kinnock, still a backbencher, brought his family in to see the show there; that was when Kinnock became a 7:84 supporter. Shortly after he joined the English 7:84 board, and did what he could when he was needed. On the night *Six Men of Dorset* opened at the Shaw Theatre, Neil was there, along with Glenys, and Norman Willis, standing up at the end, singing with the best of them, 'Raise Your Banners High!' But when the big push came in 1985 it was, alas, not enough.

7:84 England had three months in which to appeal. Bob Rae, the English 7:84 liaison person, tireless and dedicated, drew up a very impressive appeal document with hundreds of distinguished signatories, trades unionists, artists and individuals, and an account of the company's recent achievements and critical successes.

We remained closely in contact with the English company during this period, and various attempts were made to support them by one means or another. Most people in Scotland seemed to feel, 'Oh, it won't happen here – things are different here. Scotland is a socialist country. People won't *take it*.'

I was not so sure. Worried about complacency I felt we must watch our deficit and our profile and support all the time. 7:84 Scotland would not be allowed the luxury of one failure. For every two or three mediocre productions that the average rep slips on and off unnoticed or poorly attended, our *every* show must be a winner. Yet no company can manage that, however hard they try. In the next couple of years there were one or two shows which did not reach our highest standards. A new young director perhaps – there are different reasons. But, as Richard Eyre said later, 'Like any theatre company, their fortunes may have been variable, but they have always seemed to me to provide at the very least what everyone would define as "a good night out" – an evening of lively and informed theatrical entertainment.'

But we know that now, more than ever, our enemies would show no mercy.

Twenty: New Structures in Scotland. 1985

As artistic director John decided to formalise what was already happening: to divide the work of 7:84 Scotland into three broad areas:

1. Highland Touring, Foreign Tours and Publishing, which he himself would continue to run and develop.
2. Large-scale Theatre Shows like *Ragged Trousered Philanthropists*, which David Hayman would take responsibility for, and where possible direct.
3. Small-scale Industrial Belt Tours and Community Shows which John Haswell, as associate artistic director, would take on.

In Spring 1985 John adapted *The Albannach*, by Fionn MacColla, and asked Finlay Welsh to direct it. It was an ambitious show, with a lot of music from the band Ossian, and a total cast of eleven. John was determined that the audiences in the Highlands would not be short-changed, just because they didn't live in Glasgow. This tour also had dances after a lot of the shows, and late-night concerts from Ossian at several halls. It was an exciting and full event when it arrived in a community, and greatly loved. It played in twenty-eight villages in the Highlands and islands to record attendances, and to equally enthusiastic crowds when it was revived in the autumn.

At the end of the year the Scottish Arts Council drama officer of the time said: 'You took a cast of eleven on a Highland tour. You must be out of your mind.' It became a black mark against us – a sign of lack of New Realism!

John had inaugurated a series of publications to follow up the work of the

Clydebuilt season – seven books covering popular theatre in Scotland in the first half of the twentieth century. We published the complete Joe Corrie plays and poems. The book of *Men Should Weep* was already selling well. Strathclyde Region's education committee put our previous publication *Blood Red Roses* on their Schools' Book List. We were delighted, and sold 1,000 copies in one week. We were about to produce *The Gorbals Story*, by Robert McLeish, which amazingly had never been published before. Pam Strachan undertook a great deal of this work in addition to the demands of publicity. We investigated the further possibilities of desk-top publishing.

John had invited David Hayman to do a production of *Ragged Trousered Philanthropists* for the company in 1984. It was beautifully adapted by Archie Hind, with a strong cast, and had a critical success and big audiences at Mayfest, followed by a tour of big theatres.

Now, in Spring 1985, he did *In Time of Strife*, with many of the same actors, in a new production. It too went well during a similar tour. These productions were very different in style from our previous 7:84 shows, more conventionally theatrical, and heavily influenced by the Citizens Theatre, where David had worked for many years. They pleased some of the Arts Council pundits, and restored a lot of people's confidence in 7:84; we were proud of them.

John Haswell started with Ena Lamont Stewart's new play, *High Places*, which we had persuaded her to write and had already tried out in a reading at the Tron Theatre in Glasgow. It had a rather mixed reception which was disappointing. Then as a Christmas show he was to direct an as yet unperformed piece by Matt McGinn entitled *The Incredible Brechin Beetle Bug* which would tour to places beyond the reach of conventional panto, like Fort William and Wick, involving local children as well as the cast, wherever it went, with Alistair MacDonald as the Dame.

Twenty One: The New Realism

The idea of the triumvirate of directors met with a lot of suspicion from the Scottish Arts Council – they were looking for one head to chop off, not three. That might be more difficult. They had already insisted on us appointing an 'outsider' as chairman of the board. I think they would have preferred an active *opponent* of our ideas, but now they got Robin Worral (who had actually played the bass in *The Cheviot* tour dances) and they seemed to think he was reliable because he ran a small business and wore suits. Later we had Bill Speirs, Assistant General Secretary of the STUC, friend and long-time supporter. So reluctantly the Scottish Arts Council accepted this arrangement and turned their beam onto Admin – the Tories' answer to dissent: question 'Efficiency'.

As part of *their* 1984 plan, 'The Next Five Years', a firm of management consultants was engaged by the SAC to find ways of 'rationalising' the production and overheads of all their 'clients'. The management consultants at one point suggested everybody should *merge*: 7:84 with Wildcat, Tron with Traverse, Lyceum with I'm not sure who – maybe Dundee – in the same way they thought it would be a good idea to merge Dundee and Aberdeen Colleges of Education.

So what's sixty miles? Presumably to 'regularise' administration and reduce or standardise output. It was happening all around. During the *Women in Power* period our overheads had risen to sixty-five per cent of our annual budget – an imbalance with which I for one was vociferously unhappy, as was John, but for rather different reasons from those of the Arts Council. We wanted to see the money spent on the stage, not on offices, and people producing figures for Arts Council wall-charts. It began to seem as if the money was THEIRS and not entrusted to them by all the taxpayers – not only the seven per cent. . . .

Our annual grant had now been at a standstill for several years, a way to cut it, in real terms. It had always been our policy to put our money on the stage where the public – who after all regard 7:84 as a theatre not an illustrated world history of approved budgeting methods – will get what they came for. This met with some opposition both within the SAC and the office itself. The office staff grew larger, and the casts grew smaller. John pointed out this anomaly forcefully in a number of policy documents, but on the whole these met with resistance; indeed, on one occasion the paper he had written on the subject was actually withheld from the board.

What was called a GRID, a TOURING GRID, was being set up in the Grampian region. An old friend from Aberdeen, then on the Arts Council, was on that committee: the GRIDMAKERS. I suggested, tentatively, that our expertise might be useful to that committee. After all, many of the places they were talking about (not termed *venues*) had been opened up by 7:84 in the first place. Of course, he said, remembering our original searches for places to play, what a good idea. I'll suggest it. Silence.

When the SAC first set up meetings with company boards to discuss their plans and problems in the early 1980s, ours were usually conducted in our office, quite friendly for the most part, atmosphere informal. Now the artistic director, the administrator and chairman were *summoned* to Charlotte Square and it became an inquisition, punitive and without respect or concern for the artists or really for the audience. During the report back on one such meeting after *There's a Happy Land* Pam Strachan, who went with John and was doing admin and publicity for us at the time, said she was shocked and found it, 'the most horrifying meeting she had ever been at.'

In essence we had begun to *react*, rather than *initiate*, to defend our position against the next stages in bureaucratic control of our popular theatre. Even within the people involved in *running* the company, or being employed by it. It became evident we were moving inexorably towards one of two positions: confrontation or compromise.

My own position was unchanged in principle, only the nature of our intervention might have to change. People know what 7:84 stands for – and they relied on that position being maintained. What was phenomenal about the 80s was the extent to which organisations of all kinds were being moved away from opposition and into compromise, and were being made to think it was all *their* fault!

In June 1985 this had reached such a crisis point that John drew up and submitted to the board an emergency restructuring plan. We had just finished a successful Highland tour of *The Albannach*. But it looked as if the company – apart from a community project in the spring to be financed totally by Edinburgh District Council (*Victorian Values*) – would have to cease touring for the rest of the year.

The restructuring was overdue. We needed to find other sources of income, a cheaper office, to use the computer and computerised accounts (which John had initiated), to strengthen the board, and the company's democratic participation in decison-making, to organise a trades union fund, and to reduce overheads to at most twenty-five per cent of our budget.

In his report, John wrote:

'The £70,000 plus earmarked for overheads is now firmly committed and there is no chance of making any of it available for production in the current year. It will go towards the wages of administrators with nothing to administer and a production manager with no productions, offices, accounting, insurance . . . with no great purpose. A difficult and painful reorganisation is necessary if the company is to survive and develop . . . We are settling into old orthodoxies . . . we will lose the creative, open and if necessary dangerous atmosphere in which proper rethinking can happen. I personally think that huge sections of the labour movement are in this difficulty . . . The first thing is to learn lightness and mobility . . . I believe we should crew up the office from project to project as we do the stage management and cast. This will save a lot of the £40,000 (i.e. one third of our total subsidy) we spend on admin wages, and liberate the money for performers' wages and an overall increase for administrators *while* they are working. It will also make it possible to bring in freshness and enthusiasm for particular projects.

We must take the option very seriously, without recourse to simple protectionism . . . this can have a very conservative and restrictive effect on the parameters of thinking about artistic and political output.'

This document, while being taken with the seriousness it deserved by the board and indeed reflecting doubts held by the finance committee, created a storm of indignation at the office.

There *was* a deep misunderstanding of the nature and job of artistic director; they would only have been satisfied if he had either devolved *all* power to the office *or* been there to act as general manager himself, sitting in the office, not out getting plays together, writing or directing.

At the board meeting called to discuss John's proposals he reiterated he did not want to head up 'an institution': he had got to be able to think, to keep writing, to find new forms. Alan Lundmark (finance committee) said in support, 'We have created a bureaucracy which does not allow us to create theatre any more.' Annie Inglis commented, 'John McGrath is a great writer and his commitment to the company and its success has made his desire to develop as a writer less likely to succeed.'

John then offered his resignation. David Hayman turned down the offer to replace him. After fourteen years and twenty or so plays and productions, John was now having to spend his time writing 44-page policy documents to explain why he could not write for the company as it stood, why we needed a revolutionary and flexible structure to produce revolutionary and flexible theatre.

I spoke at the meeting. These are some of my notes:

'The SAC are keeping our money at a standstill. The proposals outlined by John for *General Gathering* have been taken up by theatres all over the country, but we are denied the opportunity. Does 7:84 want to use John

McGrath's reputation, respect, contacts – and money – to enable them to remain static, immovable, a dinosaur?

There are people who question his availability and seriousness.

Last week when John's mother was terminally ill in Merseyside, when his brother had already sent for him, he drove to Bettyhill on the far north coast to a company meeting to avert a crisis of confidence in the office which could well have been dealt with by any of the admin team. From Strathy he drove immediately 400 miles to Liverpool, stopping only to pick us up, to let Kate out to be sick on the side of the motorway. His mother died two hours after we arrived. No one seemed to notice his distress when we returned a few days later after the funeral.

For *years* now he has not been paid *what is his due* according to his union, the Writers' Guild, for plays written by him for 7:84. No commissions have been received. He would be the last to object, but I find it very sad. He has *consistently* boosted the image of 7:84 at the expense of his own – often at times when there *was* no 7:84 except in the mind and aspirations of the public.

The current struggle is a clear conflict which recurs again and again in the company's history, between the revolutionary and the reformist mentality. Between the desire to change things and to conserve what we have. This is a problem not of *our* making but inherent in the process of incorporation which we have undergone. Just now we can only stand still, or move backwards. John is no longer able to write or direct for the company as it stands.

We are playing into Thatcher's hands. We have become the old war horse, not the guerrilla. We cannot do justice to our audience.

What is being suggested is a different, more flexible way of doing things. Are the board willing to discuss? Suppressing the proposals makes me pessimistic about the possibility of working well with our present set-up.

Everyone in the movement is over-extended at this time. We have to help each other, not fight. We have to have mutual respect.'
11 July 1985

My comments were 'noted'. The part about John's mother I edited out, as being too painful. By the next board meeting in August the entire administrative team had departed. John had to agree to stay on. We advertised for a new administrator, to try again.

Diary – April to May 1988

Monday 18 April
John is in Glasgow looking at sheds and possible bases. He is excited about an office and rehearsal space at the top of Buchanan Street which he wants to pursue.

Danny, now back from Carrbridge, is helping out at the Freeway office.

For me, work on the appeal. Today the STUC Annual Conference at Ayr passed a motion of support for 7:84 demanding the restoration of the grant.

Weekend up north in Rogart. They are lambing at Achork, in beautiful, mild weather. Kate and I go round with Jan, keeping an eye on developments. Kate gets to feed the pet lambs – there are already three – with the bottle. Desperate for one to arrive while we are here, but no luck.

John goes to speak at a Youth Theatre conference in London. He talks to Pamela Howard about designing Border Warfare. *She is excited by the ideas, and the script.*

Kate swam twenty lengths (one kilometre) to raise money for Ethiopia. I felt proud. She is eight.

Monday 25 April
Rehearsals start for No Mean City.

6.30: 7:84 board meeting. Jo Beddoe, potential new administrator, comes up from London to meet the board. She said she felt bad about turning down the job when we offered it in January. We are now offering more money, the first concession to the New Realists. She seems energetic and keen and quite tough. The meeting is good, full of practical support and suggestions; some new names are suggested, a sympathetic accountant in Glasgow etc. John points out that our deficit is not as bad as our last chairman had suggested to the SAC. He has in fact reduced it this year from £34,000 after The Gorbals Story *(an expensive show) to £18,000, and done our tour of* Mairi Mhor *in the Highlands and islands, which came in on target and opened up more Highland audiences.*

Saturday 30 April
The Celtic Story *opens at the Pavilion, presented by Wildcat. An extraordinary event. I wish the Jonahs of the English left theatre had come – the Glasgow popular audience was there in force (excluding, I presume, the Orange element, or at least the more rabid).*

The Mayday March in Glasgow, 1983. *From left to right*: Dennis Charles, John McGrath, Mary Picken, Irini Iglesias, David MacLennan, Patrick Hamaway, Cecile Mikroutsikos, Kate MacGrath, Elizabeth MacLennan, Simon MacKenzie, Thanos Mikroutsikos, Linda Muchan.

The show, although it must have been tempting, was no empty catalogue of triumphs, but – especially in the first half – a serious account of the circumstances in which Celtic football club began its not unchequered history, and an uncompromising stance on the question of sectarianism, which the audience took, apparently on the chin, even appreciated. I felt proud of David, my brother, who wrote it. Some wonderful songs, certainly one or two for the next album, and a lot of warm comedy and feelings of celebrating the popular culture that makes the city what it is.

The entire team were there, and many, many folk who had not been inside a theatre before. I felt sure they would be back for more as that audience streamed out into the night. It was the start of Mayfest, with lots of friends meeting up, delighted with Wildcat for taking on such a big venture; we were all proud of them.

Sunday 1 May
The heavens opened and it sheeted rain all day. The May Day March meets in George Square in Glasgow. It is a big annual event. We always go unless working away at the time. It is always on a Sunday, and many well-kent faces and friends are around. John Haswell has brought the 7:84 banner as arranged. There are one or two actors from the No Mean City *company. Caroline Paterson gives big hugs and rushes around with leaflets. John is feeling tired and looking strained. Kate holds his hand tight. Her boots have started leaking. Linda McKenny is here to support us, and Dave joins us. We always meet up on these occasions, and this time I'm particularly glad to see him. We all distribute leaflets for* No Mean City *at the Kings – it opens in the last week of the Festival. 'I'll be there!' people say, smiling. The march starts to move off. David Hayman appears with his wee boy Davie, well wrapped up against the weather, in his pushchair.*

I think of all the marches Kate has been on. Thanos and Irini Mikroutsikos came with us with their two wee girls in '82 when we were planning Women in Power; *we picnicked in Queens Park, heard Tony Benn speak and watched the porformance of* On the Pig's Back, *our street show done for and paid for by NALGO as part of their campaign against the cuts.*

Today a sense of chill and isolation in spite of the numbers. As we move off, passing the City Chambers where the red flag always flies on Mayday, I notice with some shock that today the Union Jack flies in its place . . . Look, I point it out to John and David. Glasgow, City of Culture. We move on. I am uncannily aware of the ending of the film Blood Red Roses. *Defeated, but still marching. Will this be the last Mayday march for 7:84? I take photographs. It feels like the end of something. It rains all the way. The Stop the Poll Tax Campaign is well in evidence.*

Kate is sad; she usually enjoys these occasions; today there is an overwhelming sense of melancholy. We stay to the end, to hear speeches in the muddy tent. Trampled leaflets, banners resting, badly amplified singers, comrades.

The SWAPO singing group Anampondo bring some warmth and resilience to the proceedings. David tells us Celtic Story *is packing them in. Great.*

Back home, John continues his research for Border Warfare.

Elizabeth MacLennan
in *The Baby and the
Bathwater*, a one-woman
show by John McGrath,
staged between 1984
and 1987.
As Chuck Eagleburger;
as The Storyteller;
as George Orwell.

Twenty Two: *The Baby and the Bathwater.*
1984-1987

'How George Orwell invaded Grenada in 1983, and where will he invade next?'
It was against this evolving background that John and I had started to work
on *The Imperial Policeman* or *The Baby and the Bathwater* back in 1984.

What had been planned as a small, highly articulate but deconstructed
piece with a Latin American band, became a one-woman show. It was curious.
To be faced with perhaps the biggest and most difficult challenge of all – the
One-person show – almost by default. At least, that was almost how it felt at
the beginning, and we started from very low and worked up very painfully.

We felt there were people all over Scotland and Great Britain having
similar and worse problems: teachers, nurses, the civil servants, the unemployed, children, let alone the miners; all those faced with cuts, redundancy,
marginalisation of their lives and their culture. They wanted a response to
these disasters in their own lives, they needed support. But we ourselves were
already marginalised by a hostile theatre establishment.

We had a lot of heavy board meetings.

* * *

When you have spent years trying to become a good ensemble performer it
is quite difficult to suddenly do a one-person show, although I had originally
been a bit of a cabaret-type performer – very extrovert and show-off.

The circumstances of the previous year – artistically and politically – had
made me feel quite small and helpless. I heard Maureen Lipman talking
about preparing her one-person show about Joyce Grenfell on the radio. She
talked about familiarising herself with the script for at least six *months*! Our
show, although we had been researching it for some time, was written and
rehearsed in four weeks flat. When we opened in Cumbernauld I could only
just manage to do the changes in time, let alone remember all the lines. The
second half was only completely written the weekend before we opened. But
we did open, and that show grew and developed over four years into something
I am quite proud of. It has done a good job, both in Scotland and England
and in Canada.

We were sustained and given moral support in rehearsal by a loyal and
hardworking team: Jenny Tiramani the designer; Ali MacArthur, lighting;
Alistair Fraser, unruffled stage manager; Margaret Miller – her first job in
theatre – dresser; Ian Courtenay, sound. Also attending rehearsals were
David Diamond, a colleague from Headlines Theatre Company in Vancouver,
who since then has done a show in the far north of British Columbia with
the native Indian people about their land rights. It is being used as part of a
test-case land claim which could set an important precedent. He plans to
take it to New Zealand to compare notes with the Maori people.

I got used to them watching John and me argue it out on our feet, a process
it would take some other, more objective person to describe. Where does the
script get changed, lightened, the comedy sharpened, the attention focussed?
It's a two-way process and we were working as if our lives depended on it.
In a sense they did – at least on our ability to work together and to try out
new ways of saying things.

We worked in Belford Dance Centre (since cut), a big, boomy hall, often freezing cold, near the Dean Village in Edinburgh. Sometimes we worked in a side room at the 7:84 offices in Albany Street, but that was slightly inhibiting. It felt as if we were taking part in frivolous exercises, not really part of the company's *real* work, i.e. dealing with bureaucracy. . . .

We had accumulated a huge amount of information; about George Orwell and about the operation of the US in Central America. It took shape and the characters began to emerge. At first I really *disliked* George Orwell. I read everything he wrote and books about him. As our situation in Britain becomes more Orwellian by the month, I now feel he might have been a friend and a fascinating companion. He would have had a terrible time in the 80s and maybe arrived at a rather different definition of Big Brother.

We were interested in the uses to which his anti-communism have been put. More children in this country read George Orwell than the Bible. Why? What do they make of it? What are they, more to the point, *expected* to make of it? In the US too he is a standard classroom text book. Very recently they decided to publish *Animal Farm* in the Soviet Union, but not *Homage to Catalonia*, his attempt to define another socialist way forward. It is not standard reading in East or West – why not? .

Rigoberta Menchu provided the missing link. We read her extraordinary book about her own life and people, the Guatemalan Indian people. It is a towering testament to their endurance in the face of the biggest holocaust since the last war, which is still going on. It was impossible to read aloud, at first, let alone *rehearse* the catalogue of horrors that happened to her family in the name of 'freedom' and Westernisation. It is living proof of the horrors of imperialism. The destruction of a gentle, rich culture, a language, a people. It has resonance for all the Third World and for us too in Scotland.

The book is called *I, Rigoberta Menchu*. It has since been translated into ten languages and in September '89 she was nominated for a Nobel Peace Prize.

By now Carlos Arredondo had joined us to play and sing the songs – some traditional from the Chilean Araucano Indians, some from Nicaragua today, some with new lyrics by John, music by Carlos. Carlos grew up and worked in Santiago, and fled via Peru to Glasgow in 1973 when the military coup overthrew Allende. He now lives and works in Edinburgh.

Carlos, new to theatre, but *not* to committed activism, beautiful voice, fine guitar player, to become the best of comrades. We struggled to make the show happen. For him to sing in English was difficult, especially pronunciation of 'Nobody's Backyard', a song John wrote for him about the 'ordinary' US citizen's paranoia about preserving the 'hemisphere' from 'communism'.

Later, almost at the end of the play, John wrote him a speech which was very powerful, and particularly so coming from someone who had experienced what he had.

Carlos's Speech

(with Quatro musical accompaniment)

'It is very sad that in the United States many words have come to mean their exact opposite. It is sad because people suffer and die because of it.

When they talk about Chile, for example, they call Allende, who was democratically elected, a Marxist dictator. And the fascist dictator, Pinochet, is called a 'friend of democracy'.

In Guatemala 'democracy' means massacre. 'Freedom' means death.

And still when they talk of Big Brother they don't mean the Pentagon or the CIA or Reagan – they mean the Soviet Union.

Perhaps I cannot speak English as well as you. I must try harder to understand this language – I must read George Orwell.'

It was Carlos' job, apart from the music, to validate what we were saying by his presence, his solidarity. At the end of the show we play and sing 'No Pasaran' – it is a statement of Internationalism. The phrase *No Pasaran* (they will not pass) of course comes from the Spanish Civil War, but has been taken up today in Nicaragua in this song by Mejia Godoy.

This show, above all the others so far, has given us the opportunity to make links with theatre workers in other countries and to express that Internationalism. On a personal level Carlos is one of the most supportive people I've ever worked with; we made many friends on our travels, by no means always 'the converted'. I like to think that the questions the show raised, and in particular the problems of Guatemala, El Salvador and Nicaragua, were brought to the attention of a wider audience.

Certainly we raised several thousand pounds for the Nicaragua Health Fund. And for the miners. But that too varied enormously. After the show in Banchory – which had been well enough received – there was the record sum of 2p in the collecting bucket for the miners! But a week later at a packed performance in the Marryatt Hall, Dundee, sponsored by the Dundee Research Centre for the Unemployed, we raised a handsome collection from the unemployed. It was a demanding ten-week tour: frantic changes, a two-hour show, five performances per week, driving myself and Carlos all over the country and keeping up with home and children in between. But it was a friendly, warm little company all of whom treated me so well that I felt very secure.

In this version I played, apart from myself, A sixteen-year-old schoolgirl from a rough part of Edinburgh, George Orwell, Mrs Cartwright (a middle-aged English civil servant), a tabloid journalist (male), Jeanne Kirkpatrick, who was US Ambassador to the UN under Reagan, Rigoberta Menchu, Chuck Eagleburger, now stationed in Central America, and Pope John Paul II.

In a solo show it is an exhausting physical and intellectual exercise to remain alert, free to ad lib and adapt to the widely changing responses. Some nights they were spookily quiet. For example, a capacity audience (102 per cent at Springwell House Community Centre) laughed only *once* in the first half. At the interval I thought they must be *hating* it. But in the second half – magic. The jigsaw was coming together and they laughed, clapped and wanted more. Audiences are a mystery, thank goodness. They are a permanent source of wonder and keep us going.

During the last week of evenings in the Lyceum Studio we went during the day to some of the strike centres within reach of Edinburgh and did sections of the show for the miners and their families – usually after their lunchtime in the canteen.

We joined the picket at Bilston Glen Colliery and watched the scab shift coming off duty get their dues from the women in the support group. We made a lot of friends. Carlos got a warm welcome with his stories about the miners in Chile and his haunting Nicaraguan songs. As the GI, Chuck Eagleburger, I used to go looking for 'Marxists' in the audience.

'Marxists! That's what. You get 'em!
This place is fulla unAmerican activities!
So what you gonna do about 'em?
You got students,
peaceniks,
teenagers,
unemployed,
deviants,
women, women deviants,
Blacks, Indians, old people,
old people deviants
old Black Indian people deviants!
– babies!
    In short – you got Marxists –
the outfit that runs this hall is infested with Marxists like some people got crabs. (*Scratches*)
Hell, sorry I mentioned that –
And we have got sensitive installations in this country!

The audience would help me out: he's one! Over there! Behind you! At Fishcross they all pointed laughingly at George Bolton's dad, a veteran of the Spanish Civil War and a really delightful man. George is a senior official in the Mineworkers' Union. The spirit and determination of the whole mining community at that time was unforgettable. Changing in the kitchen I would get talking to the women – many of whom would have been on the picket line at six that morning.

That Christmas the STUC and Alex Clark ran a huge benefit for the miners' families and children at the Kings Theatre in Glasgow. Carlos and I were on the bill along with Ann Lorne Gillies, John Cairney, Wildcat and many others.
    The rest of 7:84 Scotland were touring *In Time of Strife* at the time. I met Alannah O'Sullivan in the wings and asked her if she would look after Kate, now five, while I went on.
    I conveyed messages of solidarity from the English 7:84 Company who were working on their play about the Kent miners, and from John who was with them. The reception was typical of a Glasgow labour movement audience – warm, intelligent – determined to win.
    But the strike was crushed and the movement in Scotland – and everywhere else – is still staggering from the blow.
    The following Spring, April 1986, we toured *The Baby and the Bathwater* in aid of the *English* Nicaraguan Health Fund, with the enthusiastic support of their branches in Norwich, Brighton and Crawley, finishing at the Shaw Theatre in London.
    But the show really came into its own in August 1985 when we did it in a tighter version, without interval, and with new material about the press, about

official secrecy, and the strike in the Edinburgh Festival Fringe. This time we had to do it on our own – that is, *without* 7:84's blessing.

For this revival we called ourselves 7:85. Why 7:85? Because the office refused to do it as 7:84. Too risky, they thought. (Although the board subsequently supported us doing the show on our own; good for 'profile', and keeping in the public eye.) The show was cut, sharpened and reassembled with the help of John Haswell. Suddenly I was working for nothing again. Carlos and the crew got paid the current 7:84 wage. *I* could be crazy if I liked, but not impose it on them. I could *just* afford to do it – because I was about to start six and a half weeks' filming of *Blood Red Roses*.

I was surprised and a bit hurt by that decision. We played for three weeks. And broke even. And played to very good, and most appreciative audiences. Many of them joined the Guatemalan and Nicaraguan health and support groups as a result. I could see the shape of things to come in August '85 – were we to continue to make theatre or to satisfy the changing demands of our paymasters? Was it possible to remain oppositional and do that? Probably not.

Diary – May 1988

5 May
The Day of the Writer. Part of Mayfest, a Writers' Guild event. I attend the evening session. They talk about Satellite, about structures, about 'looking closely at the market'. Nobody mentions the death of 7:84 – what's £135.000, our current annual grant, to these television executives? It would pay for ten minutes of The Singing Detective *or 1.8 video editors' yearly wage.*

The thousands of people who came to see Men Should Weep, *for example, are a marginal audience in terms of TV ratings. Whose culture is it anyway? A teacher on my left says she cannot teach respect for their own culture to children who have it de-rated every day and believe in* Dallas. *Normal Buchan, sitting by me, speaks eloquently on the dangers of censorship and Clause 28.*

It is now seven weeks since we were given notice of the cut. I have written hundreds of letters, leafleted, organised, lobbied. 'Not working' (this is all unpaid) is a full-time job. Mostly I have worried and been depressed, stunned, angry. We have received some wonderful letters however, all stressing the high standards of the company's work.

Our planned visit to Edmonton has had to be cancelled. They are most disappointed and sympathetic. I am really sorry.

With all this trouble, John is behind, hardly surprising, with writing Border Warfare. *His confidence is at a very low ebb. He has taken Pamela Howard on, to design. I liked her when we met at a theatre conference in Oxford last year. A clever woman; her enthusiasm for the project will be a great boost.*

John thinks it would be unwise for me to be in Border Warfare – *hostages to fortune, etc. He is probably right. I am very sad.*

Our lives are about to change radically. I will need all my strength.

Monday 9 May
Sun in Edinburgh. John in bed all day, headache, depression, unable to write.

The daisies in the garden are huge and beautiful. Columbines in bud. Shining green grass after the rain. Narcissus. Seagulls from the river. Noisy blackbirds. My maple seedling, a present from John McEwan, is a sturdy eighteen inches now.

Kate and her friend Grace are skipping happily outside with a rope tied to the railings. I can see them from Danny's window.

To Glasgow to see the Maly Theatre of Leningrad play Stars in the Morning Sky *by Alexander Galin, at Mayfest. A brave, passionate and committed performance.*

12 May
Ian McKellen's one-man show to raise funds for AIDS at the Kings Theatre, Glasgow: a wide-ranging, informal wander through his passion for Shakespeare, very accessible and skilled and much appreciated. Big reception. At the end, in his fund-raising speech, he mentioned 7:84's 'present troubles', and his admiration and support for the company, and it got a big response. We were very pleased.

Monday 16 May
Preview of No Mean City, *David Hayman's production.*

It is not good enough for the company at this critical juncture. Stylish, good-looking, bold. But not ENGAGED. Hard and glittery. The production is not standing outside *the central figure, the hardman; almost excited by him. Still, it WAS a preview – time to get the emphasis right.*

The women were all male projections, except Pat Ross's character. They didn't let us in to their *tragedy. The mother bottled, battered, frightened – she nonetheless remained strangely unmoved by it. The broken girlfriend, with her aborted child. Where was the pain? They were essentially decorative, well-protected, fading into the wings when the main story, the MEN's story, took over.*

The character Peter (a good actor) who becomes a socialist – his was a shamefaced, subdued, sedentary version. Yet, at the same time, in the same city, large, public events were taking place – strikes for the forty-hour week, tanks in the streets, rent strikes, unemployed marches. The audience would expect 7:84 to relate to these. Where was the dialectic?

Alex Norton's adaptation had set this up well at the beginning but this section has been cut.

By Wednesday it will have been sharpened up. The cast were obviously tired.

In the afternoon there was a well-attended press conference. Mark Fisher (Labour Shadow Arts) came up specially and spoke extremely well. He stayed with us and seems keen to help. We discussed playing the Labour Party Annual Conference at Blackpool this autumn – perhaps with my Rees Mogg monologue and some songs. Today Mogg's appointment as head of the 'Broadcasting Standards Council' was made official. Yet another government job.

Tuesday 17 May
Among today's letters of support, one from Joan Littlewood to the Arts Council. Philip Hedley rang, delighted, to read it over the phone. It's a cracker.

16 May 1988

Dear Sirs,
So what is wrong with 7:84 now? Too good? Too bad? Or just not orthodox? I passed my working life in the UK to the accompaniment of noises from a long line of Arts Council directors telling me my work wouldn't do for them.

The truth being that they would have liked to see Theatre Workshop in hell since it challenged all the standards they held high.

I know enough of John McGrath's work to suspect that 7:84 is in the same boat. One expects mediocrity from your London Branch. I would have been happy to know that Scotland had produced something better by now.

Yours faithfully,

Joan Littlewood

A few years ago, obviously familiar with the work he was doing with 7:84, Joan came round to our house and asked John if he would take over at Stratford East. He felt unable to abandon his commitment to our audience at that time, but it was a great compliment.

In the evening drove through to Mayfest again to see Leonard Bernstein's Candide.

This performance is sponsored by the STUC. We sat in the gallery surrounded by Scottish trades unionists who all stood up when the band played 'God Save the Queen'.

Wednesday, 18 May

No Mean City *press night. Clearer, the points made, less rushed, even some contact. The man inside the Razor King is emerging now. Caroline is strong, and Pat Ross, and Mandy Matthews, the young actress who plays Lizzie. How can the Arts Council destroy all that potential?*

We must not become marginalised.

Friday 20 May

OXFORD. *The Union. The subject for debate: The Arts Should Not Have to Depend on the Private Sector for Funding. John invited to propose by the Scots President of the Union.*

Opposing were Colin Tweedie from ABSA (the Association for Business Sponsorship of the Arts, set up by a Labour administration) and a media-seeking don – actually Scots, but now almost racist in his views on Scotland – called Stone. Arrogantly Philistine he displayed a typical Thatcherite scorn for the real needs of theatre workers and *audiences.*

It was a lively debate with some good interventions from the floor, including several women. John won the motion by 195-93.

The whole event turned out to have been sponsored by Beck's Beer! They flew us both down and presumably paid for the dinners and for a silver quaich for the best student speech – which was won by an Aberdeen supporter. A curious interlude.

Saturday 21 May

Before we left we saw Beverly Anderson, now teaching at the Poly, and John's friend Roger Lonsdale, still teaching at Balliol. Beverley says the Oxford Playhouse is closing. The University, for all its wealth, will not support it. It is extraordinary to think that a university town of the size and with the reputation of Oxford should even CONSIDER having no theatre – it would be unthinkable in other parts of Europe, East and West.

Tuesday 24 May

Letters today from Sam Galbraith, MP, and several more union branches. We must have at least 300 letters already and a number of petitions. More coming in every day.

A very touching one from Joan Jara in Santiago. 'It would be a pity if Scotland could be suspected of following the example of General Pinochet.'

Finn has two weeks till his exams – Medieval History, Modern History and Politics. He hates exams, but now he can recognise the symptoms and laugh at them a bit.

Dan is being very supportive. I could not have coped with the last two months without Finn and Dan and Kate's loyalty, objectivity and love.

Wednesday 25 May
No Mean City in Newcastle for a week, at the Palace Theatre. The reviews have been only fair, the attendance figures good in Glasgow. I wonder if any of the company there now know anything about 7:84's previous visits to Newcastle? The English 7:84 played there frequently till its demise, as did the Scottish company.

Thursday 26 May
Today we had a letter of support from Ritzaert ten Cate, longstanding innovative director and founder of the Mickery Theatre in Amsterdam, home from home to 'alternative' European, English and American theatre, his mind so broad it meets at the back of his head.

The English 7:84 caused a big stir at his theatre with Lay Off *and* Yobbo Nowt. *We played David MacLennan's show* Honour Your Partners *there too in 1976 which celebrated the American bicentennial in a somewhat different way from the stars and stripes waving that was going on that year.*

Thursday 9 June
Dan left to spend the summer in the US. I'm no good at partings, even after so much practice. But I'm delighted for him. As Kate says stoically – 'People have to make their own decisions. If they're wrong they'll find out. Of course you can always advise me about policemen and things.' But I'm going to miss him.

Sunday 12 June
A bewildering series of developments: John is now thinking perhaps 7:84 would stand a better chance of survival without him as artistic director, given all the hostility in the arts establishment and the caution within the company itself. Is wanting to discuss this option, as a way forward. I am very dubious.

He arranged a series of discussions with Jo Beddoe, Bill Spiers, Christine Hamilton of the STUC and Alan Lundmark from Glasgow District, hoping for some support, understanding. David Hayman still non-committal. He seems totally dismissive of John's contribution to the artistic management and survival of 7:84 for fifteen years. This worries me. What about continuity of policy? If he took over, partnership is OUT. He made it quite clear that he would not welcome or commit to any further plays or productions by John. He now suggests putting off Border Warfare *(planned to coincide with the appeal) until 'some time next year'. The discussion was far from helpful.*

The proposed move to Glasgow appears to have been shelved. Jo is not keen. The timing of the appeal is not seen to be a priority. We are in the hands of the managers. They have a very different 'over-view'.

Surely if we are to maximise our impact we should open with a big show –

and Border Warfare *is going to be BIG – in Glasgow, with fanfares, just before we put in our appeal. It seems staggeringly obvious to me, and unfathomable to the office. After all, we* are *a theatre company. How else should we properly make our impact?*

The board is to be re-designed at the board meeting on Thursday, 30th. I'm laying bets with myself as to who will be pushed, including me. . . .

We have a two-week cheap flight to Greece booked to go away as soon as possible after the meeting.

Saturday 25 June In the Highlands.
In Rogart. We bring in some peats with our friends, Jan and Ray Davey. Kate helps. It is quite hot, midgy and hard work, but good to be away from all this for twenty-four hours, to be out in the open.

Thursday 30 June
The meeting was marked by a decisive shift in our chairman, Bill Speirs' position. Heavy going. John had decided to recommend postponing further discussion of the artistic directorship till after Border Warfare *is on, mainly on grounds of the impossibility of him doing any concentrated work or serious writing under all this pressure. He made this clear to Bill whose response was impatient. Aonghas MacNeacail, himself a writer, clearly understood the situation. 'The office' were hostile, flinty.*

All present (except 'the office') were surprised to receive a completely unheralded statement from John Haswell, associate artistic director in charge of three productions in the last two years, tendering his own resignation and demanding John's.

David MacLennan, anxious to get on with our more concrete and pressing problems, clearly angry, proposed a vote of confidence in John McGrath's artistic direction which was seconded by Linda McKenney. Bill Speirs from the chair refused to take it, or rather recommended it be dropped. The rest of the board were uncomfortably silent. We felt very isolated suddenly. Equally suddenly, bearing in mind the initial resistance, the move to Glasgow is now approved, a date to be fixed at a later meeting with Jean McFadden to which John was not invited. 'Oh yes, we're moving to Glasgow; it's just a case of when.'

John explained the current position on Border Warfare. *The money Freeway had been offered for the project from Channel 4 – roughly two-thirds of the entire budget – was in place. At this point all that 7:84 needed to put up for this very big show with a guaranteed three-hour showing on TV was £3,000. Not a bad deal! £15,000 sponsorship money was also to be raised by Freeway, hopefully to be matched by ABSA if the office got around to applying for it. No one said, 'Nice one, John, that's a fine piece of artistic management,' although the meeting began at 6.30 and dragged on till 10.30 pm. Hayman's disinterest in John's work seems to have soured their previous enthusiasm.*

The appeal was pushed to the end of the agenda. I attempted to generate some warmth towards the efforts of our many valuable friends and allies by reading out a representative one or two of the hundreds of supportive letters I had received, copies of which they sent to the Arts Council. I was told, 'Let's leave that to some other time.' Perhaps they write to support something these people are afraid of; no longer want.

Bill Speirs' alarm at the thought of Border Warfare *being a three-hour show in which the audience might have to* stand, *or walk about a bit! I reassure him there will be some seats for disabled and geriatric trades union officials! The others look vaguely irritated, bored or non-committal on the whole subject of the actual* production.

They are offended that John – or anyone – should make even a mild criticism of any aspect of No Mean City. *Is it impossible to talk openly? To exchange ideas with comrades, or colleagues (the preferred word these days).*

Friday 1 July
My interview in the Third World Publications Quarterly, Links, *arrived. An account of our tour to Cape Breton Island and Montreal last spring. They put in a Stop Press up-date about the cut. It says, 'this is a direct reversal of the Arts Council's arm's length policy to* extend *the availability of the arts.'*
I began:

'We're into agitation, changing the situation, rather than reinforcing the middle-class values that conventional theatre is all about. We're into celebrating the values of the working class in Scotland, in Britain and overseas.

Working with 7:84 I have discovered that our problems in Scotland are not unique and that we are very much part of an international cultural set-up. I'm interested in finding the connections. We spend our time between tours of Scotland – playing in small Highland communities or in big theatres with large working-class audiences like The Citizens in Glasgow – and tours abroad, where we find a great sense of solidarity and increasing confidence, especially from our comrades in the Third World.

People in this country are constantly being told that they've got to settle for Thatcher's way of looking at the world. But there are many other ways of looking at the world and we have experienced some of them at first hand.

The connection between cultural identity and language in Scotland is very important: we are witnessing for instance a strong revival of the Gaelic language and the folk tradition. People are realising that it is something they must hold onto, that it shouldn't be colonised out of them. There was a Celtic film festival recently in Inverness, which happens every two years in different parts of the Celtic world, and this year our play There Is a Happy Land *won the top prize for the film most embodying spirit of the festival. That gathering represented a large group of cultures that are normally regarded as* fringe: *the Welsh, the Irish, the Bretons and the Gaels from Scotland. If you put all the* fringes *together, there is probably more of them than the so-called "centre", and this is an ideological struggle that has been underestimated.'*

Two days later, unbelievably, Kate and I are on an island in the Ionian Sea. Channel 4 having managed to mislay John's passport, he is now on his way with a new one.

We have found a small room to rent, not expensive, in a house covered with bougainvillea and jasmine, and made new Greek friends already. We are eating souvlaki, beans and Greek salad among the brilliant dahlias. The sea is fifty yards away. Our luggage has gone to another island . . . *we'll get it back eventually. I've got my passport, a few drachmae, and two T-shirts between us. We have already been swimming. There are mice in the vines overhead. It is hot, with a gentle warm breeze. We will sleep well.*

Next day we go to the airport to see if John is on the one daily plane – no sign. Miraculously I spot our luggage in the open hold and run across the tarmac, past two gun-toting policemen, to grab it before it goes straight back to Athens.

A couple of hours later John appears smiling on the beach. He has been to Athens, across the Peloponnese, by boat, by bus and by car, and he has found us – 'Ah, you mean the one with the little girl who has lost her luggage and her husband!' Great merriment and speculation; come, I'll show you! We are all three glad to be united and together after the hassles of the last six months.

Thoughts that wouldn't go away on holiday
After that board meeting we both knew it was a matter of time before John must leave 7:84 in order to be able to work properly.

So many things we have fought for over the years are threatened.

The division between office and artists is bad, both end up being patronised, and where are the performers in this hierarchy? Paid less, for one thing. Are they to be treated like troublesome children (who don't understand about money and things) again? Not allowed responsibility? Do they want that? What do they think 7:84 means?

So many other thoughts won't stay behind. But I leave John in peace to read, to decide for himself, sitting in the shade.

Tuesday 19 July
Kate's ninth birthday. Back to Edinburgh.

Finn is off to Spain on a working holiday with two friends, Larry and Hamish. Young men now . . . I wave cheerful goodbyes, hope they don't crash. We feel stronger, fit and brown after our holiday. It is raining.

Twenty Three: Good Times, Bad Times. January 1986 – December 1987

January 1986 began with the 'winter shoot' for the film, *Blood Red Roses*. I acted out the birth of the baby girl in the Southern General Hospital in Govan. A brand new baby arrived in the next ward just in time – perfect – and of the right sex (for the story) and strong enough to take part; starting young! There are times when the process of filming can be extraordinarily intimate and these tender scenes at the end of the film gained a lot from the atmosphere of trust and co-operation that had grown up from filming together over thirteen weeks. Oonagh Fraser – at two and a half weeks the company baby – even managed to burp and smile on cue.

Then we froze in a snow-bound churchyard in Glenlyon, filming the funeral scene till the tears came, not from grief but from imminent hypothermia. Fittingly, the last day was the picket-line scene.

Finn, the eldest son, started work with Sue Timothy in the English company office provided by the TUC in Transport House, on their bid to save 7:84 England with *All the Fun of the Fair*, John's funfair show of Tory Britain. There was enthusiasm for the show and the promenade setting. Money was promised from the GLC and at the eleventh hour it was forthcoming. Chris Bond was to direct and Ellen Cairns did a fabulous funfair setting. John describes the cliff-hanging nightmares of getting this show on in his book *The Bone Won't Break*.

Meanwhile David MacLennan started rehearsals of Sean McCarthy's new play for 7:84 Scotland about sectarianism; *Beneath One Banner*. It was to tour to many difficult new areas. Sean knew the audience well, having toured with us as an actor in *Trembling Giant* and with the 7:84 England in *Serjeant Musgrave Dances On*.

It was a hard, snowy winter. John's father was very ill in West Kirby and he was travelling up and down to see him and to attend Byzantine meetings over the English company/GLC involvement. *Beneath One Banner* opened at the Lyceum and set off on an arduous tour in thick snow. I worked on dubbing *Blood Red Roses*.

In March John Haswell directed a new community show for 7:84 Scotland in Springwell House in Edinburgh – something we felt could be developed by him in other areas. It involved the company in teaching workshops on a number of theatre skills which were enthusiastically attended. Pam Strachan played a big part in making it all happen. The whole exercise involved the community for about three months and the show that emerged was called *Victorian Values*. The writer was Donald Campbell.

Meanwhile I toured with Carlos for the Nicaraguan Health Fund in the south.

In April 1986 John's father died, just one year after his mother. Cancer again. For John a sense of finality, a wrench at his Liverpool roots.

Twenty Four: Back in the Highlands

We were by this time working on a new 7:84 Scotland production called *There Is a Happy Land*. This was intended as more of a concert, subtitled somewhat ironically the 'Entire History of the Gaels', again by John McGrath.

The band was Ossian, a folk group who had toured with us very successfully the previous autumn in John's adaptation of *The Albannach*. They were arranging the music, to be sung by Tony Cuffe and our own Catherine Ann McPhee, who had also been in *The Albannach*.

The story – or narration as it came to be called rather functionally and at times quite dismissively – was to be told by Simon Mackenzie, partly in Gaelic, partly in English, and by myself in Scots and English. Simon also sang a number of beautiful Gaelic songs, but this time I took no part in the music.

It was a beautiful spring when we opened on Friday 25 April 1986 at the Churchill Theatre. After a week there we set off on our travels. It was a short Highland tour, by 7:84's previous standards. The alarming deficit built up by our administrator had not been revealed to us, and the high costs of Highland touring made it only *just* possible to do four weeks. For obvious reasons, this time we concentrated on the Gaeltacht, the west Highlands and islands, and in the course of the tour Freeway filmed the show for Channel 4 as the first part of John's trilogy on the 'History of the Scottish People'. Part Two (*Border Warfare*) was at that time scheduled to be filmed the following spring. Without Freeway Films' financial support we could not have done the tour at all. It was very much appreciated by our audience, both 'old' and the communities we visited for the first time. 7:84 and Freeway later made an LP of Cathy Ann singing which included many of these songs.

The West Highland location – the hall on the shores of Loch Eilort at Acharacle – was a truly lovely place to be paid to be working. We made the most of it, staying in beautiful Ardnamurchan surroundings, stuffed full of delicious location catering. It made a change from some touring circumstances we had experienced. I had learnt a thing or two from my mistakes in *Blood Red Roses*. There is a kind of directness and simplicity about this film that we were pleased with and the music and scenery were superb.

Our man at Channel 4 being Michael Kustow, an old friend, relationships were good. His enthusiasm for the project was infectious. Producer Steve Clark Hall had also worked on *Blood Red Roses* and there were no hitches. It was a remarkably smooth running exercise.

An excerpt from Kate's diary of the tour (aged seven).

June 3 1986
'We went to Arisaig on the beautiful west coast. There are yachts and islands in the bay. We had tea at Jacks cafe with the company. I had fishfingers and chips and ice cream. I got a glass elephant and a glass donkey. Then we went to the hall and helped put up the show. There was a baby at the show and I helped Lynn sell tickets and programmes and the books, records, tapes and badges. The hall is made of wood. We stayed in a hotel with bendy floors. After the show I helped take down the set then we walked down by the water to the hotel.'

The last ten days of touring included Achiltibuie, Lochinver, Dornie and Applecross – a gentle, wonderful night. On the way there I picked up some boots for the Old Hen – her costume having 'disappeared' – from a lady who worked in the tweed shop in Broadford who said she had some in the shed for throwing out; they were just right. Then a rush to Glasgow to do a speech from *Little Red Hen* at a commemorative show for Spanish Civil War veterans on the Sunday. Monday night off, to do washing. Then to Arisaig, then the Gaelic college on Skye, to Strontian, Corpach – a very big house all joining in the songs – Kate getting very tired, Fort Augustus, end of tour, ready for a break.

There was the Edinburgh Festival to look forward to, with *Blood Red Roses* opening the Film Festival, Inti-Illimani playing a concert, the Abbey coming from Dublin and the Market Theatre from Johannesburg.

The film of *Blood Red Roses* was well received at the Edinburgh Film Festival, and was picked up for a short run in the West End. It has since been shown in many regional film theatres, festivals all over the world, and repeated on TV.

168

Just before it opened I felt very optimistic and wrote sitting in the Botanic Gardens:

> Autumn 86
> Rowan bright
> Sunlight
> Jumping heart
> New start.

Mairi Mhor 1987

In the autumn of 1987 I was involved again in a Highland tour, this time *Mairi Mhor, the Woman from Skye* – John's tribute to the life and songs of Mary MacPherson, an epic Gaelic song-writer of the 1890s whose story touched us and connected up with our work over many years. It was her song 'Eilann a Cheo' which ended *The Cheviot, the Stag and the Black, Black Oil*, sung with such fierce passion by Doli MacLennan. In fact the most militant verse of that song was not widely heard prior to *The Cheviot*. We picked it up from Sandie Fraser of Achiltibuie, who was at that time working as a radiologist at the Hammersmith Hospital in London; a fine Gaelic singer with a big repertoire.

Now we went into the full story of Mairi Mhor's life. She was wrongfully imprisoned and only began writing as a result of this traumatic experience at the age of fifty. The songs poured out. She became the bard of the Highland Land Leaguers and was passionately involved in the land struggle which we had recorded in several of the Highland plays. 1986 was the centenary of the Crofting Act of 1886, and we wanted to celebrate her part in the struggle for land which is still a central, unresolved issue in Scotland.

The play was not a straightforward historical drama. At the beginning I appeared as a caricature version of Mairi's ghost to set up the story and there was much merriment. But it dealt in a very flexible way with the problems she experienced and some of those still faced in the Highlands today. Parallels with other countries were drawn. At one point I appeared as Sir William Rees Mogg himself, the Scourge of Dissent. I outlined for our audience, who after all had a right to know, just what the official plans were for the future of subsidised theatre.

People were amused. Highly. Then shocked. Can this be true? The centres of excellence theory – is it going to be at the expense of all this? Surely not. Surely that's what the Arts Council is there for, they said. To bring 'art' to 'the regions'. Ah yes, but it depends what you consider to be art — and, incidentally, *which* regions. All arts are equal but some are more equal than others. And the same goes for 'regions'. We're just letting you know, we said, that we are being scrutinised.

Catherine Ann MacPhee played and sang Mairi Mhor, Simon Mackenzie played a number of parts and sang some beautiful songs and I played several parts and did some story-telling. Rab Handleigh arranged the music. He also gave a very funny characterisation of one of the 'Fierty Fifty' Scottish Labour MPs. Once again, costs dictated a very small company.

We toured for four weeks, mostly in the north-west, but also in Edinburgh, Glasgow, Dundee, Inverness, Aberdeen – I enjoyed playing keyboards again and meeting so many friends on our travels, old and new. Many said it was the most interesting show they'd seen for ages.

The Gaelic college, Sabhal Mhor, is in Skye, Mairi Mhor's birthplace, and there particularly the audience joined in with the singing and gave us a standing ovation. We would not have been surprised to see her *real* ghost that night. We were surprised to learn that the Arts Council 'assessor' who was in that packed audience gave the evening a most hostile report, which contributed greatly to the fall of the axe.

On the small boat which took us to play in Eriskay, a tiny Hebridean island with a population of about 100, we hit a severe storm. While we set up, John and Kate cooked the whole company a huge Sunday dinner. (There was no cafe or pub on the island.) As we sat down to it all around the table together we took a lot of photographs, almost as if we would not be back. . . .

The previous three years had taken their toll on us. I was aware of being older suddenly – never having given it a thought till now. But we were no longer a collective group, just a working company on the road, going back to face hassles from the Scottish Arts Council, with a legacy of administrative problems, not enough money and a very hostile government and arts establishment. It was somehow fitting that the last performance of that show was among old friends in Achiltibuie on Saturday 17 October 1987. This was the last 7:84 Scotland show I was involved in. My diary for 1988 now takes up the story.

Diary July to November 1988

Thursday 21 July
After an unsuccessful attempt last night, John wrote his letter of resignation as artistic director of 7:84 Scotland this morning. Six pages. I no longer want to dissuade him. I feel very tired. Kate stayed at the office with Susie, armed with crayons and books.

We arrange to meet David for lunch prior to John's meeting with Glasgow District to cement arrangements for 7:84's move to Glasgow. We take the train to Glasgow, me feeling as if under sentence, John quite cheerful on the face of it, to be met by Dave and taken to lunch at a piano bar. He doesn't eat. Says he thinks John is doing the right thing. There is a sickening feeling of inevitability in my stomach like before a funeral. I ask for a drink – unheard of for me at lunchtime – and push my spaghetti round the plate.

We talk merrily of future plans: about Ariane Mnouchkine's play *1789* which John is planning to produce at the Old Transport Museum. I am thinking about the coldness in Edinburgh. John leaves for his meeting, we go to Juliet Cadzow's flat and I meet her properly for the first time. I had admired her work, her boldness, wit and beauty. In Liz Lochhead's adaptation of *Tartuffe* she was a wonderful jocund soubrette. She and David are in love. I'm delighted. Her flat is very elegant. I feel like a very warm-welcomed refugee. Will the rest of my family get out alive. . . .?

We talk a bit. Juliet, tactful, goes to swim. We talk some more. 'I'm in bad shape, David, these months have eaten away my confidence. Is it a betrayal?' 'Of course not, John is right. But it's going to be a big gap in all our lives. A terrible sadness.' We talk about plans. The audience. The minutes tick. Dave says he needn't go anywhere, this afternoon's a write-off anyway. He gives me his sweater; I'm now shivering with nerves. Ring Kate at the office. 'Everything's fine, Mum, are you all right?' 'Yes, I'm fine, David sends his love.' 'When is he coming to see us?' 'Hopefully in Rogart next week.' 'Oh good!'

We talk about the different consciousness of people working in theatre between now and when we began. I read about the American Group Theater's rise and demise while I was away. They were often impoverished, sleeping on floors, on low or half wages, working part-time. But when they went on their summer schools up in the New England countryside – about thirty of them, young, with friends, girlfriends, some children and an intractable Franchot Tone (the Victor Henry of the outfit) – they took along servants! Black, of course.

I was struck by many parallels. Not the servants! Clifford Odets wrote *Waiting for Lefty* in a week. Like John wrote *The Bofors Gun*. Odets worked first as an actor with the Group Theater. Then like us, determined to reach a working-class audience, although they were centred on Broadway, he worked on *building* that audience. When they became involved with the unions (notably the taxi drivers) it started to happen; so when he started to write, he could write *for* both – for those actors, and that audience.

My own position quite like that of the actress and co-founder of the Group, Stella Adler. 'Involved' with the artistic director and driving force (Harold Clurman, in her case), both with clear ideas about what they were trying to do, within a collective context.

When they went to Moscow to visit Stanislavski (their professional guru) she told him about a current acting problem she had and how his memory technique didn't seem to help it. 'If it doesn't work for you, forget it – don't bother! Just do what you think best,' he told her cheerfully. Very Russian. On her return to New York she told this story gleefully to her director, Lee Strasberg, who comes across as rather owlish and unduly solemn about Stanislavski. He took quite a huff. Clearly Stanislavski was an unpredictable extrovert, cheeky fellow! Like Brecht, he was not the best behaved guru.

Fashion and the wind of change blow hot and cold, relentlessly. But the popular theatre forms are hard to kill; they are too adaptable and too well loved. When the great 'English' clown Joseph Grimaldi died in 1837, the press were already saying the *clown* and his friends in the harlequinade had had their day. But they survived the onset of Victorian sensibilities, albeit with subtle transformations. A hundred years later Bernard Shaw wrote, 'Grimaldi is dying an intolerably slow death' – and today his descendants are still happily to be found in pantomime. If we adapt, expand, and defy predictions, into new, maybe necessarily bigger forms, and we take our audience along with us and expand it, *we* can defy the onset of the new Victorian sensibility waving its cultural death rattle.

John McGrath resigns

The 7:84 board meeting began at 6.00. It was held in Christine Hamilton's room at the STUC offices in Glasgow. David Hayman opened the door smiling.

Present: Aonghas MacNeacail, Bill Speirs (chair), John, myself, David MacLennan, Ray and Catherine Burnet from Benbecula and, from 'the office', Jo Beddoe and Liz Smith and David Hayman. No performing company.

Bill reported on the afternoon's meeting with the Glasgow District after which he and John were hopeful of receiving a £20,000 grant, to be confirmed in August.

John's resignation letter was 'tabled'. In it he said:

'It has been increasingly difficult for some time for me to work properly in the 7:84 that now exists; not because I am "tired" or "jaded" or "lack energy" – I think my work in other areas indicates that the opposite is true. But basically because 7:84 began as a way to liberate creative energy, as a way to break new ground, to create new structures, to make things happen. The situation we now find ourselves in stifles my creativity in a welter of the SAC's bureaucratic procedures, and an atmosphere of managerial fear and timidity is inhibiting as far as new ground is concerned; we have been forced into very old, very Victorian business and personal structures.

Under the circumstances, I have felt constricted in my creative imagination, politically compromised and unable to "make things happen".

This is due in the last resort to the political disasters of 1979, 1983 and 1987, but these have been mediated through many social organisms before reaching us. It would only be someone who had not read Gramsci who would say that our present malaise is "not political".'

Bill asked him to speak about it, more.

Quietly John explained that his idea of standing down in favour of David Hayman had been a genuine part of his strategy to ensure the political survival of the company. Since then the vagueness of the plans proposed, David's unwillingness to discuss policies, and his reluctance to allow John even one production a year had made it more difficult. John maintained his commitment to do *Border Warfare* for 7:84 in October, but asked that he retain his projects outlined in the three-year plan, including specific Highland projects. He indicated his intention to remain on the board for the time being, as an indication of general support for the company's survival. He concluded by wishing his successor 'joy in the future and victory in the coming battles. It is time we started winning.'

From the chair Bill Speirs paid tribute to his 'irreplaceable' work and looked forward to working with him on *Border Warfare* and again in the future as a writer and director. Aonghas MacNeacail, clearly upset by the situation, spoke about John's contribution to the Highlands, his anger, his sense of history and wide knowledge, in quite a touching speech: it was the only human, emotional response. Nobody else spoke or said Thank You.

Bill agreed to liaise with John about the timing of his withdrawal, and the way the press was notified, which seemed to be his main anxiety.

David MacLennan stressed that while the SAC had criticised the structure of the board, the administration *and* the artistic policy, the board had not accepted the last, and he would like it stressed in any press statements that John's resignation was not a response to that criticism. John said he would make his position clear by publishing his letter of resignation. There being no further comment on this, John then left the meeting. Nobody looked up, or said goodbye. I stayed.

David MacLennan asked David Hayman to clarify how he would work with his general manager, if he got the job, and would he be living in Scotland? No. They would act as a group. 'We have a shorthand.' He wasn't available on a full-time basis, but Gerard Kelly (also resident in London) could be around as part of the 'package'. He (David) would not be available from January to June, due to other film and TV commitments. Jo Beddoe, the General Manager, said she had no aspirations to be 'an artistic director manqué'. Serious discussion needed. David Hayman said, 'There are a handful of good Scots around. The board should have me as an associate, not as artistic director.' I pointed out that in any case the SAC would insist on interviews, it being part of their conditions of funding to advertise such posts.

Aonghas proposed that David Hayman should be made *acting* artistic director from the end of the week. David said, 'Do I have to be called *acting* artistic director; couldn't I just be associate director for the time being?' I said, 'No, we can't have a rudderless ship. Let's face it, it's a Lyndon B. Johnson situation.' It was proposed a sub-committee would advertise and interview Gerard Kelly in the first instance, others later, and inform the SAC.

David MacLennan and I walk to Juliet's. A stiff drink. I can't speak. Then by car to John Cairney and Alannah's where John has already gone, with champagne it turns out.

Alannah cooks four pounds of spaghetti and insists it's a celebration. I wish Kate was there. Dear Liz, says Cairney, is there going to be a lament? No, no, John, no laments, onwards and upwards. I take photographs. I can feel myself disappearing through the wrong end of the telescope.

Over dinner conversation ranges around projects to be done. The nature of audiences. Highland touring. We drink to freedom, to Alannah's cooking, to the two Johns. John McGrath says he feels liberated. I am exhausted. Bereft. It is like a merry emotional wake.

All the way home to Edinburgh I cry silently in the back seat of the car with no Kate to hold on to.

We get to bed at 3.00 am. One boy's in Spain, one in the States. Kate at Fiona's house. The end of an era. Seventeen years. The page turns very quietly, and so far, for me at least, the next one is blank.

Friday 22 July
The morning after. John spent all day at the office handling the press release and working with Ken Logue on research for *Border Warfare*. I made aioli for tea. Kate looks after me with a bright, vigilant eye. She sits on John's knee. He is getting his papers together. In the morning he will go to London to pick up our car. I fall asleep on Kate's bed.

Saturday 23 July
The *Scotsman* carried banner front-page headline: '7:84's McGrath quits with blast at Scottish Arts Council', full front page and inside coverage, including Sir Alan Peacock's remarks about the cut being political as 'evil nonsense' and the full text of John's letter. Allan Wright, the arts editor, did us proud.

Monday 25 July
We went up north for John to continue writing, if possible, in peace. Stored some more peats for the winter.

Thursday 28 July
Finn finally rang. From Bilbao. His friend Larry (twenty-two) is deperately ill having undergone a brain haemorrhage on Saturday, spotted by my cousin and his doctor friend with whom they are staying. We are appalled. Finn says he is putting up a magnificent fight. They have arranged everything.

Larry is in intensive care. If nothing deteriorates they will operate on Tuesday to by-pass the damaged artery.

Thursday 4 August. London
Larry recovers consciousness briefly and recognises his mum and dad who have arrived from Scotland. We are thankful. We are in London for a 7:84 England board meeting. Clive Barker, Sue Timothy, Eve Bland, John and me. We try to sort out what's left (mostly an overdraft) and plan a cabaret evening. We hear from Sue about the state of funding in the south.

Sue and Eve stay to supper with me and Kate. We gossip, giggle, and exchange clapping games.

KATE'S CLAPPING GAME:
I know a little Scottish girl called
Hi Susie-Anna!
And all the boys in the fitba team go
Hi Susie-Anna!
How is yer faither?
All right!
Died in the fish shop
Last night
Whit wis he eatin'?
Raw fish!
Whit did 'e die like?
Like THIS!

to mum
with love
Kate

Later she falls asleep on my knee.

Friday 5 August
The Stage came out with an editorial after their usual fashion, saying, 'John McGrath has run out of steam . . .' I faxed John's reply:

The Editor
The Stage.

August 5 1988

Dear Sir
Thank you for your leader of August 4. It was touching to find such concern for the future of political theatre from such an unexpected quarter.
Would it be churlish of me to make two small points?
1. I am far from 'ignorant' of 'today's tastes and economic circumstances.' I oppose them – which is a different thing.
2. I have not 'run out of steam'.
Watch this space.
Toot Toot.

Monday 8 August
Back in Sutherland.

Wednesday 10 August
John is writing with good concentration. I climb with my brothers, Kate

and her cousins to the Glas Loch in the hills at Ben Armine. It is a bit
of remaining wilderness where my father first took us to fish. His favourite
spot. On the way up we see hen harriers, mountain hares, the bogmyrtle
scent strong beside the peat-brown river.

The children catch thirty-eight trout. They tumble back down through
the steep heather, singing most of the way. Hector dreams of his first salmon.
Kate and Beattie still chattering, sway fearlessly across the wire bridge,
with the river tumbling below.

Thursday 11 August
I have encouraged the folk group The Boys of the Lough to come and
play in the Rogart hall. It is packed with the best kind of Highland audience,
faces intent. Aly Bain plays as well as I've ever heard him. His father is
dying of cancer at home in Shetland. He is sad, vulnerable. They come
around to the cottage after. A great night, music, drams. Cathal teaches
the children 'Old Dunn, Young Dunn'; they sing it again and again.

Friday 12 August
They are off early in the morning to play in Wick. We drive to Edinburgh
to the press show of Freeway's new film, with John's script, *The
Dressmaker* which is being shown at the Cameo to mark the start of the
Edinburgh Film Festival.

Then drove to Glasgow airport to meet Finn and Larry. Finn has fixed
everything up. There is an ambulance waiting to take Larry, on a stretcher,
and his parents straight from the plane to Edinburgh. Larry has a huge
surgical wound in his shaved head. He manages to smile and greet us
and his friend Scott, who came with us, apprehensive. Amazing
determination. We're proud of them.

Saturday 13 August
The Dressmaker opened to the public. A fine prolonged reception. Very
heartening for John. The whole Festival starts today – a good beginning.

Monday 15 August
Adrian Mitchell's play at the Theatre Workshop is a one-woman show about
the life of a Hampstead poet, lover and feminist (1884-1947), new to me; *Anna
Wickham*. The ending makes me cry. Kate mops up patiently. 'Oh Mum
always cries'. I bought a book of her poems. 'So the play worked,' says
Adrian, pleased.

The Ninagawa Company at the Playhouse. I saw their *Medea* last year,
with Tokusaburo Arishi's powerful interpretation of Medea's scene prior to
the murder of her children. Sandy Goehr sat next to me smiling and
muttering, 'Pure kitsch,' but I loved it. The actor (a man) embraced both
children and rolled across the wide stage embracing them, back and across,
and back. Then sent them up the stairs, waving. Then turned. Seized
the sword and mounted the stairs after them.

Their *Tempest* is a more rumbustious affair with clouds of dry ice,
cymbals, loadsa-magic, a Christmas tree fairy Ariel, and a demonic Caliban
with livid demon-red make-up. (Not a bit like my interpretation at age
thirteen in a sack.)

176

Annie Inglish, 7:84 friend and board member, rang at 11.30 pm. Can she stay the night? I go to pick her up from the station. Ten days ago she had a heart attack. How dare these bureaucrats question the efficiency and commitment of our board? Since 1971 Annie has fought for us; for money, beds, bottles of whisky, meals, love and sustenance. She came from Aberdeen to Glasgow for the board meeting, and from there to see how we were managing. She is expert, in her field, promoting good theatre in the face of much Philistine opposition. On Cape Breton Island we saw a company of Innu actors (Eskimo) from Labrador. They did a play about the erosion of their way of life, the low-flying jets, the nuclear installations, their enforced move to the cities. I'd like to have seen it with Annie.

Thursday 18 August
Demo in Czechoslovakia, in remembrance of the Prague Spring. BBC describes it on Radio 4: 'The security forces moved forward in a grey wave.'

Monday, 22 August
Kate back to school. I am preparing for seventy visitors. Our friends, the Cinema Actors' Company of Tbilisi, are doing their version of *Don Juan* at the Festival – thirty Georgians, forty of us. One very large turkey. Three large haggis. (Ah Scottish caviar! Very good!) Piles of neeps and tatties. Puddings. Wine.

Simon, Jane, Kate and I make salads, Penny Thomson and Pamela arrive with more. John is sick with a migraine, trying to write. Finn returns from the hospital, jubilant, to report that Larry, until now paralysed, has some movement in his left leg. Relief. Even jollity.

We borrow a Georgian flag from Gill Connan who is helping with preparations. Nancie, our neighbour, makes two cakes. We put two candles on each to signify our two visits; us to Georgia in 1982, then to Edinburgh now. Amiran (Sganarelle in the play) holds one, I hold the other one, and we all (seventy of us) blow out the candles, making a wish to return.

The Georgians sing in five- or six-part harmony. Walking songs from Cathy Ann, John Samson on Kate's recorder, Rab on Dan's fiddle. Poems in Gaelic from Black Angus who nearly didn't come because he had work to do, but didn't regret it. John Peter from the *Sunday Times* turns up. He is intrigued. There are toasts, Georgian dancing, and tricks. A long toast from Zarab (Don Juan himself) to Kate (shy), Finn and Hod watch smiling, John toasts *their* visit, then I get on the accordion and we have waltzes and Gay Gordons with Georgian and Gael and Scot, and a couple of young Glasgow actors boggling in the corner.

Long farewells, taxis, presents exchanged, more farewells, lots of washing up.

Tuesday 23 August
After clearing up I wrote a report with recommendations for 7:84 on the procedures they might follow to maintain and extend the archive material lodged with the Scottish Theatre Archive. Sue Timothy arrived from London for the 7:84 board meeting. We drove with her to Glasgow.

The New Brooms already occupied one side of the table facing the door. I felt like a naughty child as I sat with John and the others, facing them. Where is the collective spirit?

The drift of the discussion of plans for the rest of the year seemed to be that since David Hayman, now re-titled artistic director, had now – with no apparent reluctance – turned down *Border Warfare* somehow John was responsible for 'landing 7:84 in the shit' as Bill Speirs put it. Instead they plan to revive Hector MacMillan's *The Sash* with an as yet un-named director and then do Gerard Kelly's (first, I think) theatre play about 'a young Glasgow guy who runs a chip shop'. For this they will 'transfer' the commission earmarked for John's adaptation for the Highlands of *The Silver Darlings*. It seems a rather unadventurous programme to front the appeal for survival. But confrontation is out and negotiation behind the scenes is under way.

Anna Stapleton, the Scottish Arts Council Drama Officer, is there. Smiles of understanding and knowing looks pass between her and her old friend, our new general manager, Jo Beddoe as the meeting progresses. They are the 'professionals'. 'The SAC are prepared to hear your appeal any time of course, but would prefer to see two more shows before coming to a decision.'

The question of the artistic director arises. 'We need a job description.' *I* could have done with one, John smiles. It is agreed to advertise. Jo makes it clear that she, Hayman and Kelly are to be considered 'a package'.

She smiles at Anna. They worked closely together before – Jo worked for the English Arts Council and Anna for the Greater London Arts. They know each other really well. (Sue Timothy also once worked for the English Arts Council, indeed has taken over Anna's job at GLA, but Sue had ended up on our side of the table. She was asked to resign from the board a few weeks later.)

'Let's see what Nanny says; maybe she'll let us have a *few* sweeties. She looks stern, though, boys and girls don't laugh at grown-ups. Nanny will decide. Turn over and go to sleep. Don't cry in the night. You might wake the other children, and then where would we be?

Don't forget, seven per cent of the theatre companies get eighty-four per cent of the money and *they* do what Nanny says, don't they? Yes. Don't play with those dirty children. You might catch something. Stay on the path. Don't wander in the long grass. There are snakes in the bracken, you can't climb steep hills, Nanny knows best.'

After the meeting we burst into the beautiful evening sunlight over Glasgow from Hillside Crescent. We take refuge at Juliet's.

Juliet is doing Lady Macbeth for Ricki Demarco on Inchcolm Island in the Forth. John Bett is playing Macbeth, and the audience will arrive by boat. It sounds very adventurous.

The Barra McNeils from Cape Breton are playing tonight in Edinburgh. Very attentive audience. The distinctive Cape Breton fiddle style. The girl singer recognises my voice from the tape they have back home of *Happy Land*. We are delighted to meet up again.

Friday 26 August
Dan is back from Indiana, sunburnt, with stories of adventures and
presents. I tell him about John's resignation. 'As long as you're happy,' he
says and one or two less noble expletives, deleted. I am delighted to have
him back safely.

Saturday 27 August
The TV Festival is now in full swing. John and the committee have
arranged a Russian delegation of programme makers to discuss the
impact of *glasnost* on Soviet TV. (Last month our government cut the
department of the brilliant Edinburgh University Professor Erikson,
instigator of the Edinburgh 'conversations' between Soviet and Nato
defence experts. No longer considered 'cost-effective', though their
impact has clearly been felt this year. Another bad piece of government
timing.)

In the morning John chaired the session in the Physicians Hall. I sat
in. The audience of TV professionals was interested in the technical
problems (lack of good film stock, for instance) experienced by Soviet film
makers, envious of their leisurely and thorough schedules. I was struck by
their ability to criticise their own practice without apparently objecting to
the lordly tone of many of the British producers present.

Alexander Proshkin from Moscow Cinema speaks in English about
their old-style TV being a 'spiritual sleeping pill'. This type of viewer (he
says) finds difficulty in accepting new things after years of sleeping sickness.
Our technology is the same, but we have fifteen times more bureaucrats
(laughter). There is competition for new books. We work fourteen months
on a six-part film. Three months' editing. (Envious sighs from the Brits.)

The Uzbec head of studio says he is no longer writing. He says it is
difficult to know how to react given the new freedom. 'The young people
are bolder, braver. We can learn from them. They *help* me to achieve my
personal *perestroika*.' Can I imagine this from a British television
executive?

Question: (from the audience) Do you have soap opera in the Soviet
Union?

Answer: This is not a problem! We have a shortage of soap!

Proshkin tells a story about *glasnost*. In the new atmosphere of freedom
a man goes around sticking up protest leaflets everywhere. But they are
blank, have nothing written on them. He is asked, 'Why do you do this?
Why don't you write up what you are protesting about?' He replies,
'Everybody knows!'

The most important thing, he says, is our children and grandchildren.
'We don't want them to live as we lived, think as we thought. Let them
see it in the cinema. The wealthiest people are those who have the
information.'

Meanwhile at the George Hotel, TV executives and Sky men were
drinking champagne at £3 per glass.

I went to the session on 'Black Actors, White Writers'. Nothing much
seems to have changed in this sphere in my thirty years in the business. It
required a black CBC producer to remind us gently that until black people

have as powerful a political lobby here as they have in Washington, black performers will not get their fair share of work. One casting director complained of the shortage of black actors, others seemed to be saying: don't know many, I'm afraid, and not sure if I want to go to all that trouble. Jonathan Powell (now Controller of BBC 1) was asked, 'What are you trying to say?' and replied, 'I'm trying desperately not to say anything.'

Tuesday 30 August
I saw the model for *Border Warfare* made by Pamela Howard and her assistant Margaret Miller. The sheer scale, energy and challenge of it is impressive. John is very pleased. Allan Ross is to build it.

I climb the stairs to the 7:84 office in Albany Street. The posters that were on the walls all the way up have been taken down.

Wednesday 31 August
John talking to Neil Wallace of Glasgow Festivals Unit about doing *Border Warfare* in the Old Transport Museum: it would be the perfect setting. I meet Gunter Klotz from East Berlin. He has edited five of John's plays in a German edition, and knows an impressive amount about modern British theatre. We take him to the Botanic Gardens to see the gentians.

We go to *Lady in the Dark*, a disinfected version of the Kurt Weill score performed, in the English Rose manner, at the Usher Hall. Rapturously received. Especially the schmaltzy bits.

Thursday 1 September
In a speech today about the recent IRA bombing, Thatcher compares Ireland to the Falklands. In Gdansk Lech Walensa tells the strikers to stop. He is in talks about the legalisation of Solidarity. Nelson Mandela is confirmed as suffering from TB, and removed from prison to a private white clinic.

John is talking to Wildcat about possible co-production.

Dinner with Pamela Howard and Bob Potter. She has worked a lot at the National and RSC. They talk about changing institutions 'from within'. It's a line of argument that always makes me feel uncomfortable. Like putting on your sweater inside out and trying to turn it without taking it over your head.

Sunday 4 September
The *Observer* published a secret blacklist held by the ultra-right wing 'Economic League' since the mid 70s. John's name and picture featured prominently. We know these things exist of course. John exposed their activities first in 1975 in *Lay Off* and again in 1981 in *Blood Red Roses*.

Jeremy Isaacs, Head of Channel 4 TV, asked us for a Sunday morning drink. There Gus MacDonald was complaining that *he* wasn't on the blacklist!

Thursday 8 September
The cruise missiles left Molesworth. The US ambassador said on radio the withdrawal was 'nothing to do with well-intentioned idealists having made a fuss'. Perhaps we can decide about that for ourselves.

Thatcher launches 'Enterprise Scotland' – the only launch the Clyde is likely to see for a while.

Saturday 17 September
Back in Rogart, we loaded some more peats. The hill is very wet. Returned to Edinburgh leaving John still writing *Border Warfare*.

Thursday 22 September
An invitation arrived for the Traverse Theatre's twenty-fifth anniversary 'Silver Ball' in the presence of someone or other royal. Such stunts are the hallmark of the 80s cultural scene. Quite a contrast to the Traverse's origins in the 60s. . . .I can't see us there. La-di-da.

Saturday 24 September
Bought Kate her first fiddle – very pleased.

Sunday 25 September
Wildcat's tenth birthday party. Big celebration. The atmosphere unique to Glasgow – dressy, pzazz, loud, difficult to hear – in spite of lots of old friends being there, I'm struck dumb.

Thursday 29 September
Talked to Elspeth King, curator of the People's Palace, Glasgow, about maybe exhibiting the *Cheviot* pop-up book there. She says they are grossly under-funded. They get more help from the Australia Council than the Scottish Arts Council, are permanently threatened with floods, falling masonry and annihilation.

She says 'I'm really sorry. I *wish* we could, but it would be under an unacceptable risk.' She cheered up considerably when I told her of John's bouncing back to write and direct *Border Warfare* in the Transport Museum. Thank God for Channel 4, she says.

Friday 30 September
7:84 moved from Albany Street to Glasgow.

Saturday 1 October
Finn and Dan spent all day with their mate Starsky packing up Freeway with a hired van and moving things to George Street, after a fairly abrupt notice from 7:84 to quit the shared office when they move to Glasgow – Freeway's new premises are up four flights of stairs.

Monday 3 October
Labour Party Conference
Drove with John, Rab Handleigh and John Sampson to Blackpool to do cabaret for 'Arts for Labour' after their meeting on arts funding. Situated in the Grand Hotel in a subterranean night club BESIDE an indoor swimming pool. Felt a bit like *Bedknobs & Broomsticks*. Rab sang and he and John Samson played some good reels and jigs. I did Rees Mogg speech in the presence of the Arts Council's Anthony Everett who was plugging their Urban Renaissance to some apparent effect. He talked a lot about Access.

Some quotes from his speech:
'All those who wish to should have access to the creative process.'
'Alliance is needed with the local authorities in what is essentially a commercial partnership.'

'We are a-political at the Arts Council.'
'Our purpose is to identify "good practice" and disseminate it.'
It all sounded very 'caring'.

People in the Labour Party seemed too polite or confused to object. Ann Hollinshed from Liverpool chaired the meeting and Norman Buchan was there – saw most of the Scots MPs, all busy doing something else; John Smith, preparing his major attack on the economy for the morning, wished us well.

Wednesday 5 October
Chile goes to the polls. We wait with bated breath. Ron Todd issued warning to Kinnock about defence policy. The media delight in a split.

Thursday 6 October
Chile said No to Pinochet. Wonderful. Carlos is a happy man, and so are all of us – what next, however, is the question. Pinochet will not go without trouble. We celebrate the result with our Chilean friends.

Saturday 8 October
The Labour Party Conference voted decisively No to nuclear power.

Monday 10 October
Finn to Glasgow to matriculate for the third year, reading Modern History (Hons). Dan on the train to London for an interview for this season's work.

Kate to reconstruction of 'school in the 1930s' with her primary class at the local history unit at Nelson Hall. She was fascinated by all of it; slates, inkwells etc – we had read up about the 1930s last night. I told her how, when her grandfather Hector went to school *first* in Glasgow in 1910, he was one of the few children in his class with shoes. I told her about children dying of TB in the 30s, and she said – the best way to learn history is to talk to people who were around at the time, or read what they say.

Headline in The *Scotsman*: 'The End for Bishopton'.

Bishopton is a Royal Ordnance factory near Glasgow.

During the latter part of the war my mother worked there as one of the two factory doctors. On Saturdays we went there with her in the car across the Renfrew ferry. She was a regular to the ferrymen and they liked her.

We were parked at the house of the other doctor's lady friend, Margareta. She used to wear long, floaty dresses – often from HER mother's 'dressing up trunk' – to cope with rationing, she maintained cheerfully. So you could expect to be met one week by a land girl in wellies, a baggy fairisle sweater and straw hat, and the next by a pre-Raphaelite vision in taffeta flounces and chiffon. We were immediately caught up in some ploy she had arranged, sometimes collecting or even stealing apples or cooking tarts and pies, sleeves pushed up and us standing on stools in the kitchen.

On one occasion she decided to transform the kitchen into a fairy 'dell' and we were allowed to paint the stools white with red spots like fairy amanita toadstools; but of course they didn't dry *before* they had imprinted large red spots on the back of my dungarees.

She and the doctor were very musical and played almost any instrument you cared to name. It was in their house I first saw a clarsach. The doctor spent a lot of time learning it while my mother dealt with the dreadful effects of a large explosion at the factory which I wasn't told about, being too young. My mother said the best part of the workforce there were the women. The men were 'a problem' because of the risks they took.

Margareta decided one day to bring some order into the 'music' room. She proceeded to drive nails into the walls of the rather elegant, high-ceilinged drawing room and hang the various instruments from them with bits of string. Then – a bold stroke – we helped her paint, in brilliant white *around the edges of the instruments*. 'Now we'll know where everything is!' she declared triumphantly. But of course when we returned within a couple of weeks, they were all in different places, and the room took on a surreal, and to my mind then, delightful disorder: flute hanging within viola's place, trumpet on cello, bagpipes on contra-fagotto (one of his specialities).

We dressed up as well. I was very partial to a large glengarry combined with a flowing plum-coloured silk skirt of Edwardian splendour, and would wait in this to see my mother return from work and show her all the destruction we had enjoyed. Our hostess once tacked a plank of chip-board onto the polished mahogany dining table to save buying an ironing board. My mother was very exasperated by this vandalism, but it kept us amused while she was at work.

The little girl who waited for her mum to finish work at Bishopton in those slightly bizarre circumstances has become the adult who opposes the closure of Bishopton. I suppose that is what is meant by politicisation.

Tuesday 11 October
At the Tory Party Conference on TV, Paul Channon enthuses about privatising the Channel Tunnel, and introducing toll roads.

Hospital ancillary workers walk out.

I bought a dress for David's wedding to Juliet – when did I last buy a dress? And new shoes for Kate to be bridesmaid in.

Thursday 13 October
Heseltine announced, 'The coal mines *will* be privatised.'

Friday 14 October
Half term. Took Kate to London for a break. Explored in the autumn sunshine: St Pauls, museums, markets, peacocks in Holland Park.

Thursday 20 October
Saw Harold Pinter's new play *Mountain Language* at the National Theatre. I was interested to see what he'd come up with, having chatted to him at a benefit for Nicaragua last year. He had seemed to be on the move, leftwards. This was a very intense short piece. Felt like he is starting out on some difficult new work. I hope he follows it up.

The lobby of the National feels like an airport lounge. I watch out for marauding luggage trollies to bite my ankles. The lighting seems very dim, befitting the onset of a serious artistic experience or a bereavement.

I expect a solicitous voice to announce the departure of production number 257 from gate number such and such; have I got my passport, the currency of the country visited? Not many people seem dressed up, although there are two first nights happening. Maybe they are suitably dressed to evacuate the building quickly in the event of terrorists.

Monday 24 October
Back in Edinburgh for school again, made Kate's costume for Halloween (the ghost of a Turkish belly-dancer!). Dan cooked us delicious tandoori chicken.

Sunday 30 October
John came home from Cambridge at the weekend; he is working well. The house is full of young people. Larry – up and walking now – called round for Finn.
   I made a turnip lantern with Kate.

Tuesday 1 November
No school. The EIS teachers' strike. Big support marches in Glasgow and Edinburgh.

Friday 4 November
David and Juliet's wedding at Oban, reception on the island of Luing. Dancing, fireworks, family gathering. They had transformed the working barn into a Highland palais de danse – beautifully. Kate, Beattie and Kirstie look lovely dancing in their silk dresses with beautiful flowers.

Monday 7 November
Big GCHQ demo in support of civil servants rights to unionisation, ironical in the light of Thatcher's much publicised display of 'freedom' in Gdansk.
   A wee poem:

ST MARGARET MEETS LECH
'I do think solidarity is so, so important, don't you?'

Wrote to Bill Speirs expressing unease about their putting our good friends, the Labour MPs Norman Buchan and Gordon Brown, off the 7:84 board. They have been extremely helpful. 'Norman has done a great deal of lobbying for the appeal . . . spoke at the debate (in April) in the House of Commons on arts funding (specifically on our behalf) – it would seem a bit of a snub in my opinion. Gordon Brown, flying high as he is at this moment, might also have his uses . . . or do we not want *any* Labour MPs on the board?'
   I wished them good luck with the appeal document (which I haven't seen) and in the new offices.
   Note: he replied, very speedily (on the 15th):
   'I take the points you make about Norman Buchan and Gordon Brown, and it was after considerable discussion and hesitation that we came to the view that it would be best to ask them to step down – at least in the meantime. The thinking is that we do not want to give the SAC *any* ground for criticism, however spurious . . .'
   Self-censorship now operating.

Wednesday 9 November
George Bush elected President of the US.
   Linda McKenney resigned from the board of 7:84.
   In her letter of resignation she wrote:

'I have been very unhappy with the way in which the board and the office have abandoned 7:84's artistic policy. . . .

The relationship between a popular drama group and the state as a funding body is bound to be difficult. It seems to me that the relationship between 7:84 and the SAC is about to undergo a massive change with the introduction of new administrative structures which will bring 7:84 into line with bourgeois theatres and facilitate greater Arts Council control of the company. It further seems to me that even before those structures have been introduced, there have been a number of compromises *vis à vis* our artistic and political stance . . . I see the adjustments which 7:84 is making as an unacceptable compromise with the authorities, a compromise against the long-term interests of popular theatre in Scotland.'

Thursday 10 November
For Jim Sillars, the Scottish Nationalist candidate, a sweeping victory in Govan.

April rang from Wildcat's office. Kirstie took ill immediately after the wedding. She died suddenly yesterday.

I cannot believe it. After surviving so much, born with severe spinal difficulties, so much to contend with. How on earth will Tina and Dave cope with this?

I put off telling Kate. When is the moment to tell a child her friend has died?

Finn came home – he suddenly got a lift for which I was very grateful. 'Mum, I loved that wee girl.'

Monday 14 November
John, the boys and myself went to Glasgow for Kirstie's funeral.

My brother Dave spoke well and managed somehow to give hope. The church was packed. They buried her on the cold Lambhill hillside. In the Ledgowan Hall with Maryhill towerblocks all round, friends and neighbours met to gather strength, to try to help Tina and David; the community of popular theatre in Scotland. A close-knit group. Her wider family. And from London Terry Neason, Feri, Alex Norton and others, still part of that group.

THE DEATH OF A CHILD
A Wednesday, August 1975. Little Red Hen in rehearsals, Dave Anderson's first 'proper acting' role. Dave was late that morning, and McGrath: glad to see you could join us. Dave jumps on the table, scattering research and ashtrays – exultant arms outstretched in characteristic let-me-tell-youse style –
I am gonna be a daddy!
Jubilation at 7:84! Round about seven months later Kirstie was born, defying all odds, triumphantly, ever since. She seemed living proof that nothing is insurmountable. We hoped that some of her fighting spirit would rub off on us, because she had determination, courage and wit to spare. She taught us that out of struggle comes joy and fulfilment, solidarity. At nine she thought nothing of coming on the whole May Day march – in pouring rain when many fainter hearts stayed at home. We shared many celebrations with her. She had the gift

185

of celebrating life. As a bridesmaid at the wedding last week her beauty was luminous; delighted with the occasion, dancing, a celebration after her own heart.

That is how we will remember Kirstie.

After the funeral, walking across George Square, Glasgow, with my tall son Danny, now nearly twenty-one, to catch the train. Listen to the starlings – d'you know what my first memory of this place is? He listens patiently.

VE night: my dad got us out of bed and took us out at night through the crowded streets. He put me on his shoulders and we walked with the jubilant arm-in-arm crowds, hugging and running across the square. There was dancing in the streets and lots of lights – because it had been all blackouts then, you see.

I remember a bonfire, fireworks, and searchlights in the sky swirling round, and my dad said, 'We'll never forget this will we?' Today particularly, I remember that night, the jubilation and the smell in the streets of my childhood Glasgow. And we got the train back to Edinburgh together, me and Dan.

Twenty Five: New Beginnings

Touring abroad in the 80s

In Autumn 1986 we were invited to take part in an International Brecht Festival hosted by the University of Toronto. We decided to take two contrasting shows: *The Albannach*, very local, Highland, musical and Scottish, and *The Baby and the Bathwater*, small, unashamedly intellectual. Internationalist in perspective.

Due to lack of funds we were to travel each with *one* suitcase for ourselves and *one* for the costumes for *The Albannach*. The sets would be rebuilt from what we could assemble there (Annette Gillies, designing with characteristically positive thinking). I had visions of the entire company stepping off the plane in the weightiest costumes, heavy black coats and homburgs, as required in the Free Church scene. We were spared that, due once more to Kris Misslebrook's organisational skills. My *Baby and the Bathwater* show fitted into just three suitcases.

We were billeted with friends of the Festival and our university hosts. We met John and Mallory Gilbert and fell on our feet – or rather on their hospitality and subsequent lasting friendship. Kate adopted their cats.

We played in the Harbourfront Theatre.

The Festival was abuzz with theatre companies in the one corner, academics in the other. Every day seminars were held to prove the ubiquitous influence (agreed) and importance of Brecht (in whose honour we were assembled) and every night plays were presented which had not a lot to do with him. Including the Berliner Ensemble whose production of *Threepenny Opera* was a sadly disappointing museum piece; but we loved their *Caucasian Chalk Circle*. Kate sat through the German version (three hours) happily, and thought Ekkerhard Schall was *wonderful*, but that the child was best.

We enjoyed meeting the French Canadian group, Theatre Parminou, who came to John's master class and stayed to talk. Based in Victoriaville in Quebec they have been going almost exactly as long as us, and we felt like old friends instantly with no language or cultural barriers. The specifics of Quebecois culture are proudly different, but they share with us many preoccupations about the struggle for language, about being culturally colonised, and many ideas of how to deal with it imaginatively in the context of a popular working audience.

However, at the same time almost exactly as we got cut, I had a letter from them saying jubilantly that *they* have got more money for a new centre, and *expanded* facilities in Victoriaville. Perhaps the government of Quebec has got different priorities . . .

In Montreal we watched a dress rehearsal of their very funny show about pornography. A really tricky subject but they negotiated it with such skill and good taste. Very effective too.

I performed *Baby and the Bathwater* in this Festival to a very heartening and interesting response. Many people stayed to talk about Canada's responsibilities for refugees and their so far, relatively enlightened treatment of Central American immigrants. This was all set for trouble from the newly-elected right winger, Brian Mulroney.

The second performance went really well and I finished on a high note. Annette Gillies had assembled a superb set out of thin air, and helped me with the changes. Carlos and I met a number of Chileans and people from El Salvador.

I was at the two first performances of *The Albannach*, and lovely they were. Fionn McColla wrote the book. We met his daughter Teresa and her family, now living in Toronto. They came to the first night and were thrilled with it. After the show the first of many spontaneous ceilidhs developed with fiddles, guitars and informal dancing in the bar. Here we met Chris Brookes again, founder of the Newfoundland Mummers Theatre, step-dancing spectacularly.

Thereafter, happy with the reception, the company scattered to enjoy the sights and friendship of Toronto people and when we all met up again on the plane it was with determination to return to Canada.

We did. The following spring, May 1987. We were invited to the Festival of Popular Theatre held by the Canadian Popular Theatre Alliance – that year it was to take place in Sydney, Cape Breton, Nova Scotia.

It was almost as if the story that we began with *The Cheviot* was to go full circle fourteen years later. There, where so many of the Highlanders were driven by the Clearances, as we had described in *The Cheviot*, we had two memorable weeks.

Sydney is an economically depressed, worked-out mining town, with steel workers facing redundancy, and a strong labour history. The Cape Bretoners are implacably independent and reminded me so much of people I know in Sutherland.

First stop for John, Kate and me was the Pier Legion Hall, past the carcinogenic lake, in downtown Sydney. This was to be where I played *Baby and the Bathwater* for the next two nights. Before that there was a Welcome to the Festival concert and party. Quickly I taught Tony Cuffe the words of 'Solidarity Forever', we devised our programme, and the full company – Carlos, myself, John, Kate, Simon, Catherine Ann, Tony C and Iain Macdonald, our piper, set off.

The first half was another one-woman show, this time about an early and distinguished Canadian MP, feminist and reformer, *McPhail*, played by Diana Gordon, and then we were into songs from Scotland, Zimbabwe, Nicaragua, Jamaica, India; indeed from all the companies who had so far arrived.

Apart from these preformances, there were two weeks of intensive workshops from several animators, or 'originators', including Augusto Boal (Theatre of the Oppressed), the women's group Sistren from Jamaica and ourselves.

Everyone was busy all over the town with concerts, workshops, chats – our group disappeared to St Peter's Bay to ceilidh with Iain's brother who is the doctor there, and with the Gaels from that part of the island. Kate, John, Carlos and I did *Baby and the Bathwater* on our own quite happily for the first night. The audiences were very warm.

On the second night the bouncy actress Kelley Edwards came to my rescue with the changes, and it was the best show I've done to date. Almost the entire audience, including locals, pier legionnaires, Ukranians and Scots, young Nicaraguans, students, Boal and disciples and, yes, Theatre Parminou – who turned up! – stayed behind to talk afterwards. Kate took 120 dollars on the bookstall, everyone wanted posters. It was the best show yet.

Next day we rehearsed *Happy Land* with a rather lethargic company who had been ceilidhing the night before, and saw the Sirens' *Working People's Picture Show* – a feminist review on women's rights within the unions structures, work, day care, done in a sparky, review-type format. Then to Sistren from Jamaica – twenty-two of them, a sort of black female Wildcat, plus five-piece band. Loud. Colourful. Very good physically. Then we set up at St Andrews Hall for *Happy Land*. Marauding sound man nicked my mike just before the show. A varied, big crowd, aged six months to ninety-five years. Ed Macleod's granny, whom I welcomed in the introduction, was one of quite a number of Gaelic speakers in. Some had travelled from Glace Bay, and Soldiers Cove, and Iain's family came in force. We talked to the Nicaraguan company, Teyocayanni, who *loved* it. Carlos acting as translator for them, delighted. The show went well, especially with the Gaels. 7:84's standing high.

On one day we drove past Kelly's Mountain and Dingwall with its blasted trees. Walked on the shore and we went to the North Side of the island to the French village of Cheticamp. I saw a bobcat, eagles, loons and what looked like an old (1880's) croft house.

About twenty-five people came to our workshops including three Gaelic singers from the 'Highland village' and people of different backgrounds from all parts of Canada. They were struck by the intellectualism of *Baby and the Bathwater* and its demands on the audience. They wanted to discuss style, methods of research, Gaelic culture, working-class audiences, differences from the English 7:84, Thatcher's onslaught on the arts, the role of the left. They wanted to know how we manage in the present harsh political climate, and about land struggles and Mairi's role in it in the 1880s. Aged fourteen to thirty, the Teyocoyanni Company work frequently in the war zone 'with guitar and gun'. They wanted help to buy a drumkit. People from the Catalyst Company in Edmonton, Alberta were interesting. They feel passionately about the *land question* given the present crisis in farming in the Corn Belt; many of their farmers are facing bankruptcy due to monopolies of seed merchants and fertiliser producing companies, and the big banks calling in the huge loans on which they depend. We discussed the mega-industrialisation of land. A Saskatchewan girl got very heated.

Charles Macdonald from the university raised the townsperson's point of view – who cares about the land anyway? So long as they can get bread at the store, they don't care what happens, or to whom, to produce it.*

We discussed the EEC's policy towards 'marginal' land. The 'decorative' role of landscape, in relation to crofting. We watched *Jagran* Indian street theatre from Bombay, directed by Aloke Roy. It raised the issues of black-marketeering, drugs and, bravely, forced or arranged marriage. Aloke ran his company like a real patriarch. We talked to the performers afterwards.

Later we drove across Grand Narrows to Iona, a beautiful spot, to do an extra show in the church hall – requested by the McNeills; McNeills are everywhere, and MacLennans, and Mathiesons. This hall looks out over the Barra Straits and could easily be in the Highlands – great fishing country.

A very moving experience for us. The hall was full. Thirty to forty per cent of the audience were Gaelic speakers, including young ones. The music, the stories, everything received rapt attention. Like a cross between Bonar Bridge (for laughter) and Achiltibuie or Barra for the songs. Many people living around here were originally from Barra. We made $250 and gave it to the community to help make another record. After the show most of the audience stayed to talk and ceilidh and dance. There were set dances, Cape Breton step-dancing, waltzes, Gay Gordons, three fiddles, accordion, a fine piano player, flutes, bhoran.

Finished about 2.30 and then on to further songs and music at the McNeills' house. Back in Sydney we made plans for the next Popular Theatre Alliance festival and watched Lib Spry's film of her play about the Spadina Street (Toronto) garment workers, with Chinese and Philippino actresses.

Thoughts about this Festival

The various groups and individuals were strong on commitment to *individual* issues – peace, equal rights, native rights, jobs, sexism, but weak on analysis, particularly economic analysis.

The Eastern bloc has no reality for them – it is very far away.

They take *process* very seriously – perhaps too seriously. People were surprised how much time we spent on the *content* of the show.

Perhaps skill is seen as a threat to democratic participation, rather than a necessary tool.

Michel Cormier from Parminou came to all of our discussions and was very good on analysis. He was preparing a play on the French (Quebecois) land patriots who were 'cleared' by the English in the 1780s. Interesting parallels for us in Quebec. We arranged to see them in Montreal. Nicole (also from Parminou) talked about some of the contradictions they have to deal with: they 'respond' to requests for shows, performances. A factory making warheads

---

* This workshop was highly contributory to Catalyst's further workshops on the subject of Food and World Scarcity in May 1988, to which we were invited, but which we couldn't attend because 7:84's life was in crisis.

wants a show from them. Do they play? Should they play in a non-unionised oil-works?

We saw *Peacing it Together*, Parminou's play/exposé on the arms race, with deceptively simple and hilarious clowning from Rejean and Nicole. The ideas were magic.

Final cabaret party at Pier Legion with Ras Mo from Jamaica singing 'Gimme back ma language and me cul-cha!' Simon sang. The Nicaraguans sang 'our' song from *Baby and the Bathwater* – 'No Pasaran'. It has become the key song of the festival. The Nicaraguans were obviously the most politically aware, and left a lot behind them, as well as songs. Will the multi-national, central world swamp all the marginal cultures with its monoglot consumerisation?

The Innu (Eskimo) play we saw here was moving – about the effects of the NATO presence in Labrador.

There is to be a further big NATO development in either Turkey or Northern Canada. I told the Saskatchewan Irish 'development' education person at breakfast, 'Well, they won't put it in Turkey, will they? Too unstable. A lot of communists in Turkey!' Says she, 'There's a lot of turkeys in Northern Canada.'

A few weeks after our return to Scotland we received this letter from Cape Breton from Rod and Helen McNeill who had been at the show we did in the village of Iona:

'As an old neighbour of ours said, "In all our years we've never seen such a show, and there's a great possibility we'll never see another quite like it. Thank you so much for the tape. You people are special. Suffice it to say, we'll never forget you. We wish you great success.

In years gone by our home reverberated with the sounds and music of young people. As we and our friends get older and our youngsters go further afield, the sessions become more and more scarce. Every once in a while an occasion such as our ceilidh in June comes our way and we glow for months after.

It takes much to keep Roddie from getting his sleep. He went directly from the kitchen table to the barn to milk the cows. In our life together that was my first experience of seeing him do this. He was quite willing to stay longer at the table but the singers and musicians had to get some sleep.

Beannachd liubh le gael, (Bless you)
Rod and Helen'

At Christmas they wrote again. 'I wish every Celt in Cape Breton could have heard you. The audience was unanimous. We hope you will come again. Much love from all of us.'

East Berlin

In February 1987 we were invited to East Berlin to the Festival of Political Song and played *There Is a Happy Land* in the home of the Berliner Ensemble. We felt honoured. Several of us who had been to the USSR were on that trip and found it interesting to relate to our experiences there. We were very well treated – their technicians are superb, their lighting resources, their co-operative help brilliant.

We had met many of the same company and crew on our trip to the Toronto Brecht Festival and in many ways felt we had developed a special relationship.

Although the Berliner Ensemble tour a great deal and clearly are a big earner for their country, they still feel like a small repertoire company with strong personal interconnections within their own theatre buildings. Both front and backstage are very institutional – unlike the Deutsches Theater which we also visited. The Theater am Schiffbauerdam has that almost besieged feeling which I associate with most good Living theatre and we were very happy there. The reviews were excellent.

When the SAC tried to cut 7:84 the following year we got a letter from their great actor, Ekkehard Schall and his wife Barbara Brecht:

'We are truly shocked to hear that 7:84 has fallen victim to a financial cut; how are such things possible? And that in a time when the arts are one of the few things that pass all borders and divisions. And speaking practically, as far as I know, your theaters are a bigger source of revenue (being a tourist attraction) than North Sea oil!

We surely hope that the Scottish Arts Council will reconsider – and soon.
Sincerely,
Ekkehard Schall. Barbara Brecht-Schall'

The Diary ends. November 1988 – February 1989

Sunday 20 November – Edinburgh
A big student demo in London against the replacement of grants with returnable 'loans'. The police, on horses, seemed very brutal. I fear for this generation.

Monday 28 November
7:84 appeal document arrived, penned by the New Brooms. It has already gone in to the SAC. It seemed flimsy, mostly packaging. The actual shows on offer, pretty conventional. Safe. No plans for Mayfest. None for 1990. Strange for a Glasgow-based company.
The tone of the document is placatory, anxious to appease. The proposed Highland tour feels like tokenism. A revival of The Sash – *a hit of the 70s about religious bigotry in Glasgow – seems not to be tackling the late 80s with too much rigour.*

Thursday 1 December
Busy with arrangements for Dan to go to France to work in the Alps till April. He has been offered a very good job. We'll have a celebration before he goes.
John is working on music with Archie Fisher and in Cambridge the rest of the time, finishing Border Warfare.

Wednesday 7 December
The earthquake in Armenia – unbelievable horror which clouds Gorbachev's historic speech at the United Nations offering a major disarmament initiative. The first really hopeful move in a long time. He flies back to Moscow.

Thursday 8 December
7:84 board meeting. John went, to find places had been reserved with name

tickets, as in a formal Board Room, for all the new (and the few 'old') board members, but no place earmarked for him!

He was able to clarify one or two points arising from yet another set of rather slanted minutes. The appeal has gone in to the Arts Council, and they all seem very confident about it, John said.

THE OLD YEAR ENDS, THE NEW YEAR BEGINS
The last three weeks of the year are clouded in horror. On one level I am preparing for Christmas, seeing Danny off, his bag packed with presents and fingers crossed, welcoming Finn home, cooking, clearing and polishing for the New Year, going to the zoo with Kate's class, worrying about where the money is coming from for Border Warfare. *Will it come through in time, panic on the 12th, relief on the 15th when, just before Christmas, the Festival Unit agree to pay the £25,000 shortfall, just as John went to tell Channel 4 it wasn't going to happen. Now it will. Soon.*

Trips to the panto. Dan's farewell supper, Finn's birthday and Christmas. At the same time thousands of people are dead, mutilated, homeless, starving in Armenia.

Then, as if that were not terrible enough, the Pan-Am crash at Lockerbie. Just down the road bodies are raining out of the sky and what is a personal tragedy for so many becomes a lasting terrible metaphor for all the destruction of human potential in 1988.

Monday 2 January, 1989
John is hard at work with David, for a co-production between Wildcat and Freeway of Border Warfare *– it is going to open on 23 February at the Old Transport Museum in Glasgow. Time is short for such a big, ambitious production. No contracts could be issued before Christmas because the money was still in the balance. Now it's full-steam ahead with an enormous design assignment and a company of eighteen to be firmed up. I hope to finish this book by the time they open.*

Finn goes back to university and Kate to school. Glasgow (Labour) District Council chose Saatchi and Saatchi (out of several contestants) to promote 'Glasgow City of Culture 1990'. No wonder they took down the Red Flat on May Day. . . .

Strathclyde (Labour) Region turn down a request for funding for Border Warfare *in their own words 'on political grounds'.*

Monday 16 January
Rehearsals start for Border Warfare. *John is nervous, but well prepared. The music is coming together, the set, costumes, publicity. It is a huge undertaking.*

Tuesday 17 January
The new 7:84 poster for their revival of The Sash *is up around town. It does not bear the logo: '7 per cent of the population of this country own 84 per cent of the wealth'. Omitted for the first time from any 7:84 poster. Ominous or mindless?*

Friday 20 January
7:84 has its annual grant restored for a 'trial' two-year period with a twenty per cent increase and an extra £5,000 earmarked for 'new writing' (any new writing, so long as it's not McGrath's). They have not done any of the performances or

shows which were demanded by the Scottish Arts Council before they could consider restoring the grant.

As John said, 'It begins to look rather personal.'

In the SAC's press release, circulated by the New Brooms at 7:84, Sir Allan Peacock describes the changes that have taken place, and the others that are promised within the company, as a 'very positive response'.

Gerard Kelly, the new associate director, says in a newspaper interview that he and David Hayman, having taken over 7:84, are like 'two weans with a new toy . . .'

Wednesday 25 January

Letters are being sent out to all our supporters by the SAC proclaiming their support for the New 7:84, with New Artistic Director, New Policy, New Board and New Everything, and Peacock's letter concluded: 'I hope that you will find the outcome a satisfactory one and will give 7:84 theatre company your continued support in the coming years.'

Adrian Mitchell, the poet, wrote back to the SAC:

'I don't understand how you can say that the company has responded in a most positive way when its artistic director, John McGrath, who with his own energy and talent and funds was the initiator and creator of 7:84, has resigned in disgust.

I don't understand the details of the New Look 7:84 which you attach. Because:

(a) You tell me the names of the new artistic director and his associate director, but nothing about their work in the past or their policies for the future.

(b) You tell me there's to be a new artistic policy but not what it is.

(c) You tell me there's to be a new board with new structure and expertise but not who's going to be on the board, what the structure is or who the experts are.

Now the new 7:84 you speak of may well become an important part of theatre in Scotland as you suggest and I hope it does. But I don't think you can expect those who have supported 7:84 in the past to be interested until we know what they're going to do, where they're going to do it, how they're going to do it and who they're going to do it for. Maybe you'd let me know.'

John is away rehearsing all the time. There is a high anticipation of the show, a lot of support from people and in the press. The advance booking is very good indeed. Wildcat are excited about it.

Wednesday 15 February

Salman Rushdie death threat.

The government says there are now only two million and seventy-five thousand unemployed, so that's okay.

Thatcher, in Glasgow, says she will have 'no truck' with Scottish independence, and we've never had it so good, so stick around, the market force is coming your way, whether you like it or not.

Thursday 23 February

Border Warfare opens at the Old Museum of Transport in Glasgow. Full. Standing ovation, A great piece of theatre.

Sunday 26 February
The Observer *greeted* Border Warfare *as a 'theatrical triumph'.*
    Scotland on Sunday *said: 'McGrath's pithy comedy, his proud rhetorical touch, and flair for large-scale manoeuvring have the power to galvanise even the most dormant of Nationalist sympathies. In* Border Warfare *the victory is his.'*
    It is one year since my diary began.

A Change in the weather

In the early days of 7:84 actors had argued intensely about the 'hegemony of the pen', of the band, about collective power and responsibility of playing to working-class audience, about sexism, differentials, about the struggle for language and about the nature of comedy. At the start of the 80s single issues became obsessive – women's rights, gay rights, the community, the Bomb, pollution. People began to shie away from global analysis. Key words began to mean something else – words like freedom, and the right to choose. Debate was out, market forces and performance art in.

When Thatcher was asked in 1988 what she would do about people who might disagree with a particularly repressive piece of legislation she said, 'You simply say Naeo. No.' Kate and I went around saying it for days afterwards – Naeo. You Simply say Naeo. Naeo to the miners, to the nurses, to the ambulance workers, naeo to dissent, naeo to popular theatre, and naeo to the Scottish Assembly. Naeo to the ANC, to Mandela, to Daniel Ortega, Yes to General Jaruselski, to Pinochet, naeo to the Argies, naeo to the BBC, to comprehensive schools, naeo to most universities, naeo to Europe, naeo to immigration, yes to privatisation, naeo to imagination.

Harry McShane gone, Oscar Mazaroli, Raymond Williams, Simone de Beauvoir, Sartre, all gone. Another Thatcher government; the fear of speaking out in universities; the absence of a strong oppositional press.

Nevertheless, when I met the Chilean actor, Hugo Medina, in March '88 and he asked me, 'What's happening here?' in spite of all that, and without underestimating the difficulties we face, I said, 'I think we can make it.' He asked me what I meant by that. I said, 'I think, for all that, there is a huge potential for struggle, for change and for success in Scotland. Our theatre does reflect the people's lives. It may be flawed, but there is energy. Look at Mayfest; okay, maybe it's becoming safer, but still – look at Glasgow, look how many artists now don't have to go to London, look how the audiences are growing. But what are we going to do about England?'

A week later we received notice of the cut.

Of course it was not a surprise. But it was a shock, no matter how much I had prepared for it. John was thousands of miles away. I had to act, carefully but to some effect. It was a very lonely experience. 'Pessimism of the intellect, optimism of the will.'

That was in March '88 where my diary of that crucial year began: it is by no means a full account, any more than my selection of events and feelings over the last seventeen years, but it may help to throw some light on the changes that have taken place since we set off with Victor Henry and Mike Wearing, Dave MacLennan, Gilly Hanna, Sandy Craig and the others in 1971, at the start of 7:84.

At any rate as the years unfolded it confirmed my growing suspicion that the story is not over yet. For me, at any rate. Or for John McGrath. What happens next is yet to be resolved. But it's going to be interesting.

The audience who wrote to protest against our abolition is still there. They have not been answered.

Some Conclusions

When I started to work as an actor in 1959, plays were still being submitted for the approval of the Lord Chamberlain. There was Variety with its summer seasons and its winter pantos, there was the West End with its number one and number two tours, there were the 'provincial' reps and that was about it. There was the odd one-off tour. But now, thanks to people like Jenny Lee and Lord Goodman
and the Arts Council in the late 6os and early 70s, and to the enlightened support of some local authorities, and to a very great deal of hard work, there are hundreds of new theatre buildings, halls, theatres and companies.

Performing in some of these new places a whole new generation of actors, musicians and technicians have grown up who are accustomed to being paid the same to do strikes and get-ins, to travelling out of London, to being responsible for the material which they are putting across, and for taking part in decision-making processes. They of course are part of a popular theatre tradition that was strong in the 20s, 30s, and 40s and goes back a very long way.

In my experience, the drama schools do not really reflect these changes, with the possible exception of the Rose Bruford, which they are trying to close down. They tend to prepare students for a theatre where Shakespeare is still the Bible and requires a special voice, where Olivier is god, and Peggy Ashcroft his mother. Where women still perform a largely decorative and stereotyped function. So it is not surprising that many 'ordinary' people still regard the likes of us as 'students' needing a proper day job and not really part of the *proper* acting world where acting skills once more equal the ability to wear long dresses and cloche hats, to cross your ankles decoratively, to speak posh and earn a lot of money – at least if we're to believe quite a lot of what's to be seen on stage, television and film at the moment.

I too have had a university education and a middle-class background, and been to the Royal Shakespeare Company and the National Theatre, and *admire* Peggy Ashcroft and Olivier, and what John Gielgud did to sustain a classical repertory tradition. But that is not the *whole* story. There are other skills. Other forms of commitment. Other forms of training required.

As things stand, many actors who are on a one-way ticket away from their own class are encouraged to think there is only one way of performing, to sustain only one set of values. But the range of popular theatre styles within the European tradition *alone* – quite apart from those of India, China, Japan and the rest of the *world* – is as various as the culture of the peoples they reflect. We have still a lot to learn.

The kind of performance I became familiar with in 7:84, as it was, is subject to and conditioned in the main by a series of specific pressures. It relates to these very vital questions: who is putting us on here? Is it self-financing? What happened today that relates directly to the content of the show and do we make changes or updates? What was the last show we played here? Did they like it? Did our ad appear next to the one for the sheep-dog trials? Have the audience been waiting long? Are they queueing? Is there a bar? Will it be open during the show? Is there coffee? Is there one toilet for the audience and the players? (Do not flush during the show.) Who's doing the raffle? Is there any heating? The audience certainly won't laugh if they're huddled in their coats, though I do vividly remember one woman on such a cold night on a Highland tour, producing her husband from under her arm and a set of broken false teeth in her hand saying, 'He laughed so much he broke them – are you going to pay up?'

Then the more serious questions: are we in a big theatre tonight or is the stage, as in most town halls, too high? Should we use the fore-stage – more work in the get-outs? Is there anywhere to do the quick changes? Can I get round the back? Shall we start late to allow the bus to arrive from the oil rig? – at Kishorn for instance – or the bus party from Govan, or the local works outing. Is there a dance to follow? Are we playing it? Should we play with or without an interval? Is there a storm, are the boats in? Will the fishermen come or will they stay in the bar? Are there Gaelic speakers in? Are there more women than men in the audience, children, any babies? Is that a drunk or is he trying to say something? What time does the evening mass finish? Remember to check with the priest in Barra. Are there people standing? Have they come far? Should we say thanks at the end? Are we raising money? Are we drawing attention to, or supporting, a local strike, a demonstration? Is it my turn to make a speech? In what language?

Under these sorts of circumstances it is often very hard to tell where the event finishes and the performance begins.

For this and other reasons, I have found it is pretty disastrous to employ anything other than the epic acting style. By epic I mean larger than life, but fiercely true to it. The performer must engage the audience's attention by music, gesture, speech or action.

Of course this is only my experience with 7:84 and there are many other touring companies who respond to these circumstances in different ways. Some favour social realism, some stand-up comedy, some recreate the small scale experimental theatre wherever they go in terms of seating, ticket prices, publicity and so on, and by adapting their performance style to suit the requirements of their particular audiences. Many other admirable companies have sprung up who work even more closely with, and as *part* of a community. From these companies we can all learn a great deal.

In fact the originality, zest, sensitivity, talent and variety of skills developed by such companies and their influence upon each other and their interaction provide today, to a very large extent, the life-blood of the mainstream theatre and account for most of the new audiences, in my opinion, throughout the whole of Britain and certainly in Scotland.

However, today, far from being encouraged, this tradition is fighting for its life.

I've come to the conclusion that there are five things that really matter in this kind of work as a performer. All are discouraged by funding bodies, as they are by many drama school teachers. They are:

Holding onto your roots.
Using your brain and your critical faculties.
Development of all kinds of comic skills.
Class awareness.
Not being afraid to try something new.

At drama school you're told, don't be too intelligent, forget your roots, join the middle class, learn their language, underestimate and patronise the popular comedy skills and don't bother to learn an instrument – leave it to the musicians who should stay in the pit where they belong.

If you play in a play in a theatre building in one place in, say, the West End, for a run, the performance will vary of course from night to night, reactions, running time, and so forth, but the range of variations is quite narrow. You more or less know if it's going to be a success or a flop. And I've done it.

But if you take a show on the road it can be the biggest success in one place and the next night it can be a total flop. This throws an enormous responsibility onto the performer, particularly as many touring companies travel without a director. And the responsibility has to be shared among the crew and the working actors. Because each night is the first night for THAT community – they may not see the company, or *any* company again that year. So there is a lot of danger and excitement and the touring audience will realise that and share it. It's also one of the practical reasons why such companies need some form of internal democracy.

*   *   *

A few years ago I was sitting in the kitchen thinking about what I would say at a conference held to confront the difficulties faced by touring alternative and political theatres, and my son Danny was doing his biology revision. 'Mum,' he said, 'what are the characteristics of all living organisms?'

'I don't know, you tell me,' I said.

'Respiration, excretion, feeding, growth, reproduction, sensitivity and movement.'

By that definition I think the alternative theatre is a living organism. But it is fast becoming an endangered species.

The time since 1985 seems to have been one of constant struggle and increasing isolation, reflecting in many ways the similar struggles of so many working-class and progressive cultural organisations at this time. For although we are all struggling together, it has been the success of the Thatcher mind-machine to make us all feel alone. In England this is particularly striking, which is largely why the English 7:84 has been so hard to resuscitate.

The period has also been characterised by struggles against the growing powers of administrators. When they appointed new administrators at the SCO and SNO recently, they got full page coverage. It was seen as an event of major artistic significance. It was. But where was the interview with the new conductor, or the players? The rise and rise of the managers. The same was happening in the universities with some tragic results.

What kind of ghastly priorities do we all face?

Outside the school, waiting to collect our children, everybody is feeling the pinch – those who are battling to keep nurseries open, those who work in the social services, nursing, education; the story is the same – cuts, cuts, cuts. Petitions, fund-raising, the sense of powerlessness as we watch these vital things being taken away from us. Women are always the first to feel it.

The birth of my daughter Kate on 19 July 1979 signalled a new era, a new burst of energy and hope. She was born on the same day exactly as free Nicaragua. The two events marked, for me, a new beginning; certainly both demanded an energetic participation. My friends in the Teyocoyanni company started to call her Nicaraguita. At five and a half months she was in a pushchair on the March for Jobs with me and I remember 'Haven't you got a home to look after?' being shouted from an office window.

Well, amazingly, I still had a home, and two grown sons, none the worse for it all – maybe quite a bit the better. At least they have minds of their own.

While 7:84 is under such heavy scrutiny by the arts establishment here, and in trendy disfavour in certain quarters, it has become in many ways the *model* or example for companies all over the world, in Australia, New Zealand and Canada; or at least it is warmly regarded as a close relation in practice and potential and sense of common purpose, and I am in touch with sister companies all over the world.

My involvement in the research for shows over the years, and an awareness of the transitoriness of theatre fashion made me decide in 1984 to start to maintain some sort of personal 7:84 archive, and this I have endeavoured to do since then. It has made me painfully aware of the persistent undermining effects of under-funding and lack of support.

It also reminds me of the vital role of central government in ensuring provision for the arts, and of Jenny Lee in particular for the popular arts. Not until we have another arts minister of her conviction and determination will the arts – and the new popular arts in particular – flourish as they should.

My diaries for this decade are full of fund-raising, benefits, rallies, arrangements for babysitting, letters from abroad, board meetings, requests for support; from Lee Jeans, Caterpillar, the nurses, ANC, the civil servants, Amnesty, Chile Solidarity, Nicaragua Medical Aid, the Poll Tax campaign, the demand for new shows growing as the money becomes tighter.

Now, in the bright new world of sponsorship that is being projected, the 'partnership between public and private sector' that everyone is clutching on to, the Noah's Ark for the 90s – will any of these groupings have priority? I doubt it.

In the Scottish Parliament favoured by all the interested groups, would education and the arts have *cabinet* status, or merely be there (a) to produce suitable entrepreneurial fodder or (b) to decorate the corporate image of private companies?

Wind will not cease, even though trees want rest

When I set out to try and recreate for myself some of the events and sensations of my own involvement in touring popular theatre, it was perhaps at the lowest point of the last seventeen years; the announcement, or rather the surreptitious letting-us-know of the SAC funding cut to 7:84. Many people on the left are exhausted, dispirited. 'What can we do? We feel so powerless. It's happening to everybody, you just can't take it in.'

Under these circumstances, it has been quite difficult to recall the energy and optimism and effectiveness of so much of our work, because we are constantly being told by the New Realists that things are different now and that sort of thing won't work any more. But we know from our experience that this is not true, and from history that they are defending their own powerful interests once again.

Like the teachers, the doctors, the nurses and every member of the caring society who remain, we have to stand up and fight for the things that are being taken away from us. And that includes popular theatre. The profession must take on the battle and recognise the steps that are being taken to standardise and sanitise people's lives and experiences. There is a big cultural battle going on. We are engaged in it. We must cherish and support our writers and artists and they must recognise their strengths and speak out and we must make sure that they are heard.

'It's very important that there's somewhere people can learn to speak to an audience directly. That place, as far as I'm concerned, is small-scale, it's subsidised and it has the absolute right to fail.'
Drew Griffiths, writer and co-founder of Gay Sweatshop

If a society destroys its artists it destroys itself. They are reflecting the hopes and fears of our children. They must resist; and the forms of resistance must be as available to us as the current enterprise culture that is pumped into us intravenously every day.

Theatre needs money. Touring theatre needs subsidy. Oppositional theatre needs a strong opposition and they need each other. The audience is there. The road is open.

Song at the end of *Blood Red Roses*:

Now that is our story
A tale that goes on –
Is it true or a lie or a fiction?
Is it right or mistaken the story we tell:
Is it fit to be tellt tae your children?

Appendix: 7:84 England

It is impossible to list all the performers, administrative wizards and technicians who have contributed to 7:84 England. Many are now 'household names', gracing the 'big houses', running festivals and theatre departments.

Among them:

Writers
John McGrath
John Arden
Adrian Mitchell
Barrie Keefe
John Burrows
Shane Connaughton

Trevor Griffiths
Margaretta D'Arcy
Jim Sheridan
Peter Cox
Claire Luckham
Steve Gooch

Directors
John McGrath
Pam Brighton
Alan Dossor
John Burrows
Jim O'Brien
Gavin Richards
Jim Sheridan

Richard Eyre
Penny Cherns
Roland Rees
John Arden and Margaretta D'Arcy
Adrian Shergold
Rob Walker

Designers
Jenny Tiramani
Geoff Rose
Paul Dart
Adrian MacAlpine
Annette Gillies

Di Seymour
Gemma Jackson
Claudia Mayhew
Ellen Cairns

Ex-members who have founded or helped to found their own companies:
Gavin Richards – Belt and Braces
David MacLennan – Wildcat
Gillian Hanna – Monstrous Regiment
Jim Sheridan – Project Theatre, Dublin
Feri Lean – Founding Director of Glasgow Mayfest

In addition to these companies directly influenced, there is obviously a whole theatre movement which draws its inspiration from the work of 7:84. The number of young actors, directors, writers and students who have written to us for help and information in setting up companies runs into hundreds and there are many all over the world who have taken 7:84 as their model.

The other audience

Apart from visits to the Sheffield Crucible, the Shaw Theatre, the Half Moon, the Liverpool Everyman and the large city halls, Speke in Merseyside was typical of the communities which grew to love and trust 7:84 England. These are the communities which the English Arts Council has now abandoned.

'Who went to see the two plays by 7:84 at Speke Community Centre on 14 April?

If you did then you were lucky enough to have been watching a national company on tour – performing right here in Speke! What's more you will have done so for the unbelievable price of only thirty-five pence.

Yes, 7:84 deliberately wanted to keep the cost down for folk in Speke as a special concession, because one of their plays, *Jimmy Riddle*, was about the closure of the British Leyland Plant here in Speke just a few years ago.

Jimmy Riddle, an active trades unionist made redundant from British Leyland and living in Speke, revealed the reality of a father/husband faced with redundancy and the prospect of long-term unemployment. A brilliant play, brilliantly written, and acted out by the lone performer who kept his audience riveted to their seats in appreciation, while he convinced them that his two kids, Sandra and Barney, his wife Maureen and his numerous workmates were right up there on stage with him – powerful acting that drew such comments from those who watched as, "My dad would have really enjoyed that – he should have come too," or, "I wish I had told our kid this was on tonight; he used to work at Leyland, and he hasn't worked since either . . ."

Still, if you did miss this particular performance and wish you hadn't, don't despair – there will be other plays to see in the not too distant future. The community centre aim to make this a regular feature of local events.'

Speke Independent Press

This article refers to 7:84 England's visit to Speke in May 1983 with Peter Cox's plays. The *Speke Independent Press* is the local newspaper produced for the community by the community. Speke was suffering an unemployment level of around seventy-seven per cent of those able to work, appalling housing and precious few services. It was the dormitory for the workers of Speke Boulevard, now the site of empty and derelict factories.

7:84 England fight to the death

Six Men of Dorset was first sponsored by the TUC in 1934 to mark their centenary. Here is a 1934 account:

'Written by Miles Malleson in collaboration with Harry Brooks, a railwayman at Poole in Dorset, a trades unionist of many years' standing, it was produced for the first time in the Corn Exchange, Dorchester before an audience which included representatives of the Labour, trades union and co-operative movements from Great Britain, the Continent and the Dominions, as well as representatives of the county and civic authorities. On the stage where Thomas Hardy's plays have often been produced by Dorset men and women, the TUC play was presented with impressive effect.

It is more than a piece of propaganda; it is real drama with universal human appeal, and it aroused considerable interest in the outside world, and won the praise of the critics. It is historically accurate, being based upon documents of the period, and much of the dialogue incorporates actual conversations and speeches of the principal actors in the real-life drama of a century ago, which have survived in contemporary records.'

The play commemorated the Tolpuddle Martyrs. In 1937 it received its first professional performance, again backed by the TUC, with Sybil Thorndike as Mrs Loveless and Lewis Casson as George Loveless, who, along with his fellow agricultural workers, was transported to Van Dieman's Land for forming a trades union. That company won support from trades councils and striking miners everywhere it toured.

Alex McCrindle, a member of the original cast remembered:

'During the week in each town Sybil, Lewis and I addressed meetings in foundries, warehouses, and even outside the gates of Portsmouth Dockyard. I well remember Lewis speaking from a work bench in a Merseyside factory – it was like a scene from one of the early Soviet films. Sybil spoke to thousands of enthusiastic women at the co-op headquarters in Manchester.

The highlight of the tour, however, was enacted in Nottinghamshire. We were playing at the Theatre Royal while a few miles away at Harworth, miners had been on strike for months in a fight against company unionism. Members of our company fancied paying them a visit, but the management threatened we would not play in the theatre if we did. A full company meeting was held, it was unanimously agreed we should go and I was instructed to hire a bus to take us there.

The strikers had hired the local cinema and when we arrived the place was packed. With Sybil and Lewis at our head we marched down the centre aisle to cheers and stamping that seemed to shake the whole ramshackle building. Sybil was at her best and most endearing. "My dear miners, ever since I was a little girl I always thought of miners as the salt of the earth," and so on.

The proprietor said we could not perform a scene from the play because he did not have a licence for stage performances. So out we all trotted to the village green, where we performed the key scene from the play, where the farmworkers confronted the farmers under the chairmanship of the vicar. It was a huge success and afterwards it was difficult for us to get back aboard our bus. But, before we did, we clasped hands and sang "The Red Flag" together.

Tired but happy, we arrived back in Nottingham in good time for the show. And not a word was said about that threat to bar us from our stage.'

7:84 England decided to revive *Six Men of Dorset* in 1984 during the miners' strike. Again it toured to packed houses and a very similar response.

Tour Schedule

Tuesday 4 – Saturday 8 September: Crucible Theatre, Sheffield
Tuesday 11 – Saturday 15 September: St George's Hall, Liverpool
Monday 17 – Tuesday 18 September: St Andrew's Hall, Norwich
Friday 21 – Saturday 22 September: Corn Exchange, Ipswich
Tuesday 25 – Saturday 29 September: People's Theatre, Newcastle Upon Tyne
Tuesday 2 – Thursday 4 October: Pavilion Theatre, Weymouth
Tuesday 9 – Saturday 13 October: Shaw Theatre, London
Wednesday 17 – Saturday 27 October: Shaw Theatre, London
Monday 15 – Tuesday 16 October: Shaftesbury Hall, Cheltenham

Neil Kinnock, a director of 7:84 England, wrote in the programme:
'The history of the Tolpuddle Martyrs, viewed from a distance of 150 years, has a horribly familiar ring to it.

The 1980s, like the 1930s, are years of restrictive legislation, attacks on basic trades union rights – GCHO, the government's handling of the miners' strike – all show that trades union rights must never be taken for granted.

The Tolpuddle Martyrs are remembered. Because their cruel martyrdom showed that representatives of the propertied and moneyed classes, however enlightened and well-intentioned, can never be trusted to give working people a fair deal in a capitalist society. From this realisation grew the Labour Party, created to represent and fight for working people.

Under the Thatcher Government the judiciary has again been thrust into the front line of trades union repression. The events of 1984 are proving a grim echo of the past.'

John wrote in his welcome note:

'7:84 is delighted to present this play at this time. As this government renews its many-pronged and devious attacks on the trades unions and their members, it is as well to remember both the efforts and sacrifices which were made to bring the unions into being, and the conditions of life which the working class suffered without them.

Today we are seeing another great effort and great sacrifice – this time to protect those unions. And we have no reason to trust our present rulers to be any less rapacious or to inflict less suffering if they should manage to do away with them. They have shown themselves willing to return to the 1790s: starvation, child mortality and disease included.

This play shows also the ruling class manipulating the law to achieve their own ends – the difference from today is that in 1834 at least Lord Melbourne stuck to the law as it was written, and didn't re-write it off the cuff to suit his own class ends.

Above all, this play shows what can be achieved by massive organisation, demonstration of will and the determination of the working class and their allies not to be defeated.

The six men of Dorset are an inspiration to us all, men and women, today: the triumph of the movement to release them, in the face of all odds, is just what we need today, to remind us that we can, and must, win.'

Jack Boddy, the National Secretary of the Agricultural and Allied Workers National Trade Group wrote to the Arts Council on 16 May 1984:

Dear Mr Rittner,

As you may know, this year marks the 150th anniversary of the transportation to Australia of the men known as the Tolpuddle Martyrs – pioneers on rural trades unionism and indeed all trades unionism. The anniversary celebrations include a revival of the play made famous by Lewis Casson and Sybil Thorndike, called *Six Men of Dorset*.

It is, I believe, entirely fitting that the play will be staged by the 7:84 England Theatre Company.

Pioneers in their own right, the company's ability to entertain, to inform and, not least, to attract audiences of working people in England's less dramatically favoured areas, has earned them the respect and affection of our movement.

Such ability makes them the natural choice to perform such a play at such a time and our trades union, the TGWU, is giving its own grant to help the company attempt this major production.

I appreciate that the Labour movement's respect and affection will do the company little good in the eyes of our present government, but would be surprised and distressed if the Arts Council were in complete sympathy with the government's view.

After all, the Arts Council itself grew from that same Labour movement which the 7:84 Theatre Company have served so well.

It is with this in mind that I write to ask you to reconsider your decision to withdraw subsidy from the company. The thousands of us who will watch *Six Men of Dorset* will be saddened and, indeed, angered if it is 7:84's last production.

Yours sincerely,
Jack Boddy
National Secretary

Six Men of Dorset was given generous support in addition to the TGWU from the following councils and unions:

Greater London Council
Merseyside County Council
Sheffield City Council
TGWU (Transport and General Workers' Union)
Agricultural and Allied Workers Trade Group
NALGO (National and Local Government Officers' Association)
Liverpool City Council
Tyne and Wear County Council
Equity
APEX (Association of Professional, Executive, Clerical and Computer Staff)
Sogat '82 (Society of Graphical and Allied Trades)
NUPE (National Union of Public Employees)
SCPS (Society of Civil and Public Servants)
COHSE (Confederation of Health Services Employees)
NUTGW (National Union of Tailors and Garment Workers)
UCATT (Union of Construction, Allied Trades and Technicians)
CSU (Civil Service Union)
FBU (Fire Brigades Union)
ACTTS (Association of Cinematograph, Television and Allied Technicians)
TSSA (Transport Salaried Staffs Association,
REOU (Radio and Electronic Officers' Union)
FTAT (Furniture Timber and Allied Trades Union)
Rossendale Union of Boot, Shoe and Slipper Operatives
TGWU (Transport and General Workers' Union)
UCW (Union of Communication Workers)

This tour was followed up in January 1985 by a new musical play, *The Garden of England* by Peter Cox, directed by John Burrows, again with massive support from the Labour movement and the Kent miners in particular. It was hugely entertaining and enthusiastically received.

Tour schedule

January	Tuesday 29: Sheffield City Hall
	Thursday 31: Newcastle City Hall
February	Saturday 2: Digbeth Civic Hall, Birmingham
	Monday 4: Chesterfield College of Technology
	Wednesday 6: Town Hall, Manchester
	Friday 8: Parc And Dare Theatre, Treorchy, South Wales
	Sunday 10: Granville Theatre, Ramsgate
	Wednesday 13
	to Saturday 2: Shaw Theatre, London
	March:

Box office takings and collections taken were given to the Miners' Hardship Fund.

What the Press Said at the Time

'The Arts Council must be out of its tiny mind to withdraw funds from the English branch of a company as vigorous and bright-eyed as this'

Michael Billington, the *Guardian*

'*Six Men of Dorset* was performed at the Shaw Theatre before an audience which included Mr Kinnock, Mr Willis and a former secretary-general of the Arts Council, whose successors have boxed themselves into a daft ideological corner by refusing to renew the grant of an openly left-wing theatre company, the integrity of whose work is beyond question'

Michael Ratcliffe, the *Observer*

'7:84 England is the theatre company most deeply involved with socialist ideas, most integrated with the working-class movement, and the only theatre group which has achieved the real support and love of trades unions.

And that seems to me a perfect explanation of why the Thatcherite arts establishment has prepared its longest knives for 7:84, and why every one of us should rise and be counted in the fight to save it'

Tom Vaughan, *Morning Star*

'The TUC and some twenty unions have sponsored this production – I hope they'll continue. Serious provocative plays are the lifeblood of the theatre. It is misguided and wrong-headed to silence a voice which addresses itself with passionate seriousness and authoritative skill to issues that concern each and every one of us. And the money is peanuts'

John Peter, the *Sunday Times*

'If the Arts Council has withdrawn its subsidy to this company on political grounds, it should realise that is is also betraying the cause of art that it nominally stands for'

B. A. Young, the *Financial Times*

'It is an indication of the bizarre processes of the Arts Council that it has deemed it fit to axe the grant to possibly one of the finest touring companies this country has ever produced. There can be little argument that it would be a shameful disgrace if 7:84 were to be allowed to go out of business. The Arts Council planning is as weak as its policy. It airily dismisses the company with a wave of the hand. It called its recent policy "The Garden of England". It looks as if one of the oak trees in it is about to be uprooted to make way for a gravel path'

Phil Penfold, *Newcastle Chronicle*

'We've been hearing a lot these last days, and with reason, about the awfulness of trying to stifle free speech and democratic intercourse. Shouldn't the Arts Council ask itself if it isn't making its own small contribution to that same foul conspiracy?'

Benedict Nightingale, *New Statesman*

* * *

In March 1986 the last 7:84 England production TO DATE opened at the Half Moon Theatre without a penny from the Arts Council. A promenade spectacular funfair setting, it was co-written by John McGrath and directed by Chris Bond: *All the Fun of the Fair*. It was financed by the about to be abolished GLC.

John summed up in the programme:

'Over the last seventeen years, 7:84 has presented a huge number of productions of the highest quality to audiences from Orkney to Portsmouth, from Sligo to Amsterdam, from Toronto to Tbilisi. The sum of the work has helped to bring about significant changes in attitudes in British Theatre, to new forms of writing and production, to new audiences, and to the political value and values of theatre work.

7:84 works in the belief that theatre of the highest possible standard can and should spring from the lives and experience of the working people of this country, and can and should be made accessible to them in every way. 7:84's theatre has values and allegiances which are socialist. It is not afraid to recognise the existence of a class struggle being waged in this country, in which it comes down firmly on the side of the working class, the unemployed and the many other victims of the paternalist-capitalist state, which now evaluates human beings solely by reference to their usefulness to the industrial money-making machine and its instruments.

Because of 7:84's opposition to these values, which are the values of the new Ruthless Toryism, 7:84 England was told by the Arts Council that its annual revenue grant of £91,000 would be stopped from March 1985. In spite of its record of work, in spite of two hugely successful shows in 1984 and 85, in spite of many eloquent appeal from all over the world, from the Labour movement, from the trades union movement and from thousands of members of our audience, the Arts Council's mind was, in 7:84's case, absolutely immovable.

7:84 was then greatly encouraged to receive invaluable help from the TUC, in the form of the free use of an office at Congress House. The GLC also came to its rescue, with the commission to produce a summer show, to tour in a circus tent in August and September of '84. Unfortunately the first Westminster City injunction, an attempt to stop the GLC controlling its own funds, which specifically named 7:84's grant, was allowed to maunder on through the judicial processes until the show could not be done. This left the company with considerable problems, and a large debt.

Early in 1986 the GLC once again came to the company's rescue, and funded *All the Fun of the Fair*.

7:84 faces the future with great optimism and determination to continue its work, but in England they are now without any visible means of support. This government and the present state of the country however cannot go on forever. We look forward to changes. Soon.'

7:84 Productions, 1971–1988

7:84

1971	*Trees in the Wind* by John McGrath
	Apricots and Thermidor by Trevor Griffiths
1972	*Plugged into History* by John McGrath
	Out of Sight by John McGrath
	Occupations by Trevor Griffiths
	Underneath by John McGrath
	The Ballygombeen Bequest by John Arden and Margaretta D'Arcy

Sergeant Musgrave Dances On by John Arden, adapted by John McGrath

7:84 England

1973	*Man Friday* by Adrian Mitchell
	The Reign of Terror and the Great Money Trick by 7:84 England adapted from *The Ragged Trousered Philanthropists* by Robert Tressell
1975	*Fish in the Sea* by John McGrath
	Lay Off by John McGrath
	Yobbo Nowt by John McGrath
1976	*Relegated* by Shane Connaughton
	The Rat Trap by John McGrath
	Our Land, Our Lives by Steve Gooch
1977	*Wreckers* by David Edgar
	The Trembling Giant by John McGrath
	Joe of England by John McGrath
1978	*Underneath* by John McGrath
	Vandaleur's Folly by Margaretta D'Arcy and John Arden
1979	*Big Square Fields* by John McGrath
	Bitter Apples by John McGrath
	Trees in the Wind by John McGrath
1980	*SUS* by Barrie Keefe
	One Big Blow by John Burrows
1981	*Night Class* by John McGrath
1982	*Trafford Tanzi* by Claire Luckham
	Rejoice! by John McGrath
1983	*V-Signs* by Peter Cox
	Spike in the First World War by Jim Sheridan
1984	*School for Emigrants* by 7:84 England
	Six Men of Dorset by Miles Malleson and Harry Brooks
1985	*The Garden of England* by Peter Cox
	All the Fun of the Fair by John McGrath with Chris Bond, Farrukh Dhondy and others

7:84 Scotland

1973	*The Cheviot, the Stag and the Black, Black Oil* by John McGrath
1974	*The Game's a Bogey* by John McGrath
	Boom by John McGrath
1975	*My Pal and Me* by John McGrath
	Capital Follies by David MacLennan and John Bett
	Little Red Hen by John McGrath
1976	*Honour Your Partners* by David MacLennan
	Out of Our Heads by John McGrath
1977	*Thought for Today* by David MacLennan
	The Trembling Giant by John McGrath
	His Master's Voice by David Anderson

1979	*Joe's Drum* by John McGrath
1980	*Swings and Roundabouts* by John McGrath
1980-1	*Blood Red Roses* by John McGrath
1981	*The Catch* by John McGrath

CLYDEBUILT SEASON

1982	*Gold in his Boots* by George Munro
	In Time of Strife by Joe Corrie
	U.A.B. Scotland by Harry Trott
	Johnny Noble by Ewan MacColl
	Men Should Weep by Ena Lamont Stewart

1982	*Screw the Bobbin* by the company and Chris Hannan
1982-3	*Men Should Weep* by Ena Lamont Stewart
1983	*On the Pig's Back* by John McGrath and David MacLennan with Wildcat
	Women in Power by Aristophanes and McGrath with General Gathering
	Maggie's Man by Colin Mortimer
1984	*The Ragged Trousered Philanthropists* adapted by Archie Hind
	The Baby and the Bathwater by John McGrath
1985	*The Albannach* a version by John McGrath of the novel by Fionn MacColla
	The Baby and the Bathwater by John McGrath – Edinburgh Festival version
	In Time of Strife by Joe Corrie
	High Places by Ena Lamont Stewart
	The Incredible Brechin Beetle Bug by Matt McGinn
1986	*Beneath One Banner* by Sean McCarthy
	Victorian Values by Donald Campbell as part of The Springwell House Community Drama Project
	There Is a Happy Land by John McGrath
	The Albannach a version by John McGrath of the novel by Fionn MacColla
	The Incredible Brechin Beetle Bug by Matt McGinn
1987	*The Gorbals Story* by Robert McLeish
	Mairi Mhor, the Woman from Skye by John McGrath
1988	*No Mean City* adapted by Alex Norton

Index

211